How Dramas End

How Dramas End

Essays on the German *Sturm und Drang*, Büchner, Hauptmann, and Fleisser

Henry J. Schmidt

Ann Arbor

THE UNIVERSITY OF MICHIGAN PRESS

Copyright © by the University of Michigan 1992
All rights reserved
Published in the United States of America by
The University of Michigan Press
Manufactured in the United States of America

1995 1994 1993 1992   4 3 2 1

Library of Congress Cataloging-in-Publication Data

Schmidt, Henry J.
   How dramas end : essays on the German Sturm und Drang, Büchner,
Hauptmann, and Fleisser / Henry J. Schmidt.
      p.   cm. — (Theater — theory/text/performance)
   Includes bibliographical references and index.
   ISBN 0-472-10261-3 (alk. paper)
   1. German drama — History and criticism.   2. Drama — Technique.
I. Title.   II. Series.
PT628.S36   1992
832.009 — dc20   92-169
                                                   CIP

For Cynthia and for Max

Editor's Note

Henry Schmidt devoted much of his scholarly career to the writings of the German dramatist Georg Büchner, and like Büchner, he died before he could put the finishing touches on the manuscript of his own major work. During the last few months of his life, however, he did revise the first three chapters of *How Dramas End*, and he made a number of notes about the changes he wanted to introduce into the final four chapters. Unfortunately, he didn't have an opportunity to make those changes, and we felt that his own words, even in their unmodified form, expressed his intentions far more eloquently than any of us could have hoped to do. Other than correcting a few obvious typographical errors, we have therefore left his formulations to speak for themselves.

As he began to revise his manuscript, Henry was already aware of the illness that would bring about his premature death. The irony of writing about the endings of literary works at that moment did not escape him. In fact, he himself acknowledged in his first chapter that "the ultimate anxiety addressed by an ending is the fear of death." Henry had the intellectual curiosity to pursue such ideas wherever they might lead, and he had the courage to confront the meanings he discovered in his quest for understanding. Many of the fruits of that quest are contained in *How Dramas End*. For all those who profit from the book's wisdom and insight, Henry's final sentence will seem particularly fitting because it is certainly true that, as he says, "every ending makes room for a new beginning."

Notes found among his papers by Henry's colleagues at Ohio State and by his widow, C. Max Schmidt-Schilling, indicate that he wished to express his appreciation to the Department of German and the College of Humanities at The Ohio State University for a sabbatical leave and to the Fulbright Commission for the award of a Senior Research Grant that enabled him to spend the 1988–89 academic year in Berlin. He also wanted to thank those who, he felt, had offered him valuable criticisms: Leslie Adelson, David P. Benseler, Sigrid Damm, Mac Davis, Francis M. Dunn, Mark Roche, Jan Zychlinski, and Karin Wurst. He was also grateful for the help of Christian Büttrich at the Bibliothek des Fachbereichs Germanistik der Freien Universität Berlin and of Ilona Fürst at the Marieluise Fleisser Archive in Ingolstadt.

Earlier versions of materials contained in this book have appeared in *Büchner-Studien*, the *Lessing Yearbook xi*, and *Fide et Amore: Festschrift for Hugo Bekker on His Sixty-Fifth Birthday* (Kümmerle Verlag). They are published here with the permission of the editors of those publications. The original version of the chapter on Gerhard Hauptmann had been accepted for publication in the forthcoming *Playing for Stakes: German-Language Drama in Social Context*; it is also published here with the permission of the editors. Paul Klee's *Schlussbild einer Tragikomödie* (1923), the painting on the dust jacket, is reproduced with the generous permission of Culture Crossing, Inc., in New York City.

Henry himself had formulated the concluding words of his preface, and they aptly express the generosity of sentiment that permeates his writing: "To you to whom this book is dedicated: thanks for teaching me about the ambiguity of closure."

Richard Bjornson
Leslie Adelson
Michael Jones

In Appreciation

Many heartfelt thanks to those who saw where they were needed and jumped in to fill the void, who took on the responsibility for the completion of the book after Henry's death, and who in many ways expressed the loss they felt at his death. I remember Leslie Adelson's words at the memorial service, "I could use Henry's help right now to describe this ending which has come too soon."

Thanks to Gisela Vitt for her ongoing concern and support; to Richard Bjornson, who took on all major responsibility for the book's completion; to Aija Bjornson; to Leslie Adelson; to Michael Jones and Jeannine Blackwell; and to LeAnn Fields, a caring editor.

Also thanks to all those who supplied moral support, among whom are Barbara Rigney, Susan Nielson-Weiskott, Susan La Tourneau, and Susan Christy.

C. Max Schmidt-Schilling

Contents

Chapter 1

How Dramas End

Prologue 1

Many poets tie the knot well, but unravel it ill.

— Aristotle, *Poetics*, XVIII

During the performance of a tragedy in which one of the main characters died in the best of health, a spectator asked his neighbor: "But what did he die of?" "What did he die of? Of the fifth act!" was the answer. Truly, the fifth act is a nasty form of distemper that does away with many who were promised a much longer life by the first four acts.

— G. E. Lessing, *Hamburg Dramaturgy*

Endings of literary works betray literature's mimetic capacity. Fictions must have conclusions; life does not. A fictional ending, like a beginning, is an interruption. Once underway, a literary work appears to progress naively, propelled by its inner momentum. Yet as the moment of closure approaches, the work tends to become self-conscious, seemingly aware of the judgmental presence of the reader, who, having been captured, must be successfully released. Authorial anxiety increases as the writer is compelled to select one of an infinite number of possible solutions, suppress alternative courses of action, gloss over a multitude of unresolved contradictions, and legitimate the preceding action by supplying a "meaning." The resulting exertion renders art more artificial, theater more theatrical, as the literary work builds to a final flourish before it disappears from view.

A study of endings, especially drama endings, would nevertheless appear to be an exercise in simplicity. What can be complex about plot resolutions, since most are as familiar as reconciliation, marriage, celebration, and death? Normally we prize the originality of a dramatic action rather than the often conventional close that brings down the curtain or gets the actors off the stage. Yet in terms of structure and impact, endings are beset with contradictions. To commence with Aristotle: "Every tragedy falls into two parts—Complication and Unraveling or Denouement [*lysis*]."[1] According to J. Hillis Miller, the denouement is "the combing out of the tangled narrative threads so that they may be clearly seen, shining side by side, all mystery or complexity revealed."[2] Yet a denouement is also its opposite: it is "a tying up, a neat knotting leaving no loose threads hanging out, no characters unaccounted for."[3] Is a play properly tied or untied at its conclusion? The distinction would appear to hinge on the effects of closure versus those of release, both of which are inherent qualities of an ending. Moreover, endings contain a deeper ambivalence: they are both desirable and frightening. On the one hand, they contain a utopian moment, an experience of pleasure seemingly transcendent because of its apparent timelessness, a boundary that gives significance to all that precedes it. On the other hand, endings are threatening because they are finite; they merely project timelessness but do not enact it. Thus, the pleasure of closure conflicts with its arbitrariness. A happy ending is perhaps merely a willful contrivance; perhaps the curtain falls, as Schopenhauer wrote, "at the moment of joy . . . so that we don't see what comes after. . . ."[4]

The mechanics of imposing closure on an action rest on ethical choices as well as on structural logic. Aristotle stated that the effort of tragedy "to hit the popular taste" is "to produce a tragic effect that satisfies the moral sense."[5] The resolution of moral dilemmas is inextricably linked to the formal logic that ultimately breaks the chain of causality and brings about closure. Ethical and aesthetic factors interact to produce certain courses of action while disqualifying others, to highlight certain voices while suppressing others. Typically, a drama will assert its individuality as it unfolds, but its conclusion—which inevitably represents an aesthetic and moral compromise—will relapse into conformity with a dominant system of beliefs. The force that brings this about is generic convention.

By "generic" I mean not only the structural aspects of textual closure but also the "public" qualities of drama as performance. Although a drama ending has been referred to as a point or boundary, the unraveling of a plot on stage is, in fact, a process that includes recognition (anagnorisis), catastrophe, a coda (the denouement in a narrower sense), and the conclusion of the theatrical performance, which is often inscribed into the written text. Before the emergence of the proscenium stage with its front curtain, which could cut off the action in medias res, actors took their leave in accordance with prevailing theatrical practice: the formal exodus of the chorus in Greek drama, the call for applause in Roman comedy, the pageantry of medieval drama, the restoration of order in Elizabethan drama. These devices were, in their time, so self-evident that only the briefest annotation was necessary for their proper execution, which makes it more difficult for later generations to comprehend their intent and impact. Both the structure and the symbolic meaning of a conventional ending were a matter of communal understanding among author, cast, and audience—a consensus intensified by the ritualized nature of a performance's conclusion.

A group of actors performing before an audience is engaging in an institutionalized collective activity; the mutual acknowledgment between actors and audience that occurs at the end of a performance reflects the conditions that make this activity possible and desirable. The actors' bows and the audience's acclaim constitute a symbolic transaction for having entertained, namely the expectation of reward, its fulfillment through applause, and gratitude for that fulfillment. The ritual also heightens the pleasure of collective action and spectatorship by celebrating the values that unite actors and audience. More pragmatically, the actors' obeisance to an audience or to a particular patron dramatizes the theater's economic dependence. In the course of history, these factors have been embedded in a drama's ending, which contains the recognition that its performers must ultimately come face to face with their benefactors.

Awareness of this obligation not only compounds authorial anxiety but makes it infectious. That is, concluding a drama becomes not only a matter of providing adequate closure to a fictional artifact but to a public social event, often with economic ramifications for the participants. Any staging of a drama results from not one but a series of texts;[6] subsequently, the publisher, director, dramaturges, performers, and audience assume part of the responsibility for whatever the drama manages to communicate. When it is "released" from the theatrical experience, the audience's attitude is, in its immediacy, usually a far more significant factor for performers than for the playwright in deciding how to fashion the mechanism for this release. Consequently, as particularly sensitive mediation points between art and society—that is, points at which art makes coercive social mechanisms apparent—drama endings tend to be the most often revised component

of any play. The revisions often begin with the author, as he or she attempts, in retrospect, to come to terms with the work's totality and to
gauge its potential effect on a particular audience. Directors and performers, temporally and culturally often far removed from the original
work's context, may undertake yet more fundamental changes. An ending's power seems to lie in its ability to condense and intensify a drama's
affirmative or subversive social function. In effect, the drama ends up
making a statement about the prevailing moral code, ranging from enthusiastic acceptance to wholesale rejection—an act of no little consequence for the participants. The chronicle of the choices that have been
made since the drama's inception anchors the text in cultural history.

To explore further in this introductory chapter how dramas end
and why they end the way they do, I will first examine endings using
the artificially polarized categories of "need" and "difficulty"; then I will
offer a descriptive typology of endings based on a survey of dramas
from the Greeks to the present. (This typology applies, in many
respects, to films and television dramas as well, but they would require
separate analysis.) My intent here is to identify "ending strategies" as
a preliminary step to further inquiry—for generating structural categories is, as an end in itself, ultimately meaningless. In order to penetrate
beyond formalistic generalization to discover the forces that affect the
tying/untying of a particular dramatic plot, an eclectic approach is
necessary, encompassing close readings of texts, the biography and social environment of the playwright, the dominant conventions of literature and theater, as well as the nature of their respective audiences. In
short, the analytical framework must remain historical, for drama endings, as structural solutions, have social content. The generic and
thematic conventions that shape them are ideological constructs with
historically variable social functions. An analysis of endings can, therefore, shed light, from various directions, upon the relationship between aesthetics and history.

The Need for an Ending

> So one who is mortal [should] look at that final day. . . .
> —Conclusion of Sophocles' *Oedipus Rex*

Endings provide both emotional and intellectual pleasure; they address one's psychological needs while they confirm or challenge one's

Weltanschauung. To define their impact is therefore extremely difficult, because whatever categories one may develop will slip from field to field, perpetually relativizing each another. The definitional problem is similar to that surrounding the Aristotelian concept of catharsis. According to Gerald F. Else, the noted commentator on the *Poetics*, "the great virtue, but also the great vice, of 'catharsis' in modern interpretations has been its incurable vagueness. Every variety of moral, aesthetic, and therapeutic effect that is or could be experienced from tragedy has been subsumed under the venerable word at one time or another."[7] Since an ultimate conceptual synthesis is beyond reach, I can at least try to "dramatize" the problem of endings with definitional juxtapositions.

A good place to begin a discussion of the need for an ending is in the classical era, where the notion of a drama's close had a secure, unambiguous place in a comprehensive aesthetic. Although Hegel was not the first to present what might be called the classical definition of the sense of an ending, his *Ästhetik* established a philosophical justification that continues to resonate in contemporary aesthetic theory. For Hegel, a drama's conclusion represents the expression of necessity, the imperative synthesis of all contradiction.[8] The harmony produced by necessity is both structural and philosophical, balancing conflicting elements of plot and character in a rounded off, closed whole. The image of rounding off, the Aristotelian untying of complication, is in Hegel's terms a utopian projection: "The end . . . will be achieved, when it has brought about *in every respect* the resolution of contradiction and entanglement."[9] An ending supplies meaning for suffering and misfortune, overcoming terror and pity. For Hegel, this act of reconciliation after disorder is an intrinsic aspect of art, which must never lack this fundamentally positive impulse.[10] Reconciliation is a manifestation of eternal justice, which restores moral unity through the destruction of the "one-sided" individualism that challenged it.[11]

Transplanted from their philosophical context by the epigones of classical idealism, Hegel's definitions froze into a dogma reflecting the normative aesthetics of a complacent, hegemonically secure bourgeoisie. For example, Gustav Freytag, author of the influential work, *The Technique of Drama*, maintained that the self-contained unity of a novel creates, for the reader, "the comfortable feeling of security and freedom; he is transplanted into a small universe in which he surveys in its totality the rational coherence of events."[12] For Freytag, a proper

dramatic ending creates an aesthetic whole as it mediates a universal-
ized (for which one might wish to substitute "imperialistic") concept of
Bildung. An ending's truth claim is based on clarity, ruling out the
potential validity of self-reflexivity or ambivalence: "The final words of
a drama must remind us that what has been shown is neither accidental
nor unique but is a poetic artifact intelligible to all."[13] Achieving successful closure, according to Freytag, depends on one's gender and
genes: "in order to create a good final catastrophe one needs a manly
heart and a superior mind."[14]

In the twentieth century, traces of this classicist philosophy of endings survive in New Criticism and neo-Aristotelianism. By emphasizing the autonomy of art, these schools attempt to legitimate the autonomy of critical judgment. John Gassner, for example, posits a state of
transcendent detachment both for the production and reception of an
ending: "Only enlightenment . . . and an induced state of mind that
places it above the riot of passion—can effect this necessary equilibrium."[15] As with Freytag, Gassner's concept of aesthetic enlightenment reflects the privileged status of a genteel cultural elite; enlightenment is "a state of grace," "a civilized attitude achieved in the course
of experiencing the play." From the spectator's viewpoint, the experience of catharsis likewise hinges on the ability to triumph in transcendence: "the exaltation comes only if we have prevailed over the anarchy
of our inner life and the ever present and ever pressing life around
us. . . ."[16]

Contemporary criticism tends to define endings as a manifestation
of control: individual will asserts itself by interrupting continuity. Closure is considered to be:

> the principle that behavior or mental process tends toward as com-
> plete, stable, or "closed" a state as circumstances permit: e.g., an
> asymmetrical figure tends to be perceived as symmetrical, an un-
> finished act to be completed, an incomplete musical chord to be re-
> solved, a meaningless object or situation to be perceived as having
> meaning.[17]

In terms of cognitive response, closure "provokes a flash of awareness, . . . a heightened insight into human experience."[18] Edward
Said speaks of the "need to apprehend an otherwise dispersed number
of circumstances and to put them in some sort of telling order, sequen-

tial, moral, or logical"[19] — a need addressed, to be sure, by artistic beginnings as well as endings. Analogous to birth and death in nature, fictive beginnings and endings inspire hope and anxiety. Both respond to "the primordial need for certainty," compensating for "the tumbling disorder of brute reality that will not settle down."[20]

As a disjunction, an ending is a moment frozen in time from which one may look backward and forward, defining the flow of action by differentiating it from other actions. The concept of "process" could not exist without the idea of "ending." Frank Kermode mentions the need to "give [the great crises and ends of human life] patterns . . . that defy time." "We project ourselves," he maintains, "past the End, so as to see the structure whole, a thing we cannot do from our spot of time in the middle."[21] An ending is pleasurable because it fulfills the desire to rest after action, to be released from "the potency of events."[22] It is psychologically satisfying because it signifies the return of lost objects, which, according to Terry Eagleton, "are a cause of anxiety to us, symbolizing certain deeper unconscious losses. . . ."[23] We are able, nevertheless, "to tolerate the disappearance of the object because our unsettling suspense [is] all the time shot through by the secret knowledge that it [will] finally come home."[24] That is, after the desire for gratification has been aroused and repeatedly postponed, it is finally fulfilled. Confusion and pain are replaced by order and meaning, temporarily healing the rift between reality and individual desire, giving purpose to random action. Even if a conclusion is predetermined, as in the retelling of a popular myth, the ending still represents an answer to the questions raised by a particular narrative. Rather than resolving suspense, the ending provides satisfaction by confirming the rightness of the path leading to it.

The ultimate anxiety addressed by an ending is the fear of death.[25] Entering into a literary or theatrical experience means exposing oneself to the risk that the as-yet-unknown ending may turn out to be meaningless, or at least disappointing. In other words, there is no guarantee that a reader's or spectator's expectation of catharsis — itself a vicarious experience of death — will be fulfilled. Yet the flirtation with mortality remains a tantalizing, pleasurable gamble. As Jean Duvignaud points out: "In the theatre, death is something overcome and integrated, something that only remotely implies the real spiritual horror of actual annihilation, for it has already been socialized and transformed"[26] — usually in a manner acceptable to specific audiences, which therefore know that the odds in favor of satisfaction and reassurance are high.

In fact, the vast majority of readers and theatergoers actively seek out the type of entertainment that will meet their expectation of a "just" resolution. In the words of Ronald Reagan: "There is something about a detective story. You know the right people will win, no matter how tense it gets."[27] Those who stumble across an alien aesthetic often cannot cope and even construct conspiracy theories to suppress their unresolved anxiety. A newspaper reader once wrote the following to the "TV question box": "I like 'Lou Grant' but am tired of his shows being unfinished, left up in the air. I am convinced somewhere there are endings to these programs being shown at some other time. Do you agree?"[28] Like a pleasurable reflection in a mirror, prevailing conventions confirm the viewer's identity and legitimate his or her status. Experiencing a satisfying fictional resolution is therefore self-ennobling, assuring one of the correctness of one's beliefs and of the fundamental stability of one's social and moral environment. The reestablishment of order is experienced as regained security, which was temporarily and vicariously threatened before the denouement. To affirm order is to reject anarchy, which has been evoked in order to tame it. Likewise, the spectator's emotions are aroused so that they may be properly socialized.

Endings that appear to resolve all conflict are utopian projections, myths of a nonoppressive society, affirmations of the pursuit of happiness. In Ernst Bloch's words, "an unmistakeable drive is working in the direction of the good end. . . ."[29] By defining this unquenchable utopian spirit as a motor of history, he countered the tendency of optimistic conclusions to be static and mindlessly affirmative: "More than once the fiction of a happy end . . . reformed a bit of the world; that is: an initial fiction was made real."[30] The gratification supplied by an ending can therefore be more than merely momentary, more than merely culinary: it can inspire change.

The Difficulty of Ending

> Unlike mystery novels, life does not guarantee a denouement; and if it came,
> how would one know whether to believe it?
>   —last line of Tom Stoppard's *Jumpers*

As I implied in the introduction, an ending cannot be satisfying without being manipulative. Gerhart Hauptmann, master of theatrical shock effects, once reflected upon the inadequacy and violence of endings.

> True drama is basically endless. It is an eternal inner struggle without resolution. At the moment of resolution, drama breaks off. However, since we are compelled to provide a resolution for every stage play, every performed drama is, unlike life, fundamentally pedantic and conventional. Life knows only the eternal struggle, or it ceases. The ideal drama that I would like to write would have no resolution and no conclusion. . . . The last act is almost always a constraint imposed by the playwright upon himself or upon his plot. Yes, in most cases the last act represents a criminal assault upon the plot.[31]

While the fate of an individual can be narrated, human history is endless—a distinction employed by Peter Szondi to illustrate the fundamental contrast between dramatic and epic form.[32] A drama cannot evoke the reality that follows the end of narration as well as an epic; the cessation of action in drama is absolute and, therefore, more abstract.[33] The ephemeral nature of an ending requires a high degree of suspension of disbelief in order to create an impact. "The curtain must fall before the smiles fade on the faces of those grouped in the final tableau," writes Walter Hinck, echoing Schopenhauer's cynical comment.[34] Dramatists who wish to emphasize continuity rather than finality are often defeated by the constraints of their chosen genre. Eugene O'Neill, for example, tried to subvert the optimistic resolution of his drama, *Anna Christie*, after the fact. In a letter to critic George Jean Nathan, he wrote:

> The happy ending is merely the comma at the end of a gaudy introductory clause, with the body of the sentence still unwritten. (In fact, I once thought of calling the play *Comma*.) . . . My ending seems to have a false definiteness about it that is misleading—a happy-ever-after which I did not intend.[35]

One might say that the intractability, even contrariness of an ending lies in its insistence on being a full stop.

Endings do violence to the plot, as Hauptmann indicated, by over-simplifying, by sacrificing faithfulness to reality for the sake of a manufactured totality. The dramatic text is unalterable and hence unyielding; characters convert into stereotypes, and alternative lines of development are cut off, producing a solution that the reader is coerced to accept. The drama's voices (that is, its ideologies) unite in seamless harmony, dictating conclusiveness, silencing all other voices. This triumph of the whole is literally and figuratively totalitarian. By compressing the action that led to it, an ending negates the process of its production. Although the action of any drama is always unique in some way, its resolution tends to be indistinguishable from a multitude of other endings.

Theatrical conventions offer the playwright techniques to get the cast off the stage in a manner acceptable to the audience, but such techniques are innately confining because they depend not on the unique logic of a particular work but on popular taste, on what Aristotle called "the debility of the audience."[36] That is, no matter how complex the action, convention demands an unproblematical, norm-affirming ending that fulfills certain culturally bound intellectual and emotional needs. Good is to be rewarded and evil punished in conformance with prevailing moral standards. (Especially in popular culture, gradations of retribution are a remarkably accurate measure of a society's permissiveness. For example, a fictional adulterous woman may either be killed off, consigned to a life of rejection or repentance, mildly disciplined, or not punished at all.) Social and generic conventions, the usual determinants of a drama's acceptance by the public and, hence, of its economic potential, tend to produce reactionary endings even in dramas with highly provocative content. Such backsliding may also result from a playwright's inability to pursue the logical consequences of his or her insights past a certain point.[37] Endings that seem incommensurable with the preceding action may signify a philosophical crisis, conscious provocation (a technique to be examined in the next section), or an aesthetic or ethical sellout to prevailing market forces. Because of the inherently strong psychological impact of closure, endings can easily manipulate audiences into powerful yet superficial emotional responses. In contemporary mass culture, fashionably progressive content tends to be nullified by trivializing denouements that provide much cheap sentiment but no intellectual nourishment—the aesthetic equivalent of junk food.

In certain instances, endings can be indeterminate. We do not know, for example, how Büchner's *Woyzeck* was meant to conclude because the playwright died before he could complete his revision of earlier drafts – although any staging of the play must, of course, select one of the possible scenes as the final one. Whereas many ritualized real-life events such as trials and competitive sports can indeed have "dramatic endings," contemporary extensions of the concept of drama to happenings and street theater can make it impossible to pinpoint a conclusion. For this reason, improvisational or wholly spontaneous events that have gained acceptance as forms of dramatic art will remain outside my survey, which will restrict itself to "designed effects"[38] in texts that, by their nature, must have endings.

An additional difficulty of ending lies in the gap between authorial intention and the immeasurable range of possible reader response, which is affected by yet another variable when a drama is filtered through the medium of performance. Each reader or spectator creates a concrete conceptualization of the work, and it differs from all others because it is based on the intangibles of subjective experience. Even various conceptualizations by the same person will differ considerably, as initial surprise gives way through repeated encounter to the expectation of a familiar, usually pleasurable response. Moreover, the constant mutability of aesthetic and ethical standards can make dramas unperformable or, at least, diminish the potency of their resolutions. The "just" endings of yesteryear often offend or amuse today's audiences; a conclusion once perceived as being profound and moving may, in the course of time, be regarded as implausible, clichéd, or sentimental. The closural function of weddings, for example, weakens when marriage is no longer considered to be the ultimate cure-all for male-female problems.[39] In fact, the traditional concept of closure itself has become suspect, especially among French feminist critics, who tend to view it as a component of patriarchal structure that values hierarchy over the equality of parts, linearity over circularity, disjunction over flow, postponement of gratification over immediate pleasure, and language over silence.[40] A strictly essentialist (i.e., biological) view of the experience of closure tends, however, to polarize categories of gender and underestimate the influence of social determinants. To what degree my own preoccupation with closure – manifested in this book – is gender specific I cannot judge; in any case, many of the "negative" aspects of closure described in this and in following sections confirm the feminist view that endings, as expressions of ideology, can be authoritarian. The experience of their oppressiveness—and, conversely, of their utopian potential—can vary greatly according to gender, class, and race. These determinants, therefore, relativize the absoluteness of closure. An ending's suppression of the Other and its marginalization of rebellious voices can grow more or less obvious over temporal and cultural distance, proving that a drama is, in fact, perpetually unfinished.

Ways of Ending

> The poetry of the beginning and the poetry of the end must have that exquisite finality, perfection which belongs to all that is far off. . . . This completeness, this consummateness [is] conveyed in exquisite form: the perfect symmetry, the rhythm which returns upon itself like a dance where the hands link and loosen and link for the supreme moment of the end. Perfected bygone moments, perfected moments in the glimmering futurity. . . . But there is another kind of poetry: the poetry of that which is at hand: the immediate present. In the immediate present there is no perfection, no consummation, nothing finished. The strands are all flying, quivering, intermingling into the web. . . . There is no round, consummate moon . . . on the face of the unfinished tide.
> —D. H. Lawrence, Introduction to *New Poems*

The dilemma of ending would appear to be the transition from what Lawrence calls "the unfinished tide" to the "perfected moments in the glimmering futurity," from continuity to stasis. To ask where a drama's ending begins is futile, for endings are built into beginnings and middles.[41] The common idea of an ending is the triumph or death of the protagonist, but most dramas do not end at this climactic point, concluding instead with a denouement or coda *after* the tragic or comic climax. Confronting the leap from fiction to reality, most endings, especially those antedating the twentieth century, attempt to provide a "soft landing" for the spectator, blunting the shock of death, suffering, or comic confusion. These "mediated" endings seek to reassure the spectator that what has been shown was indeed unreal, thereby making the audience's reawakening to self-consciousness seem less traumatic. By emphasizing the continuity of human existence, such endings create an environment more familiar (and less complicated) than that of the immediately preceding tragedy or comedy. Many playwrights have considered this transition to be natural in a work of art and, hence, relatively unproblematical, whereas others have attempted for various reasons to portray inconclusiveness at the moment of finality.

The types of endings cataloged below are derived from a sampling of dramas from various cultures and periods, with emphasis on German drama. Since the categories are highly eclectic—encompassing moods, gestures, and attitudes as well as structural, stylistic, and theatrical devices—overlap is unavoidable. Quoting endings in translation, as many of them will be, is like photographing the tip of an iceberg through a filter. Yet incompleteness and distortion do not wholly eliminate a sense of contour and aesthetic effect. Much will remain below the surface until the subsequent chapters, when individual dramas will be examined at greater length.

Since drama is said to originate in ritual, drama's ur-ending would therefore be *celebration*. From the Greeks through Shakespeare and Restoration comedy, it was customary for the entire ensemble to join in celebrating the rebirth of the community after a period of adversity. Comedies typically ended in weddings, insuring the continuation of the social order. The symmetry of pairing off symbolized the total integration of the individual into the community, leaving no antisocial elements unassimilated. In Roman comedy, a bond between players and audience was established through *call-for-applause* endings that implicitly extended the celebration beyond the close of the dramatic fiction, in effect making the theatrical performance itself a theme of the play. The spectator's involvement in these celebrations was not always strictly vicarious: acts of communion even included the sharing of food. By acknowledging the presence of spectators, the cast extended the celebration to them while playfully manipulating them back into self-awareness, flattering them by implying that their reality was, after all, far more substantial than that of the fiction they had just witnessed. Variations of such direct acknowledgments of spectators range from blunt commands such as: "Now you folks—clap!" (Plautus, *Poenulus*)[42] to elaborate Elizabethan epilogues, often written for specific occasions and, therefore, not an integral part of the drama.[43]

The theatrical events of which Greek tragedy was a part normally ended with the revels of the satyr play, yet the choric endings of numerous tragedies were already a form of celebration. Looking back upon misfortune, these endings express a collective spirit of liberation and declare it permanent, prolonging the moment of celebration into an imagined future. The ending of the first extant Greek trilogy (Aeschylus, *The Eumenides*) articulates a fundamental utopian wish: "There shall be peace forever between these people. . . ." Similar expressions of collective relief anticipate a homecoming (Sophocles, *Philoctetes*) or sing a hymn of praise to the deus ex machina who unraveled a conflict too complex for human resolution (Euripides, *Iphigenia in Tauris*). The tradition persists in Shakespeare's histories, which celebrate particular monarchs, their military victories, and the reestablishment of order in the feudal state.

In contrast to such denouements of collective pageantry, the celebration of a *moral* victory in medieval and Renaissance drama at first appears to be anticollectivist in its glorification of an individual's martyrdom. Eulogizing ethical steadfastness as rebellion against oppressive authority, these dramas, in fact, recollectivize their audiences as spiritual communities in opposition to corrupt worldly power. Spiritual salvation may appear imminent: "Soon I shall enter the heavenly abode of the eternal Lord . . ." (Hrotsvitha von Gandersheim, *Dulcitus*); "The Eternal-Feminine / Draws us onward" (Goethe, *Faust*); or it may be achievable through penance: "I'll make a voyage to the Holy Land, / To wash this blood off from my guilty hand . . ." (Shakespeare, *Richard II*). The resolve for individual betterment is extrapolated either explicitly by the author or implicitly by the spectator to society as a whole. Inspirational visions of better worlds climax dramas ranging from German classicism and expressionism to works by contemporary black and third world dramatists.

The victory of moral idealism in the face of adversity can assume operatic proportions (analogous to the intensification of ritual through music), heightening the glorification of heroism in defeat, as in Goethe's *Egmont*.

> EGMONT: . . . Protect your own! To save what you love most, die gladly, as I now set you an example! (*Roll of drums. . . . At the same time the music of a Victory Symphony begins, which concludes the play.*)

The protagonist's final statement in Ibsen's *An Enemy of the People* is a quintessentially classical self-glorification of the individual who upholds humanistic values against corruption and oppression: "the strongest man in the world is he who stands most alone"—as is Berenger's "I'm the last man left. . . . I'm not capitulating!" in Ionesco's *Rhinoceros*. Dramas that hope to inspire revolution employ a similar tech-

nique: "FRANZ (*Eye to eye*): . . . This isn't the end, it's only the beginning!" (Wolf, *The Sailors of Cattaro*). In modern drama, anticipating
liberation can become gender specific; that is, oppression is defined not
as a sociopolitical or metaphysical but as a patriarchal phenomenon. A
well-known protofeminist ending is the sound of a door slamming as
Ibsen's Nora leaves her "doll's house" and her baffled but still hopeful
husband.

Related to the triumph of self-resolve is that of *reconciliation*, of forgiveness and harmony after conflict, which celebrates human relationships and social regeneration. The victory of love and eternal fidelity
dominates popular literature and opera; at the conclusion of Wagner's
Flying Dutchman, for example, the protagonists are literally exalted after
Senta's line: "Here stand I, faithful, yea, till death! (. . . *the transfigured
characters . . . float upward.*)" Enlightened reconciliation in German
drama is epitomized by the "universal embrace" that concludes Lessing's *Nathan the Wise*; some modern variants tend toward understatement.

> WILLY: (*Goes to Martha.*) Now you're back. (*Touches her.*)
> MARTHA: Wash yourself first. You're dirty.
>   (Kroetz, *Cottage-Work*)

The promise of perfection in all such unions is, however, always
limited by what a particular culture considers to be desirable fulfillment. In a materialistic age, a reconciliatory ending might resemble
what Henry James caustically described as "a distribution at the last of
prizes, pensions, husbands, wives, babies, [and] millions. . . ."[44]
During Elizabethan times, the obligatory celebration of restored order
demonstrated that the laws of nature and society still prevailed, yet the
stabilizing denouements of such Shakespearean tragedies as *Hamlet*,
Othello, *King Lear*, and *Macbeth* reveal a loss of substance as well. As Alvin B. Kernan points out,

> it is not the old order that is restored at the end . . . but some
> greatly diminished and more limited thing. . . . The joy, the
> grandeur, the enormous certainty of the earlier world is gone, and
> the rulers who stand at the end of the historical process are usually
> diminished, always more uneasy and uncertain, than those they
> succeed.[45]

The bland secondary figures—Fortinbras, Lodovico, Edgar and Albany, Malcolm—take power in order to establish an undramatic bureaucracy that resembles far more the audience's mundane reality than does the rich world of the departed heroes. Continuity is in the hands of those figures whose emotions are unthreateningly moderate and, hence, do not dwarf the spectator. By enacting and then exorcising fascinating yet forbidden transgressions, Shakespearean tragedy concludes with a vision both utopian and dull.[46]

In ritual, the counterpart to celebration is *lament*. As a public response to an individual's fate, celebration looks toward a better future whereas lament longs for a past prior to the tragedy that is being mourned. Like celebration, lament mediates between the fictional climax and the spectator's reality, demonstrating to the audience the "proper" emotional response to the portrayed events. Lament widens the play's focus from individual tragedy to collective grief, thereby providing a stabilizing context for the experience of intense personal conflict. The contrast itself has dramatic value, as Schiller noted: "Dramas portraying powerful emotions end more beautifully in peace and quiet than in swift turmoil."[47] The lyricism of a spoken lament approximates the music in choric epilogues. Yet mourning as a ritualized pose was not always deemed sufficient for a drama's ending because, as pure emotional expression, it is inadequate as a carrier of meaning. But if it is articulated as a requiem for a departed hero—that is, for unfulfilled ideals—a final lament has a summarizing quality that provides inspiration for the future by underscoring the exemplariness of the fallen. Goethe's *Götz von Berlichingen*, for example, ends with secondary characters mourning the death of the title figure while transmitting a lesson to contemporary audiences: "Noble man! Noble man! Woe to the century that rejected you! / Woe to the coming generations that fail to admire you!" Several of Schiller's major plays conclude with an implied lament-through-contrast, recalling the final lines of his ode, "Nänie": "There is splendor even in this—to be a lament in the mouths of those we loved, / For what has no distinction goes down to Orcus unsung."[48] The loss of the protagonist at the conclusions of *Don Carlos*, *Wallenstein's Death*, and *Mary Stuart* is intensified by the depiction of the moral vacuum that remains (embodied, respectively, by King Philipp, Octavio Piccolomini, and Queen Elizabeth).

Lament is commonly linked to the insight of *resignation*: "Now let the weeping cease; . . . These things are in the hands of God"

(Sophocles, *Oedipus at Colonus*). As a form of closure, reconciliation to fate ranges from serenity to bitterness. Chekhov's "We shall rest!" (the final words of *Uncle Vanya*) are a poignant mixture of lament and optimism, as are "We're free . . . We're free . . . " at the conclusion of Miller's *Death of a Salesman*. Often, all that remains in modern drama is lyrical renunciation: "And so I lie down once again on my back, enjoy the warmth of decay and smile" (Wedekind, *Spring's Awakening*); "Blow out your candles, Laura – and so good-bye" (Williams, *The Glass Menagerie*). Such endings usually articulate a withdrawal from the public to the private sphere – a tendency well represented by "the large, white, broad bed" toward which Kragler is heading at the conclusion of Brecht's *Drums in the Night*. The nuclear age produces more drastic withdrawals, such as the final self-imprisonment of Dürrenmatt's scientists in *The Physicists*.

This ending is, in fact, *dystopian*, an outlook that bewails the futility of human action, the apparent meaninglessness of human existence by projecting a continuity that is unrelievedly malevolent: "Here we are . . . together . . . for ever!" (Pirandello, *Henry IV*). Lavinia exits into a house with nailed shutters at the conclusion of O'Neill's *Mourning Becomes Electra*; Sartre's *No Exit* ends in perpetual mutual torment. The stage direction that concludes Frisch's *When the War Was Over* mourns the breakdown of human communication: "*. . . they look at each other as if over an impassable abyss. Silence.*" The ultimate consequence of lament or resignation is the apocalypse, often combined with a spectacular *coup de theatre*: "I'm burning up! (*The curtain falls among fire, thunder, and lightning*)" (Grabbe, *Don Juan and Faust*). The conclusion of Kaiser's *Gas II* dramatizes the Dies Irae; an immolation ends Frisch's *The Firebugs*. It is questionable, however, whether the psychological effect of dystopian closure is qualitatively different from that evoked by a celebratory ending. If they seem compellingly logical, both can inspire a sense of aesthetic and intellectual fulfillment, as long as their audiences accept their ideological implications. Under these circumstances, the emotional impact even of a downbeat ending can be exhilarating. One might, therefore, conclude that the creation of *any* work of art is an innately positive act that negates whatever negativity its final gestus may contain. Thomas Mann, for example, allowed the narrator of his *Doctor Faustus* to perceive an element of spiritual redemption in the conclusion of Adrian Leverkühn's profoundly melancholy late composition, *Dr. Fausti Weheklag*.

No, this dark tone-poem permits up to the very end no consolation, appeasement, transfiguration. But take our artist paradox:
grant that expressiveness—expression as lament—is the issue of
the whole construction: then may we not parallel it with another,
a religious one, and say too . . . that out of the sheerly irremedia-
ble hope might germinate? It would be but a hope beyond hope-
lessness, the transcendence of despair. . . . For listen to the end,
listen with me: one group of instruments after another retires, and
what remains, as the work fades on the air, is the high G of a cello,
the last word, the last fainting sound, slowly dying in a pianissimo-
fermata. Then nothing more: silence, and night. But that tone
which vibrates in the silence, which is no longer there, to which
only the spirit hearkens, and which was the voice of mourning, is
so no more. It changes its meaning; it abides as a light in the
night.[49]

For Serenus Zeitblom/Thomas Mann, this change of meaning symbolized the redemptive power of humanist beliefs amid the destruction
of World War II. As an aesthetic phenomenon, the cello's G exhibits the
affective power of an intensely focused conclusion. The final note (like
the final word or action of a drama) acquires its impact through contrast
with the silence that follows it—a silence in which the artistic event is
no longer an experience but a memory.

Like a classical symphony, a drama typically prepares the audience
for closure through intensification: the tempo increases, themes are
resurrected and blended, the medium of expression is elevated in anticipation of the resolution of dissonance into consonance, unrest into stability. In Shakespeare's plays, such rounding off occurs even at the end
of individual scenes, in which the rhymed couplet takes the place of the
nonexistent curtain. The couplet's lyric harmony underscores both climax and caesura in the dramatic action. One might say that such endings are characterized by a rhetorical overload—the poetic flourish calls
attention, at times with undisguised irony, to its artistry, to its potential
to gratify aesthetic expectation through a type of geometrical balance.[50]
A similar effect is achieved by incorporating beginnings into endings,
as in the frame narrative of a novel. Most *cyclical* resolutions of this type
evoke the eternally recurring patterns of nature and society. The conclusion of Brecht's *Mother Courage* does both while recalling the opening scene.

Christians, awake! Winter is gone!
The snows depart! Dead men sleep on!
Let all of you who still survive
Get out of bed and look alive![51]

The latent optimism of Brecht's endings links them to resolutions in
Elizabethan drama, with the difference that he celebrates the restoration of disorder, the reestablishment of the subversive power of the *Volk*
in a prerevolutionary milieu. Normally, however, the theme of eternal
recurrence tends to be cloaked in cynicism or resignation in twentieth-
century Continental drama. Examples range from Schnitzler's *La Ronde*
to the plays of Ionesco, Beckett, and Bernhard. In certain works of
Wedekind, tragedy is avoided at the last minute by a sudden reappear-
ance of anarchic self-interest, the law of the jungle. The Marquis von
Keith, for instance, decides not to shoot himself and returns instead to
a Darwinian existence: "Life is a roller coaster" (*The Marquis von Keith*).
In *The Tenor*, Gerardo throws moral responsibility to the winds and
literally steps over a corpse, saying, "I've got to sing 'Tristan' in Brussels
tomorrow." A surprising variety of dramas employ an economical variant of cyclical endings: they evoke their title at the work's close. A sampling: *Everyman*, Cervantes's *The Cave of Salamanca*, Lope de Vega's
Fuente Ovejuna, Ford's *'Tis Pity She's a Whore*, Grillparzer's *A Loyal Servant of his Master*, Nestroy's *Earlier Circumstances*, Wilde's *The Importance
of Being Earnest*, Synge's *The Playboy of the Western World*, O'Neill's *The
Hairy Ape*, Becher's *Winter Battle*, Grass's *Uncle Uncle*, and Albee's *Who's
Afraid of Virginia Woolf?*[52]

We have already noted the summarizing quality of an ending in its
fusion of past, present, and future. By "universalizing" the action, it
adds structural unity and intellectual insight to the cathartic experience. Mimesis thereby converts into a more explicit form of signi-
fication. For this reason, the ending is the moment in the work with the
highest *didactic* potential. By highlighting a drama's "meaning" and
"significance," playwrights seek to assure audiences that what they
have just viewed or read has redeeming social value beyond pure entertainment. Moreover, a didactic or explanatory ending exerts a powerful
control over audience reception; its authoritative voice legitimates not
only the work itself but a particular interpretation of it. (This is, of
course, the primary reason why endings are changed so often.) Since
ancient times, the final lines of drama have been used to enunciate the

moral, often with the ritual formality of a sermon. Referring to Greek
tragedy, Gerd Kremer calls the moralizing ending an "Ecce-ending,"
which he traces back to the lament for the dead.[53] Greek endings attempted to teach wisdom (cf. Sophocles' *Oedipus Rex*, *Antigone*, and
Ajax) or humility: "Many things the gods / Achieve beyond our judgment" (Euripides, *Medea*). Sententious conclusions are common in medieval, Elizabethan, Restoration, baroque, and of course Enlightenment drama. As the latter began to interact with Sentimentalism, its
endings not only prescribed a moral but the appropriate emotional response: "It was not love but the lover's folly that made me unhappy.
Pity me" (Gellert, *The Affectionate Sisters*). A paradigm of this education
of the mind and senses, which Lessing was to call "the transformation
of passion into virtuous proficiency," stands at the conclusion of Lillo's
influential *The London Merchant*.

> With bleeding hearts and weeping eyes we show
> A human gen'rous sense of others' woe,
> Unless we mark what drew their ruin on,
> And, by avoiding that, prevent our own.

Classicism continues the didactic tradition, which in the twentieth century includes, surprisingly enough, Ernst Toller, who ended his
dramas with such homilies as "one must help one another and be good"
(*The Machine-Wreckers*) and "Every day can bring paradise, every night
can bring the deluge" (*Hinkemann*). Brecht's conclusions to plays of the
1930s and 1940s combine didacticism with direct calls for action: "While
changing the world, change yourselves!" (*The Baden Learning Play on
Consent*; other examples include the final verses of *The Exception and the
Rule*, the famous epilogue to *The Good Person of Sezuan*, and the pointed
warning of *The Resistible Rise of Arturo Ui*: "The womb [fascism] is still
fertile, from which that crept!"). In the postwar period, variants of
Brechtian endings appear in political dramas of many nations.

    Premodern drama endings often tended toward the *Gesamtkunst-
werk* in their poetic use of language, structural closure, and employment of music and dance. Equally important was the arrangement of
figures and background into spatial art, namely into a tableau. The
tableau is the freeze-frame of drama that fixes a particular image – and
an interpretation of it – in the mind of the spectator. This does not imply
that all movement ceases, only that no more words are spoken while

the characters perform symbolic acts, usually of reconciliation: *"While all are embracing each other silently, the curtain falls"* (Lessing, *Nathan the Wise*). Hebbel's Meister Anton *"stands wrapped in thought"* to add emphasis to the line, "I no longer understand the world!" (*Maria Magdalene*). At times, playwrights simply specify a tableau without describing it (Wilde, *The Importance of Being Earnest*, Albee, *Who's Afraid of Virginia Woolf?*).[54] Its simplicity has great affective power, which, however, can easily lapse into overstatement: excessive pathos, artificial posing, sentimentality. For better or worse, the tableau's inaction anticipates the stasis of the utopia or dystopia evoked by the ending. Modern drama's dystopian tableaus include O'Neill's *Long Day's Journey into Night*: "*Edmund and Jamie remain motionless*" and most notably Beckett's works: "*Yes, let's go. (They do not move)*" (*Waiting for Godot*); "*Krapp motionless staring before him. The tape runs on in silence*" (*Krapp's Last Tape*).[55] On the other hand, final immobility can have a comic effect, creating, as in Gogol's *The Inspector*, a dumb show of surprise: "*For nearly a minute and a half the group remains in this position.*"

Like celebration and lament, the tableau belongs to the category of endings that mediate between a dramatic climax and the actual "release" of the spectator. In modern drama, however, the sudden reversal of fortune (occurring as the result of chance rather than through the influence of a higher power) may occur nearly simultaneously with recognition, followed by little or no denouement. A shock effect of this sort can be called an *unmediated* ending, wherein the spectator is not "let down easily" but rudely. A comfortable transition to reality is lacking; the shift from anonymous observer to self-conscious individual is abrupt. Moreover, the act of resolution is left to the spectator's imagination. Playwrights with didactic tendencies naturally spurn such endings so as not to leave audiences in a state of mental and emotional ambivalence. Historically, the emergence of the sudden reversal signifies the decline of the premise of rational order, the "home key" into which classical drama traditionally resolved.

Typical of post-Enlightenment dramas is an abrupt reversal from comedy to tragedy; de Musset's *No Trifling with Love* ends when a reconciliation between two lovers is suddenly destroyed by the suicide of another young girl who has been victimized by them. Unexpected tragedy, as a *coup de theatre*, was a favorite device of the Naturalists, who used it to heighten the dramatic impact of their severely mimetic art. In Ibsen's *Ghosts*, *Hedda Gabler*, and *Rosmersholm*, the tragic climax is nearly simultaneous with the fall of the curtain. In *Rosmersholm*, a reconciled couple suddenly falls into a river as an onlooker proclaims: "The dead wife has taken them." *Hedda Gabler*, Chekhov's *The Sea Gull*, and Hauptmann's *The Rats, Drayman Henschel*, and *The Celebration of Peace* end with offstage suicides or announced deaths, leaving the lament to the audience.

Distinguishing between mediated and unmediated endings would appear to be more precise than attempting to contrast "closed" and "open" forms. In Volker Klotz's influential definition, the classical closed form inevitably refers back to itself, whereas the epic open form points beyond itself to a limitless future.[56] Yet various types of classical endings — the celebration, the lament, the didactic ending — more often than not look toward the future and thereby lay claim to universal applicability. The open ending, in contrast, can be quite self-referential, resolving far more than it means to, for "to conclude that there is no solution is also an answer," as Raymond Williams points out.[57] Numerous modern dramas end with overt or implied questions: "But why am I left to live on the earth and to suffer?" (Ostrovsky, *The Thunderstorm*); "Sister, why do we do this?" (Toller, *Mass Man*); "Doesn't anyone answer? Doesn't anyone, anyone answer???" (Borchert, *The Man Outside*). Such questions can be viewed as statements celebrating ambivalence, and audiences that value ambivalence over conclusiveness may experience gratification and reassurance similar to that generated by conventional closure.

On the other hand, closure is sometimes wholly avoided if the audience is to be retained past the end of a single reading or performance, be it a serialized novel, an adventure film, a soap opera, or television miniseries. Concluding with an unresolved dramatic climax to whet the appetite for more, each segment will resort to a *deferred* ending. Similarly, dramas that exist both as separate entities and as parts of a larger whole, such as a trilogy, will moderate the feeling of closure between parts. Closure does occur, however, within segments as a kind of scenic punctuation whenever conflicts are resolved or births, weddings, deaths, and so forth take place. Gratification thus becomes literally intermittent, dispersed (especially in television serials) in carefully calculated amounts to secure maximum viewership and, thereby, to satisfy any controlling material interests. In commercial films, seemingly firmly closed endings are often "reopened" if a sequel gives promise of profit. Thus, sequels to slasher films, for example, invariably find ways to resurrect their apparently vanquished demons.

Up to now, drama endings have been discussed in separate categories, yet closure normally results from a combination of devices and moods. To reinforce finality and intensify an ending's affective power, playwrights often employ *multiple* resolutions. Since ancient times, simultaneous resolutions at various levels of social rank have been utilized for an ideological purpose, namely to transform social stability into a totalizing myth, whose premises can no longer be questioned. In communities that hold master-servant relationships to be immutable, the mirroring of "high" tragic or romantic action on a "low" comic level is common. By reducing somewhat the masters' stature and elevating that of the servants, dramatists strive to humanize both, implying that the bond between them is benevolent, not merely just or necessary.[58] As utopian as the mood of reconciliation may be, the process of achieving it nonetheless contains an element of satire. That is, the affirmation of communal wholeness is rendered more palatable by adding irreverent humor, such as that of Shakespearean clowns or servants in social comedies.

Yet in a denouement, satire need not resolve into celebration, as it did in Greek and Roman comedy. *Parodied* and *ironic* endings are genres unto themselves, enabling a playwright to express mistrust of conventional resolutions, to reintroduce originality where others have relied on formulas. This category, therefore, encompasses all those we have investigated so far, because all endings are capable of being subverted in some way. The prototype of the modernist ending that withholds resolution and satirizes conventional audience expectations is the conclusion to Shakespeare's *Troilus and Cressida*. Most of the main characters remain alive, lovers are not paired off, and the perverse clown, Pandarus, threatens rather than appeases the audience in his sardonic epilogue, an inversion of the call-for-applause ending.

> Some two months hence my will shall here be made. . . .
> Till then I'll sweat and seek about for eases,
> And at that time bequeath you my diseases.

Such parodies are legion, since they enable playwrights to avoid excessive sentimentality, pathos, and implausibility as the curtain falls.

Often the theatrical medium itself is highlighted, as in Lessing's *The Misogynist*, in which the actors reach out for the audience's help, as it were: "LISETTE (*toward the audience*): Please laugh, gentlemen, this comedy is ending like a wedding song!" The tendency of romantic writers to parody self-consciously the genres in which they wrote is well known; Tieck's *Puss-in-Boots* ends with rotten pears and apples being thrown at the author of the play-within-the-play, and, in Grabbe's *Joke, Satire, Irony, and Deeper Meaning*, several characters curse Grabbe himself as he appears bearing a lantern. The parodistic treatment of performance itself appears in many modern variants, as in Pirandello: "The management is grieved to announce that in view of unfortunate incidents which took place at the end of the second act, we shall be unable to continue the performance this evening" (*Each in His Own Way*); in Sartre: "PRINCE: Mr. Kean, you are an ungrateful wretch! KEAN: Ah, sir, what an exit. With your permission, let it be the last word of our play" (*Kean*); and, in Arbuzov,

> VICTOR: But that is another story. . . . This one ends with me standing on the road, looking after her and thinking how dearly I love her.
> CHORUS: Good luck, Victor! (*To audience.*) The end.
> (It Happened in Irkutsk)

Ultimately, of course, such generic self-referentiality can lapse into mannerism, which can in turn be parodied: "*A trap-door may or may not open; or perhaps the stage may or may not slowly collapse . . . according to the technical facilities available*" (Ionesco, *The Future is in Eggs*).

Numerous parodies of endings take aim at the philosophy or mood underlying a particular convention. (To call them "surprise endings" is too vague a term, because even highly formulaic conclusions contain an element of the unknown; conventions, after all, are skeletons that must be fleshed out.) Audience expectations can be confounded through *false closure*, in which an awaited resolution turns out not to be the last word after all. In Giraudoux's *The Trojan War Will Not Take Place*, the curtain begins to fall when peace is in view, but as the action unravels, the curtain rises again, finally to fall when the Trojan War has become unavoidable. Another obvious target for parody is tragic pathos; in Wedekind's *Pandora's Box*, the familiar gestus literally breaks down: "COUNTESS GESCHWITZ: . . . I'm near you! I'll stay near you—forever! (*falls to her elbows*) O damn it!—(*She dies.*)" The contrast between lament and ridicule permeates Bernhard's *A Party for Boris*: "JOHANNA: Boris is dead (. . . *As soon as the good woman is alone with Boris, she breaks out into terrifying laughter.*)" Less malevolent is the laughter that concludes Shaw's *Man and Superman*: "ANN: . . . Go on talking. TANNER: Talking! (*Universal laughter*)"; Stoppard (in *Travesties*) likewise spoofs the age-old tendency to moralize.

> CARR: . . . I learned three things in Zurich during the war. I
> wrote them down. Firstly, you're either a revolutionary or
> you're not, and if you're not you might as well be an artist as any-
> thing else. Secondly, if you can't be an artist, you might as well
> be a revolutionary . . .
>   I forget the third thing.

Contemporary audiences of avant-garde theater tend, in fact, to respond more favorably to ridicule of traditional forms of closure than to the conventions themselves.

Closure that appears to contradict history or that has become implausible resonates with irony. Irony restores perspective to the moment of celebration; it implies continuation after finality by drawing in the spectator as a judge. It can render a conclusion more profound and gratifying when it appeals to an audience's historical knowledge: King Edward's triumph at the conclusion of Shakespeare's *King Henry VI* trilogy, for example, offers the pleasure of superior insight to those spectators who know that the rise of Gloucester (Richard III) was soon to follow. Characters who are blind to history, to social change, or simply to the distinction between good and evil have the last word in such otherwise radically dissimilar dramas as Schiller's *Mary Stuart*, Grabbe's *Hannibal*, Ibsen's *A Doll's House*, Zuckmayer's *The Devil's General*, Dürrenmatt's *The Visit of the Old Lady*, and Weiss's *The Investigation*. By allowing morally deficient characters to dominate the conclusion, playwrights provoke their audiences to join them in denouncing a particular ideology or class. In these cases, the function of irony is explicitly or implicitly didactic.

In numerous drama endings, however, the imputation of irony is debatable, because the signals are ambiguous or contradictory. Plays that sustain a utopian moment along with its simultaneous debunking have, in a sense, one foot in the future and one in the present. Such

ambivalence—often lauded by critics as a major aesthetic achievement—is evident in the works of Molière, Lenz, Kleist, Büchner, and
Sternheim. Moreover, if we take into account the constant evolution of
literary and theatrical conventions, then *all* endings are latently ironic,
containing the seeds of their own subversion. Thus, even intentional
irony can backfire—a phenomenon not restricted to dramatists, as
Shostakovich discovered when *Izvestia* described the audience's reaction at the premiere performance of his *Fifth Symphony*.

> The powerful stirring sounds [of the finale] compel the listener to
> rise. The entire hall stands. It is enveloped in a feeling of joy, a feel-
> ing of happiness: it bubbles through the orchestra like a spring
> breeze. . . . We cannot but believe our Soviet listener. . . . [He]
> is organically unresponsive to decadent, gloomy, pessimistic art.
> [He] responds passionately to everything bright, clear, joyful, op-
> timistic, life affirming.[59]

The composer himself, however, stated in his memoirs:

> I think that it is clear to everyone what happens in the Fifth. . . .
> The rejoicing is forced, created under threat. . . . It's as if some-
> one were beating you with a stick and saying, "Your business is re-
> joicing, your business is rejoicing," and you rise, shaky, and go
> marching off, muttering, "Our business is rejoicing, our business
> is rejoicing."[60]

Shostakovich's image of the spectator-as-robot is an apt introduction to my final category, which is not, in fact, a particular type of ending but an aspect of all endings: *silencing*, or the elimination of alternatives during the act of closure. These alternatives are usually embodied
by dramatic figures who are either cast out of the collective or who are
coerced into thinking that their business is rejoicing or mourning or
simply remaining quiet. Their rebellion against consensus is drowned
out by the din of celebration or lament; they are excluded from the final
spotlight. Taking note of silenced voices raises the question: at what
price is the final gestus of affirmation, provocation, didacticism, or ambivalence achieved?[61] Denouements in any case tend to destroy the individuality of dramatic figures because they eliminate uniqueness;
reconciliation scenes of many dramas often read like extended mono-

logues, because they are, in fact, based on ritual. In societies with a strong moral consensus, the ritual of reunion and the suppression of nonconformism is unproblematic, but once the ethical foundation shifts, the justness of closure becomes suspect. Feudal drama, for obvious reasons, contains little or no self-reflection about its social judgments. Enlightenment drama contains the growing awareness that an enormous amount of manipulation is required just to get the vision of universal harmony into focus. The inspiring conclusion of Lessing's *Nathan the Wise* is a famous example of a patchwork resolution verging on the ludicrously improbable. Less known is the strained ending of his early work, *The Jews*, in which he dramatized a theme that could not be realistically resolved within the social environment of its time. "The Traveler," an incognito Jew, has performed great services for a baron, who offers him his daughter in marriage. The traveler reveals his religion, and the baron reacts in horror: "A Jew? O cruel fate!" But his daughter innocently responds with a question that presumes a spirit of tolerance incommensurable with the realities of Lessing's age: "Oh, what does that matter?" Lisette, her worldly maidservant, silences her with: "Shh! Miss, shh! I'll tell you later what that matters." The daughter says not another word for the rest of the play; in effect, she ceases to exist. The baron and the Jew struggle toward an awkward reconciliation, their anaphoric moralizing at the end of the penultimate scene sounding like condemnation rather than praise.

> THE BARON: . . . O how estimable the Jews would be, if they
> were all like you!
> THE TRAVELER: And how amiable the Christians, if they all pos-
> sessed your qualities!

The final scene — resolution on a lower social level — finds Lisette trying to probe into the background of the Jew's servant, and the play concludes with *her* silencing.

> CHRISTOPH: That's too nosy a question for a chambermaid to
> ask! Just come along! (*He takes her by the arm, and they exit.*)

From the late Enlightenment onward, numerous German playwrights become ever more self-conscious about suppressing voices to achieve a harmonious ending. The silencing of Thoas in

Goethe's *Iphigenie*, the sudden bewilderment of Alkmene in Kleist's *Amphitryon* and of the title figure in his *Prinz Friedrich von Homburg* reveal increasing ambivalence toward conventional closure. In twentieth-century drama, such suppression is no longer merely implied but transformed into a theme; numerous endings demonstrate that the restoration of order actually depends on the marginalization of the traditionally powerless: women, lower classes, other races or nationalities, socially unacceptable individuals. At its conclusion, the modern German *Volksstück* often spotlights the ironic contrast between the triumph of male dominance and the violence that brings it about. Horváth's *Stories from the Vienna Woods* ends with Marianne's exhausted capitulation to her disagreeable admirer.

> MARIANNE: I can't go on any longer. I just can't go on—
> OSKAR: Then come with me—.[62]

In Kroetz's adaptation of Hebbel's *Maria Magdalena*, Marie is deprived even of the pathos of her imminent death.

> MARIE: So that you know: I poisoned myself. . . .
> PETER: First you gotta be dead, then we'll believe it! . . . Get a
>   beer, that's more sensible. (*Pause.*)
> MARIE: Yes. (*Exit.*)[63]

Surely one of the most powerful thematic treatments of silencing in modern drama occurs at the end of Lorca's *The House of Bernarda Alba*: Bernarda's daughter has killed herself, thinking that her lover has been shot. Bernarda proclaims:

> We'll drown ourselves in a sea of mourning. She, the youngest
> daughter of Bernarda Alba, died a virgin. Did you hear me? Silence, silence I said. Silence!

But silencing need not invariably represent the imposition of a collective consensus upon the individual. At the conclusion of Monteverdi's opera, *The Coronation of Poppea*, the allegorical figure of Love triumphs over Virtue and Fortune, highlighting the lovers Nero and Poppea and silencing the society that surrounds them. The social legitimacy of the Empress Octavia has been erased by her unethical behavior, allowing Nero to dispose of his opponents and to crown his courtesan, Poppea, in her place. Amorality wins out over immorality, and its victory is neither mediated nor placed into a recognizable context through collective celebration. Instead, the lovers sing a duet, and they end the opera with a perfect musical evocation of harmony: a unison note. This ending is truly absolute: two become one, and there is no Other.

Ways of Talking about Endings

> Always historicize!
> —"Slogan" quoted by Fredric Jameson, *The Political Unconscious*

Are there good and bad endings? Surely one can try to establish criteria by which to measure their quality, yet, as with all value judgments, the outcome will tell us at least as much about the critic as about the objects being evaluated. For example, a critic may label a resolution "unsuccessful" because it is perceived to be overly explicit. This judgment may claim to derive from immutable aesthetic criteria. Its purpose in appealing to a so-called higher law of form is to stigmatize content as being transitory and quotidian, thereby elevating the work (and the critic's interpretation of it) to a transcendent plane. But by denying that aesthetic standards are linked to a particular culture and are, hence, relative, the critic's judgment fails to anticipate its own obsolescence. Instead of transcending content, the critic merely ends up denouncing it— implicitly rather than explicitly.

Older generations of critics tended to be less self-conscious about linking ideology and art than are their modern counterparts. We recall that Gustav Freytag considered a good, final catastrophe to be a reflection of certain cultural and national values. When Reinhold Schneider denounced Hauptmann's *Beaver Coat*, he presumed a natural correspondence among forms of aesthetic, moral, and judicial order. "*The Beaver Coat* is, as a glorification of the thief and a derision of justice, destructively revolutionary; the play's construction documents a peculiar human and artistic weakness in its great creator . . . the course of law within a drama must come to a proper end."[64] His polemic is based on the correct perception that a drama's form and content combine to legitimize certain social attitudes, and, hence, the fronts are clearly drawn: the conservative Schneider denounces what he perceives to be a subversive play. Although a drama's legitimation function varies with its changing context and is thus difficult to pin down, denying the existence of such a function reinforces the familiar "creative-process mystique" that obscures literature's social embeddedness. The appreciation of drama then becomes expressible only in essentialist categories of feeling that make it difficult to differentiate one's aesthetic response from that of the proverbial concentration camp guard who weeps over a Beethoven symphony after performing unspeakably inhumane acts.[65] By placing a drama's impact into its historical context (synchronically by analyzing the role of drama and theater in a particular community, diachronically by surveying its theatrical and critical reception), its subversive and affirmative potential can be clarified.

Designations such as "unsuccessful" or "gratifying" closure are, indeed, hardly more subjective than such apparently neutral concepts as "clarity" or "tragedy." The latter are commonly invested with objective validity, although they too are culture-bound rhetorical devices of ever-shifting significance. The critic who makes them into absolute terms is, in fact, documenting his or her cultural bias. One might say that accepting any such term as a universal standard is equivalent to the exclusionary process inherent in a drama's ending: when a particular theme, gestus, or character is spotlighted, alternatives are discredited, process becomes abstraction, meaning is totalized, the part becomes the whole, and everything else remains in the dark. Raymond Williams points out that an idea such as tragedy, "which is now temporarily dominant" in Western culture, is magnified to be "at once historical and absolute." Even death, he maintains, is not value-free in its portrayal and reception: "To tie any meaning to death is to give it a powerful emotional charge which can at times obliterate all other experience in its range. Death is universal, and the meaning tied to it quickly claims universality, as it were in its shadow."[66] In any particular culture, the representation of reconciliation, tragedy, and other forms of resolution is shaped by the way that culture prioritizes human experience. Modern Western art stresses the primacy of the individual; this focus, itself a historical phenomenon, both highlights and excludes. The ennoblement of the bourgeois subject overshadows the concept of social class; "free will" casts the idea of "collectivity" into the shadows. In socialist and in non-Western societies, the emphasis is usually reversed.

Understanding how experience is prioritized helps one grasp the signifying and affective potential of cathartic endings. Too often employed in a manner that reduces audience response to a few formulas, the term *catharsis* becomes historically meaningful when one asks: under what hierarchy of values is it subsumed? Is it directed toward empathy with the Passion of Christ? Is it a path toward Enlightenment morality? Is it a release from existentialist terror? Is it the emotional gratification offered by mass entertainment? The ultimate effect of the cathartic experience is usually revealed at a drama's conclusion; here a drama most obviously reveals its functional purpose and betrays its ideology. As the conclusion to a symbolic enactment of social antagonisms, an ending situates the drama within a prevailing dialectic of order and anarchy.[67] This ideological opposition occurs within the coordinates of class, gender, and race that affect a drama's creation as much as its reception.[68] Dramatic conflict is mediated by genre; that is, certain generic codes or "predisposed continuities" (such as the prevailing concepts of tragedy or comedy) that anticipate particular resolutions (social messages about rewarding virtue, punishing evil, restoring order, etc.) create guidelines for interpreting a particular dramatic action.[69] The dramatic text evokes these generic expectations, and the work's momentum is sustained by the suspense about whether familiar norms will be upheld or whether a writer will attempt to delegitimate a particular tradition by "writing beyond the [conventional] ending."[70] No matter how abstract or "timeless" a play may appear to be, its ending inevitably represents an engagement with topical moral and political issues—if only by obvious evasion. How a drama ends thus reveals its author's ideological allegiances.

An objective investigation of closure (inasmuch as that is possible) must, therefore, avoid overvaluing a particular form of it in order not to shoulder uncritically the philosophical and political baggage of that form. Yet ideological criticism alone is insufficient; dramatic affect and meaning interact in complex, compelling ways, and the quality of this interaction must somehow be reproduced in a critical discussion of dramas. Raymond Williams suggests an approach.

> If we are asked to believe that all literature is "ideology," in the crude sense that its dominant intention (and then our only response) is the communication or imposition of "social" or "political" meanings and values, we can only, in the end, turn away. If we are asked to believe that all literature is "aesthetic," in the crude sense that its dominant intention (and then our only response) is

the beauty of language or form, we may stay a little longer but will
still in the end turn away. Some people will lurch from one position
to the other. More, in practice, will retreat to an indifferent ac-
knowledgement of complexity, or assert the autonomy of their
own (usually consensual) response.

But it is really much simpler to face the facts of the range of intentions and effects, and to face it *as a range*.[71]

Critical distance thus requires maintaining a sensibility for the power
and historical significance of both conventional and anticonventional
closure, however that may be defined in a particular age.

Endings sustain a tension between utopia and reality, occupying
the space "between the two shores of the 'not yet' and the 'not *that*.' "[72]
They embody the simultaneity of need and difficulty, of affirmation and
negation, of capitulation and provocation. To allow such binary oppo-
sitions to have the last word, however, is, as Williams indicates, to erect
a monument to ambivalence. As appealing as this may be to certain critical schools, it would betray the singularity and intensity of the real
struggles lurking in a drama's fabric. The task of the critic must, therefore, be to sustain an ending's multitude of significations, unmasking
its power to legitimate dominant interests while delineating its utopian
potential to anticipate a resolution of conflict unrealizable under present circumstances.[73] To affirm, as did Bloch, that "the stupid drive to
a good end can become a clever one, passive belief a knowledgeable
and summoning one,"[74] namely as a "motor of history," is to comprehend the unceasing and immeasurable power of an ending.

Prologue 2

Declining confidence in closure is often said to signify an ideological crisis. In post-Enlightenment culture, conventional forms indeed tend to
disintegrate and overlap, a sense of openness and even irresoluteness
prevails. Sociocultural analogies are legion: in late eighteenth-century
Germany, for example, harmonious resolution in art was losing credibility as ever more radical critiques of Enlightenment rationality, once
itself a subversive force, appeared on the scene. The more that rationality was perceived to be evolving from an agent of antifeudal democrati-
zation to a servant of mercantile interests that reduced nature and society to an instrumental status, the more writers, composers, and artists

adopted themes such as disorder and wildness in their works. To be sure, having transgressed into antisocial proclivities such as passion, violence, and excessive self-interest, they tended to draw back to tame the anarchic impulses they had aroused.[75] In the temporal arts, the conciliatory gesture toward the forces of order tended to come last; it is symptomatic that Beethoven went to almost grotesque lengths to hammer home closure in the final measures of his gargantuan provocation, the Fifth Symphony.

This cultural context represents the starting point for the subsequent essays on German drama endings. Were I to attempt at this point a comprehensive historical survey of drama endings from ancient Greece to the present, or, less ambitiously, from Lessing to Heiner Müller, the method and structure of analysis would contradict the premises of uniqueness and interdisciplinarity outlined earlier in this chapter. A conventional historical survey, as useful as it might be, would apply closure to the evolution of closure in drama. I can, therefore, offer no systematic overview; the essays to come are meant as core samples from different parts of the landscape. I have limited myself to German drama because I am most familiar with this terrain. However, the analyses of German dramas are not meant to be exclusively content oriented; they hope to function as models for the analysis of drama per se. Although German drama has the reputation of being more fixated than that of other nationalities on what might generally be called a social component, I believe that the interplay of dramatic convention and innovation, the institutional factors that affect the publication and production of dramas, and the resonances between a specific text and concerns of class, race, and gender are to be found in all dramas and their endings, in various forms of disguise. In my case, the techniques to address these issues evolved from the subject matter, which is why the essays vary widely in their format. I offer a brief preview.

In Germany, revolution was, from the start, a cultural rather than a political project. The notion of rebellion against authority could be played out only in the private sphere. For a protagonist facing self-destruction, the most familiar recourse was to affirm it; the baroque legacy of martyrdom extends to the outset of the Sturm und Drang (Gerstenberg's *Ugolino*), as well as to classicist revisionism of the Sturm und Drang (Goethe's second version of *Stella*). But as self-idealization began to lose its footing, conventional endings, both comic and tragic, became unstable and ambivalent (*Stella*, original version; all the major plays of Lenz). To be sure, not every altered ending of the period reflected artistic uncertainty; at times, opportunism resolved the conflict between the Sturm und Drang playwrights' progressive social philosophy and conservative theater praxis (Wagner's *The Child-Murderess*). Much later, another ambitious playwright discovered an effective way to mediate between popular taste and social reform by merging the avant-garde tendencies of naturalism with the sentimentalism of melodrama (Hauptmann's *The Weavers*).

As cultural paradigms changed, an ending's legitimation of hierarchical order became increasingly problematic in terms of gender as well as class standing. That is, the presence or absence of women in the final spotlight no longer simply affirmed their "natural" subordinate role, but, in ways often unclear to the playwrights themselves, women tended to undermine the premises of rationalist thought and structure (Lenz). Eventually they seemed to take command of the pauses and gaps of history (Büchner's *Danton's Death*). When they functioned as producers rather than objects of art, they were obliged to cope with male-dominated cultural institutions and, as female playwrights, with a genre that seemed by nature peculiarly male (Fleisser's *Soldiers in In-golstadt*).

To clarify an ending's impact, it helps to ask *why* a drama ends when it does, rather than earlier or later. In several of the essays, I will consider alternative conclusions: those actually created and at some point rejected by a playwright (as documented by drafts and editions), as well as hypothetical alternatives suggested by the dramatic action. A drama's performance history, if it is extensive, increases the options exponentially. The transformation of an ending reveals playwrights in conflict with their own past, literary and theatrical epochs in opposition to previous trends. Furthermore, the essays are linked methodologically by the attempt to explore yet another simultaneity in an ending: the coexistence of emotional impact and critical distance.[76] The ideal of my interpretative discourse is to give equal weight to a dramatic text's synchronic and diachronic character—that is, to its affective potential as well as its historicity. At the root of this desired synthesis lies the Brechtian imperative to penetrate through signifiers back to the signified: critical distance, after all, clarifies emotional response, which nurtures a commitment to drama's humanistic messages.

Chapter 2

Altered Endings

Introduction: The Sturm und Drang

The prisons, asylums, hospitals, and workhouses of eighteenth-century Europe contained, often in indiscriminate proximity, social offenders and the socially offensive: political dissenters, victims of feudal intrigue, criminals, the insane, vagabonds, and the poor. As heterogeneous as the clientele were the motives for their incarceration. By isolating, sterilizing, and otherwise reducing undesirables to silence, society maintained its stability, guarding itself "against the subterranean danger of unreason, that threatening space of an absolute freedom,"[1] attempting to demonstrate by negative example that submission to authority served the best interests of the commonweal. As the century progressed, ever more sophisticated means were found to disalienate the nonconformist. Prisoners were subjected to forced labor not primarily to increase overall economic productivity, but to compel them to "submit [their] liberty to laws that are those of both morality and reality,"[2] to experience the legitimacy of the work ethic and thereby learn to affirm it. Conversely, the punitive aspects of imprisonment were occasionally diminished in order to induce the confined to become their own captors. Through gentle, parental reasoning they were encouraged to acknowledge their moral culpability, to internalize their stigma and their punishment.[3]

Voluntary suppression of one's rebellious instincts was by no means limited to the confined, however; it characterized the self-controlling, self-punitive ethos dominant within the German middle classes. This social stratum encompassed a vast diversity of professions, living standards, levels of education, attitudes, and life-styles, whose common denominator was simply that its members were not of the aristocracy nor of the peasantry. Locked within the feudal hierarchy, the middle classes nonetheless harbored liberalizing forces that eventually evolved into the truly class-conscious industrial bourgeoisie and proletariat of the nineteenth century. During the eighteenth century, however, feudal hegemony continued to sustain itself by what might be called the fundamental repression of the era: while expanding middle-class capitalism was furthering individual autonomy and self-confidence, especially in the cultural sphere, society's productive forces remained politically and intellectually disenfranchised. While the state depended upon the economic expertise of middle-class businessmen and granted them considerable freedom to exercise it, their judgment was inhibited, at least legally, in governmental matters.[4] In decentralized Germany, moreover, there was no definable national goal that could have drawn the heterogeneous subclasses more closely together.

Within the sphere of commerce, the middle-class citizen (here almost invariably male) cultivated a domain in which he could exert a modicum of control and promote his interests. His ultimate refuge from the state apparatus lay within the intimacy of his family. Here, the otherwise disenfranchised could give voice to grievances without the danger of retaliation and could be esteemed as an individual, not just as a producer or owner of goods. Familial respect and love offered a substitute for the unattainable "representative" stature of the nobleman. Within the family, one could nourish at least the illusion of self-sufficiency, of personality development within an autonomous sphere. Governed by a protective, compensatory morality, the family believed itself to be preserving humanistic values independent of regulative mechanisms. Thus it could foster, as a self-justifying ideal, the concept of an apolitical, egalitarian "Mensch," which it hoped would reform the immorality of the public sphere.[5]

Yet this tendency toward self-idealization masked a significant truth: while proclaiming its independence from the marketplace, the family was, in fact, its agent. Paternal authority merely reflected the authority structures of society as a whole.[6] Since the family was a training ground for survival outside itself, it acted as a civilizing influence, raising its younger members to assimilate themselves to the logic of organized productivity. In the middle-class family of eighteenth-century Germany, submission to authority was ingrained at an early age; moral and religious teachings stressed the virtues of puritanic self-denial and polemicized against counterproductive idleness. The bonds of love and mutual dependence were consciously emphasized to stabilize and

regulate the family structure, to provide acceptable outlets for suppressed emotion. Historically, the family's legitimation mechanisms
derived from both enlightened rationalism and the cult of feeling,
originating in Pietism and English and French sentimentality.[7]

Not until the Sturm und Drang era was attention called to the latent antagonisms beneath the veneer of middle-class familial harmony.[8] Particularly the Sturm und Drang dramatists began to confront
the traditional rationalization of strict parental authority with an exposé
of the repressive mechanisms by which it operated. They questioned
whether the interests of the individual family member inevitably cor-
responded to those presupposed for the family unit. An autocratic decision to subordinate the family to the assumed needs of society could
conflict irreconcilably with the emotional needs of its members.[9] In
short, the family in Sturm und Drang drama was more often than not
hopelessly caught in the intolerable ambivalence of its several roles.
Parents were shown dealing unjustly with their sons and daughters
while continuing to insist on their right to respect and affection.[10] Such
pressures intensified, often with fatal consequences, the innate emotional ambivalence that characterizes authority relationships: fear,
reverence, admiration, love, and hatred.[11] The dramatists also described ominous perversions of initially positive impulses, for example, the rational maintenance of order often turned to excess, beyond
the requirements of social interaction. Blind adherence to religious or
moral precepts impeded the recognition of weakness or failure within
the family or society. Thus transformed into an absolute, authority lost
its substance, becoming a ritualized means of subordination, often to
the point of tyranny.

The central figures of Sturm und Drang drama are characteristically trapped between inbred affirmation of authority and rebellion
against it, especially when it has ceased to fulfill its proper functions.
A father's weakness creates irresolvable contradictions and antagonisms; as the family attempts to come to terms with the *pater abscon-
ditus*, it goes violently to pieces. Beyond the private sphere, the family's
disintegration symbolizes an imperfection within society, and by impli-
cation, within the universe. Sturm und Drang protagonists, therefore,
suffer from multiple alienation: rejection of a puritanical work ethos,
institutionalized morality, bureaucratic anonymity, bourgeois right-
eousness, and vapid sentimentality, awareness of class distinctions
and, hence, of one's own political impotence. But fundamentally their

alienation derives from lack of contact with creative forces that have, or give promise of having, a visible social effect.[12] Suppressed desires produce frustration and inhibition; the need to cope with coercion generates various forms of sublimation. Consequently, the restraints upon their desire to improve their situation and realize their creative potential became internal as well as external, imaginary as well as real. As these psychoneurotic figures rebel against confinement, challenging the presumed sanity of rational order, they reveal ingrained inhibitions within themselves that are far more difficult to overcome. These tendencies are observable as well in the biographies of the dramas' authors; alienated subjectivity and internalized confinement were a part of the common life experience of Sturm und Drang writers. Rather than being merely an avocation of the cultured elite, writing became a psychological necessity.[13] Sturm und Drang works thus both *are* symptoms and *contain* symptoms of social maladjustment.

Under these circumstances, the resolution of conflict in life and art was obviously a formidable challenge. Whereas an older generation was still able to maintain its belief in enlightened reconciliation— Lessing's heroic attempt in *Nathan the Wise* to fuse warring religions in a universal embrace appeared after the Sturm und Drang had run its course—the younger authors sought alternatives to the conventional affirmations of order that contradicted their perceptions of social reality. Literary endings thus became tentative, overtly or implicitly self-refuting, ephemeral. The plays I will discuss have been selected to illustrate the diverse ways that Sturm und Drang authors coped with having to create finite conclusions to problems that, unlike Oedipus's Sphinx, would not disappear after they were identified.

Gerstenberg's *Ugolino*

Since closure had become infected by insecurity, a change in Weltanschauung or artistic motivation could readily impel a Sturm und Drang author to revise an ending. Such altered perceptions manifested themselves sometimes after several weeks, sometimes after decades. Our first example, Heinrich Wilhelm von Gerstenberg's *Ugolino* (1768), falls into both categories. The history of Count Ugolino della Gheradesca is material suitable for a High Baroque tragedy: a widely admired nobleman grew ambitious for dictatorial power and was brought to fall partly through his own intrigues. His villainy was equal to that of his archenemy, Archbishop Ruggieri degli Ubaldini, at least according to Dante, who consigned them both to the Ninth Circle of Hell, imprisoned for eternity in the frozen sea of Cocytus. Their courtly conspiracies doubtless held dramatic potential,[14] yet Gerstenberg relegated it to the exposition of his groundbreaking drama, which depicts instead Ugolino's final earthly confinement in a tower, narrated in canto 33 of Dante's *Inferno*. The drama's laconic preface announces: "The story of this drama is known from Dante," hence the familiarity of Gerstenberg's theme precluded the possibility of suspense. This earliest of Sturm und Drang dramas is remarkable because it is a work in which essentially nothing happens. In Aristotelian terms, the entire play is a denouement, a drama not of action but of reaction to a catastrophe that has already occurred. Although martyrdom was a common theme in Baroque and early Enlightenment tragedy, Gerstenberg's twentieth "Letter about Noteworthy Aspects of Literature" indicates that his intentions pointed in a different direction. He maintains that the substance of literature is not only a fusion of action and emotion but that each element may exist separately, "action without emotion, and emotion without action."[15] The latter, emotion derived from character,[16] is the essence of *Ugolino*. Klopstock's influence is evident here, especially of his dramatized lyrical requiem, *The Death of Adam*, with which *Ugolino* is often compared. For Gerstenberg, the basis of truth and nature lay in human passions arising from the heart or soul.[17] Although he lamented that "psychology cannot yet penetrate beneath the surface of the soul . . . since we grope in the blindest ignorance to discover [its] inner mechanism" (45), he insisted that poetic genius is measured by the ability to "fathom the essence of *every* object according to its smallest distinctive features" (18). Human nature reproduced with exactitude was, however, not simply to be documented but to be endowed by the poet with "a new intensity" (31, 58) in order to produce a powerful affective stimulus in the observer. Like Klopstock, he considered the ultimate object of literature to be not the moral education of the enlightened citizen but the arousal and agitation of emotion, the creation of a bond of sentiment between writer and audience. As a consequence, his many literary reviews and his Shakespeare interpretations inevitably subordinated action to character. Anticipating *Ugolino*, he claimed in his "Letters" that Shakespeare's dramatization in *King Lear* of "decline and . . . destruction of the human spirit" moves a British audience to pity and terror (34). Indeed, he was aware that an accurate representation of extreme emotions could produce experiences intolerable to conventional eighteenth-century sensibilities: "a misfortune perceived in its totality, as insignificant as it may be, will usually cause both the observer and the victim to consider it excessively severe."[18] Yet he maintained "that it is sometimes good to let the spectator who views his fellow man's misfortune suffer a bit more intensely than merely for pleasure."[19] As we shall see, contemporary reaction to *Ugolino* confirms that the drama transgressed beyond conventional codes of feeling and subsequently broadened them. The play's verbalization of forbidden rebellious passions within the family enabled later Sturm und Drang writers to portray yet more destructive familial conflicts.

Ugolino disqualifies itself as a historical drama because of its exclusive focus on the intimate sphere of the family. Severed from their aristocratic milieu, Ugolino and his three sons, who have been imprisoned with him, appear as private persons dominated by physical and emotional needs. Whereas silence reigns in Dante's Tower of Hunger,[20] Gerstenberg's figures are volubly sentimental, "striving for virtue, full of feeling, even luxuriating in feeling," concealing their antagonisms "in sentimental and mournful tears," preoccupied not with affairs of state but with intimate human relationships; their fate is calculated to evoke "tears of compassion." These phrases are not excerpted from critical commentary on Gerstenberg's play but from definitions of the German middle-class tragedy.[21] This genre is never mentioned in conjunction with *Ugolino*, most likely because of the noble standing of its characters. Yet as Karl S. Guthke and Peter Szondi have emphasized, the predominance of aristocrats in numerous eighteenth-century tragedies neither contradicts the dramas' middle-class ideology nor its function. The figures in Lessing's epoch-making *Miss Sara Sampson* and Diderot's *Le père de famille* derive, after all, from English and French nobility, and, as an extreme example, the hero of "A Middle-Class Tragedy in Four Acts" (published in 1793) is none other than Louis XVI. Its preface indicates that the genre is determined not by the presence of middle-class figures but by its middle-class perspective: "Ludwig was endowed with all the traits of a kindly private individual. He was a faithful husband, a good father, an honest friend. . . ."[22] Inner worth, the wholesomeness of the self-contained family, a humanitarian morality: this ethical basis defines the middle-class tragedy, no matter how it may be disguised. The high-born figures served to intensify the dramatic impact upon a middle-class audience, which could savor in them the literal ennoblement of its lifestyle and attitudes.[23]

Granted, Ugolino is an aristocrat imprisoned by an aristocrat and he retains traits of baroque stoic heroism. Nevertheless, Gerstenberg's acutely differentiated study of the psychological impact of confinement and imminent starvation highlights with drastic intensity the inner state and most intimate relationships of the private individual. His characters display a remarkable variety of sublimation strategies to preserve their rational and emotional equilibrium.[24] The play's five acts teem with assertions of self-denial; Ugolino and his sons are breathtakingly skilled at internalizing real or imagined guilt and radiating forgiveness with indiscriminate generosity. As their fear and hunger increase, their reassurances that family ties have not weakened in adversity become more strident. The children show that the need for a strong authority figure grows in direct proportion to one's inability to alter one's situation. But the sentiment turns out to be anachronistic if authority has already lost its potency. Submission thus becomes a perceptual distortion; suffering is not traced logically to its source, for the sons would then see the unbearable truth of Ugolino's culpability in their victimization. Prohibition of conflict within this thinly veiled middle-class family is based on the conviction that one's relatives are innately virtuous. Latent hostility, however justified it may be, is masochistically redirected toward the self. In Ugolino and his sons, self-deprecation coexists with profuse admiration of qualities one does not possess. Inspired by Dante, Gerstenberg extends this tendency to its limit when, toward the end of the drama, the second son, Anselmo, offers his own flesh to his starving father. The subservience manifest in this willingness of the young to sacrifice themselves for the old is a perversion of natural law, and it is a stark refutation of enlightened rationalism.

Resigned to inactivity, the Gheradescas sustain themselves with idyllic and heroic fantasies as hyperbolic as their suppressed despair.[25] Their heroic rhetoric, contrasting ironically with bitter reality, evokes an analogy to a politically weak and fragmented social class's utterances that glorify thoughts and actions in order to obscure their basic ineffectuality. That Ugolino is meant to be viewed primarily as a middle-class paterfamilias is evident in his self-castigating monologue in act 4. He is concerned neither with the collective welfare of his former subjects nor with the trappings of power, but instead with the lost bliss of conjugal love and the heartwarming sanctuary of the family. Having destroyed this spiritual base is worse than the most excruciating martyrdom (which Ugolino describes in pathological detail).

The characters' intense suffering alternates with soothing emotional releases induced by singing, copious weeping, and highly sentimental dialogue. When anger has run its therapeutic course and dissolves into tears, the individual emerges from isolated subjectivity to reintegrate himself into the family's spiritual community. But sublimation is nowhere as pervasive as in the immoderate tone of the dialogue itself; the Gheradescas's declamatory fervor is clearly a product of their situation. Emotional intensity functions as the linguistic correlative of suffering. Their sentimental pathos aestheticizes and makes bearable the gruesome reality of confinement. In other words, their only means of escape lies in language – a bitter irony in their situation, because the words that sustain them are all too transient and devoid of substance. Language is nevertheless to be treasured as an antidote to apathy, and it is to be used precisely; at one point, for instance, the youngest son, Gaddo, of all people, pauses to consider whether "clattering" or "rolling" best describes the sound of pebbles on a roof. *Ugolino*'s dramatic dialogue thereby displays a rationality characteristic of even the most turbulent Sturm und Drang dramas: passion is reined in by self-conscious reflection. Even hyperbolic effusions about cosmic disorder turn out to be rationalizations – stabilizing mechanisms through which the speaker comes to terms with his emotions by verbalizing them and, at times, deliberately holding them at arm's length.[26] "I fear our father's silence," says Francesco in the last act, for silence means that compensatory devices have failed and reason has lost its grip. The result is despair or violence.

In its various forms, sentimentality suppresses conflict or transfers it to an acceptable object. As such it was historically symptomatic of middle-class resignation and inhibition – in Szondi's memorable phrase, "sentimentality is the veil of tears over the middle-class family."[27] Self-generated feeling substituted for constructive action; the conversion of suffering into a virtue compensated for the difficulty of finding pleasure in meaningful activity. To the extent that sentimentality promoted social cohesion, it affirmed existing authority structures.

But in Gerstenberg's era, it was beginning to acquire another dimension: as it tended toward anarchic passion, it became socially subversive, a provocation of the established order.[28] In *Ugolino*, it appears in its double visage. Gerstenberg's psychological realism, charting the emotional trajectory from hope to despair, penetrated beyond the "civilized middle-class tears" of sentimental drama to the "cry of nature"[29]—in this case emanating from the struggle for survival. He dared even to venture into the grotesque, creating extreme effects that teeter on the edge of the comic or tasteless.[30] *Ugolino*'s intended impact, therefore, diverges from Lessing's humanitarian concept of fear to resurrect the elemental meaning of Aristotle's *phobos*. The drama is thus an early symptom of rational order crumbling into psychoneurotic disarray. Incarceration is no longer represented as allegory nor as righteous punishment but as physical and emotional torment. Cruelty is directed not against an enemy but against oneself and one's relations. Although the social context remains wholly symbolic, the Gheradescas in extremis embody a bourgeois nightmare, a threat to bourgeois complacency more immediate than that of actual confinement: the family, heretofore glorified as an idyllic refuge, could itself be a prison. The phobia it breeds is claustrophobia. The antagonisms brought to light in Gerstenberg's *ecce familia!* arise when natural covenants are not permitted to develop naturally.

From the start, *Ugolino* is a drama with a predetermined ending: the protagonists' death by starvation. Of course, this foreknowledge does not preclude suspense, as the spectator tries to predict the intended meaning of the representation: in what way will its final gestus reflect upon the human condition? As the drama draws to a close and any hope of escape has been ruled out, Gerstenberg anticipates several possible resolutions for Ugolino: despair, suicide, or heroic defiance of death. After Francesco dies of poison and Gaddo of hunger, Ugolino becomes crazed and strikes down Anselmo, believing him to be his enemy Ruggieri. Ugolino calms himself with his lute, upon which, as a stage direction indicates, *"gentle, mournful music is heard."* Here, realism gives way to operatic intensification of an internal state, preparing the audience for a climax. Ugolino recognizes Anselmo and throws himself down next to him. Anselmo dies quoting a passage from Klopstock about salvation, and the stage is set for Ugolino's final monologue. He contemplates suicide, which evokes the image—

preestablished by Dante—of himself and Ruggiero locked in eternal animosity in the afterlife. He then adopts *"a noble pose,"* the music *"ends sublimely,"*[31] and he concludes:

> I'll gird my loins like a man. I'm lifting my eyes to the Lord. My ravaged soul is healed. With you, hand in hand, you nearly redeemed one! (*Embracing Anselmo.*) And then praise be to those, who cast down this body to decay. I've nearly reached my goal!

He thereby fulfills the dying Francesco's expectation that "if he [Ugolino] can preserve his spirit until the end, he will be the greatest mortal on earth . . ." (55). His inner triumph over adversity, however, would seem to blunt the impact of Gerstenberg's psychological realism, either casting the drama backward into the genre of the baroque tragedy, reaffirming Christian values in a celebration of martyrdom, or forward as an anticipation of the classicistic endings that regularly displaced "genuine" Sturm und Drang conclusions. Yet it must be emphasized that the quoted denouement, appearing in the play's first printing, was an afterthought, the result of Lessing's moderating influence. A note in Gerstenberg's papers indicates that *Ugolino* was originally to end as follows.

> Bleeding, Anselmo moans and dies. Ugolino speaks as if in a dream of the screams of the dying. Catching sight of Anselmo's corpse, he curses the hour of his birth. He sinks exhausted to the floor, stretches out as if to embrace the earth, with which he unites himself.[32]

Presumably, the corresponding lines in the published text are:

> UGOLINO: And did I—Oh, you most horrible avenger! Lie here, murderer! (*He flings himself down violently next to Anselmo.*) Consecrate yourself to the earth forever! (*He spreads his arms over the ground.*)

The eighteenth century had provided no models for this theater of disillusionment. A falling curtain at this point would have seriously violated existing standards of decorum. Vicariously experienced suffering would have ceased without the requisite cathartic resolution. Nonetheless, Gerstenberg's plan was fearlessly consistent, faithful to the drama's logic, faithful to its source. In the *Inferno*, Ugolino's death is clearly a physical and spiritual defeat: "Therefore I gave myself, now blind, to groping over each and for two days called on them after they were dead. Then fasting had more power than grief."[33] The ambiguity of the final line does not rule out the possibility of cannibalism. To extract the Ugolino episode from Dante's metaphysical context, as Gerstenberg did, is to confront the injustice of Providence without mitigating explanations or rationalizations, be they religious, moral, or social. Had its original ending been retained, *Ugolino*'s fatalism would have had no equal in eighteenth-century drama. It would have prefigured the dystopian stasis of Beckett's plays.

Gerstenberg had sent his manuscript to Lessing, who delayed several months before delivering his verdict. His reservations were based on the impossibility of reconciling the drama with his theory of pity. "My compassion became a burden to me," he wrote to the dramatist, "or rather, my compassion ceased being compassion, becoming a wholly painful sensation."[34] He was concerned above all about the superfluousness of guiltless suffering: "Children ought never to bear the wrongs of their fathers." Only a few weeks earlier he had expressed similar views in the seventy-ninth and eighty-second pieces of the *Hamburg Dramaturgy*. Suffering without self-incurred fault, he maintained, is "horrible," "wrong and blasphemous in equal measure," contrary to the dictates of reason that enable one to sustain one's "faith and cheerful spirit" even in the state of servitude. His conclusion: "it is therefore imperative that we be reminded as little as possible of the confusing examples of such undeserved terrible fate. Remove them from the stage! Remove them from every book, if we can!"[35] His primary concern was the affective function of the aesthetic object, which cannot be "confusing" lest it lose its moral justification.

In his response, Gerstenberg at first refused to accommodate himself to audience sentiment, but it soon became evident that he had internalized Lessing's enlightened perspective. His vocabulary betrays his new direction, which was essentially a step backward into conventional aesthetics, negating his extraordinary prescience of nineteenth-century pessimism: "thus I have you to thank for a perspective, without which, as I now realize, Ugolino's character would not be developed *completely* enough."[36] Describing his addition to the last act enclosed with the letter, Gerstenberg says that Ugolino attempts suicide, but little by little his passion cools, as it seems natural to me in such a case; he *reasons with himself* over his decision, as he would be able to do as a Catholic and in accordance with the concepts of the theater audience; tears afford him relief, and the play now ends on a note of submission to fate, which leaves the spectator, who has been dreading the consequences of suicide, with a much brighter outlook than before.[37]

The capitulation to "the concepts of the theater audience" is complete: Ugolino is transformed into a pious martyr who bows to Divine Will while pointedly quoting from the Book of Job. Like Lessing's Faust, who was to escape from the devil's grasp, the transfigured Ugolino has eluded eternal damnation in the ice of Cocytus to be reunited with his family in the afterlife. His apotheosis is overtly, but only overtly, a victory over resigned passivity. The drama has already exposed the heroic pose as disguised ineffectuality; it is simply another form of submission. According to Fromm, "to submit to fate is the heroism of the masochist; to alter fate is the heroism of the revolutionary."[38] One might object that the captive Ugolino is incapable of changing or revolting against anything. Nevertheless, his attitude has social implications beyond its immediate context. Ecstatically affirming his fate, he typifies compensatory self-ennoblement while submitting unquestioningly to higher authority – a reaction characteristic of a bourgeoisie that, lacking the status to bring about political solutions to political problems, transposed the conflict to the moral sphere and proclaimed itself victor. It was thus compelled by its historical situation to view itself in images of greatness deferred.

In their correspondence concerning the first draft of *Ugolino*, Lessing had obliquely suggested to Gerstenberg yet another resolution: an unambiguous termination of the protagonist's (and the spectator's) suffering through Ugolino's suicide.[39] Gerstenberg had responded that such a suicide "would spoil everything." Salvation or enduring one's fate in the face of starvation was the "knot" of the drama, he claimed; to hack it apart through a suicide would be incompatible with the drama's intended purpose.[40] Forty-four years later, however, Gerstenberg announced that he was reconsidering Lessing's advice as he prepared to republish *Ugolino* in an edition of his collected works.[41] Looking back upon his relatively brief period of literary creativity, he realized how difficult it would be to improve works he could hardly remember writ-ing.[42] It is pertinent to our theme to note that, in the reprinted version of *Ugolino*, he preserved the text of the first edition without any alteration whatsoever—except the conclusion. To provide a necessary prop for Ugolino's suicide, Gerstenberg inserted into act 4 a monologue by Fran-cesco, in which he produces and flings onstage a dagger he has smug-gled into the tower.[43] After striking down Anselmo in act 5, Ugolino launches into a lengthy final monologue, finds the dagger-ex-machina, and proclaims that an angel from heaven is calling him.

> (*The music approaches*—) . . . I'm coming, blessed one! I'm com-ing, you avenger with the flaming sword! Messiah! Redeemer! Oh you my Savior! Mercy! Mercy! I'm coming! I'm coming! (*The mo-ment he points the dagger against his breast, the curtain falls.*)[44]

Gerstenberg apparently intended to make Ugolino more assertive and his end less ambivalent. With classical delicacy, he suggests suicide but leaves the outcome to the audience's imagination. What this mannerist resolution discloses above all, however, is Gerstenberg's waning poetic power. Dramatic intensity is gone; Ugolino is sentimental and cliché ridden. Gerstenberg may have succeeded in disposing of his hero more properly, but in the process he stripped away the uniqueness of his character.

The ending in the first published version was a similar, although milder compromise. From what we know of the original manuscript, Gerstenberg initially dared to stage the *silence* after Ugolino's (literal) fall. This silence, drowned out in the later texts by music and rhetoric, represents a void in which injustice has triumphed, mocking the idea of a beneficent universe. The difficulty of ending in any other way than this lay in Gerstenberg's appropriation of Dante's tale without its redemptive framework: after Ugolino's death, there is no longer any possibility of mediating between the tragedy and a more stable order, as in a final lament by another character. No one is left, and Ruggieri, the only figure who could conceivably have appeared in the tower, would have only intensified the horror. Thus the material's over-whelming aura of fatalism could only be dispelled if Ugolino were to utter his own requiem, and "in accordance with the concepts of the the-ater audience," to stage his fate as a Christian ceremony.

Goethe's *Stella*

As the Sturm und Drang's inaugural drama, *Ugolino* seems most obviously to anticipate Goethe's *Egmont*, one of the last of the epoch. Both protagonists are imprisoned by sinister rivals; both are sustained in confinement by visions, which in *Egmont* even become theatrical reality when Egmont's allegorical dream is enacted before the audience. Both devise "exemplary" deaths by associating themselves with a higher cause, and both experience a musical apotheosis. But if we leave aside similarities of plot, another of Goethe's dramas stands forth in peculiar kinship to Gerstenberg's monomaniacal work, namely *Stella*, "A Play for Lovers" (1776). This subtitle would seem to rule out any reasonable basis for comparison, yet there are, to begin with, close formal correspondences. Although they are five-act plays, both are so unusually brief and so focused in terms of time and place that they appear to unfold in one act, in a single rush of emotion. Both are seismographs of intense feeling, and both were ultimately transformed by their authors from innovative dramas into conventional tragedies. But before we attempt to make further sense of this analogy, let us briefly survey the contours of *Stella*, its reception, and metamorphosis.

Stella dramatizes a wildly improbable coincidence: having loved and deserted his wife Cäcilie and his mistress Stella, Fernando returns to Stella at nearly the same moment that Cäcilie arrives with their daughter Lucie, who is to be employed as Stella's companion. The drama thus hinges on recognition and analysis, aiming toward an unpredictable resolution. Goethe balances the emotional claims of Cäcilie and Stella upon Fernando so carefully that choosing one would be a drastic injustice to the other. Cäcilie finally unravels the knot by narrating the tale of the Count von Gleichen, who joined a Crusade, was captured, and returned to his wife with the woman who had freed him. Their mutual love, sanctioned by God and the Pope, "blissfully encompassed One home, One bed, and One grave." The parable's moral is quickly accepted, and the play ends with both women embracing Fernando, exclaiming "We are yours!"

Like Goethe's *The Sufferings of Young Werther*, *Stella* demonstrated upon publication that an unorthodox work not only provokes sharply differing reactions but can actually stimulate production within the cultural sphere. Some who considered *Werther* immoral, unduly pessimistic, unrealistic, or simply incomplete took to writing adaptations or sequels; likewise, in at least two instances, *Stella*'s ending was adjusted (as fairy-tale endings often are) to conform to more socially acceptable behavior. One anonymous critic produced a "sixth act" of the play, published in the same format as Goethe's text and continuing the original's pagination.[45] In this addendum, Stella's uncle arrives after Goethe's ménage à trois has concluded its embrace. The uncle has Fernando arrested, placed in chains, and sentenced for life to hard labor. Cäcilie is about to retell her parable when the uncle points out how little relevance it has to the situation. Stella departs with her uncle, and Cäcilie reconciles herself with her father. Another sequel required five acts to tell how Fernando, ultimately deciding to live with Cäcilie, sends his brother ("Fernando 2") to Stella, who marries him.[46] These antidotes to the original's alleged immorality reflected the prevailing view that Fernando's good fortune – which a profligate such as he did not deserve in any case – offended contemporary ethical standards. Commenting on Goethe's drama, Hamburg's Pastor Goeze, famous for his quarrels with Lessing, reminded his readers of the distinction between poetic and moral virtue: although the former might apply to *Stella*, God would, after all, eventually judge them according to the latter.[47] Other critics suggested ways to restore an ethical balance to the play; for example, Fernando should have killed himself, or the two women should have sent him packing.[48]

Goethe defused the controversy himself several decades later when, at Schiller's urging, *Stella* was performed in Weimar with a tragic ending. In retrospect, Goethe wrote that since contemporary morals are "inherently grounded in monogamy, the relationship of a man to two women, especially as it is shown [in this drama], could not be justified, and it therefore qualified unequivocally as a tragedy." Consequently, he revised the conclusion of the play in a manner "that satisfies one's senses and heightens one's compassion."[49] Like Gerstenberg with *Ugolino*, Goethe changed only the ending of his play: while Cäcilie narrates her parable, Stella takes poison, whereupon Fernando shoots himself.

The original version was provocative not just because it culminated in a celebration of love – many sentimental comedies ended on this note – but because its representation of love subverted rather than affirmed prevailing codes of social cohesion. The *Stella* that dared to advertise itself as "a play for lovers" reveals a profound antagonism between the Sturm und Drang and its social milieu: the impulse toward spiritual and sexual fulfillment clashes with the self-preserving mechanisms of the middle-class family that require, instead, the subordination of individual desire.[50] From a rationalistic, middle-class perspective, prioritizing feeling above social stability is a counterproductive eccentricity that, as Goethe demonstrates in *Stella* and its predecessor *Werther*, can lead to anarchic notions and behavior. Both works lift the veil of sentimental discourse to reveal that passion can override social contracts such as marriage and challenge established concepts of role and gender. The moral ledgers of the enlightened middle classes could not accommodate such subjective license. Furthermore, moral arbiters may well have been unnerved by Cäcilie's and Stella's refusal to become rivals upon discovering their mutual love for Fernando, coming together instead as kindred spirits. As rivals, embodying the wife-versus-mistress polarity that subjugates women by fragmenting them into stereotypes, one of the two would ultimately prevail, but as friends they establish the basis for Goethe's convention-flouting ending.[51] That the author appropriated Enlightenment didactic methodology (a parable) and medieval legend to secure divine legitimation for his ménage à trois may well have been, for some readers, the crowning impertinence.

Upon closer inspection, however, the dichotomies between happy ending and tragedy, irresponsible male wish fulfillment and moral retribution are not as clear-cut as they might seem. Like *Werther*, *Stella* is without doubt a form of *Erlebnisdichtung*, an opportunity for Goethe to come to terms with his experiences, his desires, and his limitations. The play is a meditation on his numerous relationships with women, an analysis of the components of passion. Unlike a sentimental comedy, *Stella* highlights the psychological rather than the moral quality of love, exploring the tensions created by sexual and intellectual attraction, possessiveness, self-denial, self-assertion, repulsion, and the desire for autonomy. As Sigrid Damm has recently pointed out, Goethe's play also reflects his inability to regulate his feelings in accordance with such social classifications as "wife," "mistress," and even "sister."[52] To attempt to find specific correspondences to Cornelia Goethe, Lili Schönemann, Anna Sibylla Münch, or Friederike Brion is irrelevant, however, because Stella, Cäcilie, and Fernando are highly stylized type characters. What is immediately striking about the women is the absoluteness of their love for Fernando. "Ah! The loved one is everywhere, and everything exists for the loved one,"exclaims Stella,[53] and Cäcilie compares Fernando's abandonment of her to the loss of a god (*HA*, 309). Their obsession becomes their destiny; their lives are split into states of utter fulfillment or nonfulfillment. At first sight, Goethe seems to have constructed a play in which man is woman's universe, but not the reverse. However, this premise (which would justifiably offend modern sensibilities) is contradicted as often as it is affirmed. As we know from *Werther*, Goethe did not consider obsessive love an exclusively female trait. Werther's infatuation makes him far more of a social misfit than is Stella, who copes with her loneliness by doing charity work, or than Cäcilie, who is a competent mother and, in Goethe's own words, a "heroine in soul and intellect."[54] For that matter, both women are more socially integrated than is Fernando himself, who, unlike them, is ostensibly free to determine his own destiny. Indeed, Goethe initially defines gender according to social role (housewife, mistress, well-to-do gentleman), but then he breaks open the stereotype to show where genders overlap. Stella, passion incarnate, is as capable of self-reflection and self-irony as is Werther, indicating that, for Goethe, these traits are not gender bound. His relativizing perspective enjoins him from valuing one life-style above another; his literary representation of psychosocial conditions therefore cannot be read as an affirmation of male-dominated social structures. As we shall see subsequently, Goethe devises, in *Stella*, a massive exposé of the sentimental-Faustian protagonist Fernando, the structural and emotional focus of the play.

The extraordinary loquacity of Goethe's sentimental protagonists betrays their inherently melancholic disposition. Like the imprisoned Gheradescas, Cäcilie, Stella, and Fernando share the same idiom,[55] experiencing language as emotional release, as a stabilizing mechanism that compensates for their inability to satisfy their desires. Stella speaks for all three when she says: "How well I feel now that my heart can open up again, now that I can blurt out all that oppresses me so!" (*HA*, 322). Although they are able to aestheticize their inner state through their evocative prose, their obsessive self-reflection is endlessly, unproductively cyclical.[56] Goethe is careful to emphasize, both in *Stella* and in *Werther*, that this trait is class specific; that is, only the socially privileged have the requisite freedom from material needs to indulge in such emotional/intellectual exploration. *Stella*'s contrast figure is the busy

Postmistress, whose husband died three months earlier, but "the likes of us have as little time to weep as to pray" (*HA*, 310).[57]

In this drama, love is the energizing emotion, yet—here the psychological abysses of *Ugolino* reopen—love is also confinement and delusion. Cäcilie pities the man "who clings to a girl. . . . I view him as a prisoner. . . . He is drawn from his world into ours, with which he has nothing in common. He deceives himself for a while, and woe unto us when his eyes open!" (*HA*, 332). At this juncture, Goethe does make a gender distinction, reflecting prevailing "essentialist" views of gender difference: it is woman's nature to be wholly focused on the object of her love, whereas man's emotional needs vacillate between conjugal happiness and self-realization. The dilemma of Fernando's "male nature" is already prefigured in *Werther*.

> A vast twilit entity lies before us, our perception is lost in it and becomes as blurred as our eyesight, and we yearn, ah, we yearn to surrender all of our Self and let ourselves be filled to the brim with a single, tremendous, magnificent emotion, but alas . . . when we hurry to the spot, when There becomes Here, everything is as it was before and we are left standing in our poverty and constraint, our soul longing for the balm that has eluded us. Thus the most restless vagabond yearns in the end to return to his native land and find in his cottage, in the arms of his wife, with his children around him, and in the occupations that provide for them, the joys he sought vainly elsewhere.[58]

After several happy years with Cäcilie, Fernando, conforming to type, felt himself irresistibly drawn away. How self-centered his Faustian urges were emerges in a dialogue with his estate manager (quoted from the first published version of the play).[59]

> ESTATE MANAGER: I remember when our good, dear Cäcilie was your wife for two or three years, how exasperated you were, how nothing could please you, how tied down, how confined you felt, how you were panting for freedom . . . and how you said to me, overcome with discontent: "Franz, I must leave!—I'd be a fool to let myself be tied down! These conditions sap all my energy, they rob me of my spirit's courage,

> they confine me! – How much lies within me! How much could
> I evolve! – I must leave – into the free world! – ." . . . We es-
> caped, we went into the free world; – and fluttered up and
> down, in – out – and with all our free spirit we had no idea what
> to do with our boredom. . . . That's how our energy freely ex-
> panded. . . . That's how our talents developed.
> FERNANDO: Do you know what you're ridiculing?
> ESTATE MANAGER: Everything you talked about so often but
> never did; everything you desired and never found, and often
> weren't even looking for.

Stella abandoned her family and inheritance to live with Fernando.
They never married – the young lawyer Goethe was careful to avoid involving Fernando in *legal* bigamy – and the daughter Stella bore died at
an early age, eliminating the further complication of having an illegitimate child on the scene. Yet Fernando's restless spirit and feelings of
guilt led him to forsake Stella as well, to search in vain for Cäcilie and
their daughter, and finally to serve in a foreign army, where he "helped
suppress the perishing freedom of the noble Corsicans" (*HA*, 333).[60]
Both women believe that Fernando's nature is torn between "male instinct" and moral sense, so they find themselves alternately condoning
and condemning his fickleness. For his part, Fernando is faced with an
emotionally and ethically impossible choice between wife and mistress. "Each one claims me totally" (*HA*, 343), he states, and the deci-
sions he makes are valid only for the moment in which they are ut-
tered.[61] At the end of act 4, Cäcilie voices the need for a denouement
(unconsciously addressing the dramatist's problem as well): "if the
knot can be untied, dear God in heaven! don't tear it apart" (*HA*, 341).[62]
In generic terms, this means the play will define itself at its conclusion
either as a sentimental comedy or a middle-class tragedy.[63] The three
protagonists contemplate various endings: flight, murder, or suicide.[64]
Cäcilie offers to withdraw her claim on Fernando in favor of Stella, but
he accuses her of self-deception: "Cold common sense will not untie the
knot" (*HA*, 344). He is correct, but only temporarily, for Cäcilie then
thrusts into the drama a major stylistic aberration, the parable of the
Count von Gleichen (clearly an appropriate name for this dilemma).
The Count's situation is, to be sure, not at all analogous to Fernando's,
but this is beside the point because the divine sanction of the wife-

mistress-husband relationship as well as the high pathos of the narrative itself converge to authorize an emotional bond as a natural and legal one. In response to Stella's "I can't comprehend it!" Cäcilie insists, "You're feeling it" (*HA*, 347), and she ends the play with a quotation ("Wir sind dein!") from her own parable.[65]

The manipulative quality of the utopian vision of permanent bliss à trois is intensified, indeed made grotesque, by its impact on Fernando. At the end of the play he, its structural center, is nearly silenced, which in eighteenth-century drama normally happens to female rather than male figures. Immediately after Cäcilie's narrative, he says with profound ambivalence: "God in heaven, who sends us angels when we are in need, give us the strength to bear these phenomenal visions!" His spoken text after that is reduced to exclamations: "My wife!" / "Stella!" / "Mine! Mine!", but what is truly extraordinary in this final scene—and casts an entirely different light on the interpretation of *Stella* as a comedy—are the stage directions Goethe specified for Fernando, commencing just before Cäcilie's narrative. He has thrown himself in a chair in despair over his situation, but, as Cäcilie begins to speak, he somehow senses that a deus ex parabola is about to occur, and he tries to flee, perhaps from the forbidden dream of uniting wife and mistress, or more likely from the imminent socialization of his emotions.

> CÄCILIE (*goes to him and takes his hand.*): Once upon a time there was a Count—
> FERNANDO (*tries to leap to his feet, she holds him.*)

. . . and she continues. During the narrative "*Fernando lies sobbing with his arms spread over the table.*" After his rejoinder, "*he collapses again.*" Cäcilie calls in Stella, and Fernando "*leaps up as if to flee,*" but Cäcilie takes hold of him again. Finally, with a woman "*hanging*" on each arm, he joins the embrace. By this time one cannot be sure whether this final embrace represents liberation or confinement. Fernando's conversion—like King Thoas's from "Then go!" to "Farewell!" at the conclusion of *Iphigenie*—is inarticulate. That is, the rehabilitation of "the center," namely the prosperous, educated male, can no longer be demonstrated through the logic of enlightened discourse. It can only be asserted as a given that requires a leap of faith to be credible. By attempting to escape, Fernando seems to have anticipated post-happy-ending disillusionment, intuiting, like Faust, that if one pauses to grasp the "beautiful moment," life is over. The happy ending may have gratified Goethe's fantasy, but at the same time he was clearly aware of its impermanence: only the briefest glimpse of a utopian solution is possible before the structure threatens to collapse.[66]

The efficacy of Cäcilie's parable becomes yet more dubious in Goethe's revised version, for, upon its conclusion, Stella is discovered to have poisoned herself, which drives Fernando to suicide. The "logic" of this tragic outcome is objectively no more nor less compelling than that of the happy ending; no historical or fictional model predetermines the characters' fate. To what degree the dramatic solution is thought to be appropriate depends on audience expectations. There was, as we have seen, considerable consensus among *Stella*'s critics that Fernando's immorality predisposed him for a tragic ending, but the young Goethe and his supporters, on the other hand, did not view him as an innately tragic figure destined for punishment.

The revised conclusion, conceived twenty years after the original version and published yet another ten years later, resembles *Ugolino*'s altered ending not only in its recourse to suicide but in the deterioration of its literary worth. Empty pathos comments on the action instead of impelling it forward.[67] Rather than focusing on the situation, emotions broadcast their affective intention to the audience. Stella delivers a series of epitaphs for herself before she ends the play "(*sinking down*): And I will die alone" (*HA*, 351)—a highly overdetermined ending, lacking only the words "pity me" to make it generically indistinguishable from that of early sentimental drama.[68] Goethe's heavy hand reveals how certain he had become of the drama's tragic character and of its impact. In their revisions, both Gerstenberg and Goethe seemed intent on eliminating all possible misunderstanding about the drama's end; hence the recourse to a didactic tone that characterize pre- and post-Sturm und Drang literature. Attempting to accommodate the moral expectations of their times, both authors were unwilling to leave contradictions provocatively agape, as they had in their earlier versions.[69] In a sense, *Stella*'s metamorphosis from comedy to tragedy bears witness, as Brecht said of Lenz's *The Tutor*, to the "German calamity": a utopian reorganization of human relationships based on a community of love had no better fate than to be shattered by its critics and, at the last, by its author.

Wagner's *The Child-Murderess*

When dramas are altered to increase their audience appeal, certainly the more common tendency is to reverse *Stella*'s progression and convert tragedy into comedy. The performance history of Shakespeare's plays, for instance, indicates that theater audiences have often seen his tragedies end happily. Sturm und Drang dramas were not immune to this practice, as our next example will show. Heinrich Leopold Wagner's *The Child-Murderess*[70] (1776) argues powerfully against a grave social injustice of its time: the ostracism of the unwed mother and the death sentence she faced if she killed her child in desperation. The theme of the seduced and abandoned middle-class girl pervades the Sturm und Drang: Goethe's Werther discourses eloquently on the motivations that might lead such a person to suicide; Goethe's Faust leaves his Gretchen to face execution; Lenz's Gustchen in *The Tutor* and Marie in *The Soldiers* are rescued at the last from similar fates; even an idyll, Maler Müller's *The Nut's Kernel*, explores the theme in order to denounce those who have caused such grief. Wagner's play begins with a witty, convincing seduction scene after a ball in a disreputable inn. The aristocratic Lieutenant von Gröningseck drugs the all-too-frivolous middle-class matron Frau Humbrecht and, toward the end of act 1, overcomes her daughter Evchen's resistance to his amorous advances. The following five [*sic*] acts reveal the tragic consequences of an intrigue to undermine von Gröningseck's promise to marry Evchen. Strong sociocritical impulses emerge intermittently; for example, the state is shown condoning the murder of a starving boy by one of its agents but condemning to death the unwed mother who kills her infant.

Wagner's drama reveals him nevertheless to be a second-rate playwright at best. Schiller's verdict of it seems accurate: "Wagner's *The Child-Murderess* has poignant scenes and interesting aspects. But it does not rise above mediocrity. It has little effect upon my sensibility and contains too much water."[71] By no means do I want to associate myself with the classicist tradition of disparaging Wagner's play because of its "plebeian" interests or its supposed lack of formal harmony. Instead, I would like to reexamine briefly the play's impact on Wagner's contemporaries in order to qualify his image as a progressive playwright among hopelessly prudish and reactionary detractors. As a whole, the drama reveals that its author is not entirely in control of his

material.[72] The abrupt transformation at the end of act 1 of von
Gröningseck from a resourceful seducer to a paragon of middle-class
virtue is unconvincing; the villainy of his fellow officer, von Hasenpoth, is largely unmotivated; the gullibility of those who are duped by
the latter's forged letters verges on the ludicrous. In short, the play's
action is transparently manipulated while it appeals to be taken at face
value. Critical to any judgment of the drama, moreover, is its most
notorious scene: Evchen has run away from home to give birth to her
child, and she is living in utter poverty with a washerwoman. Having
lost all hope, she contrives to be alone with her child and says:

> (*grimly*) – But you'll never be what I am, never endure what I have
> to endure. (*Picks up a pin and stabs the child in the head, the child cries
> out dreadfully, to drown it out she sings, at first very loudly, then more
> and more softly.*)
>   Rock-a-bye, baby!
>   Sleep, baby, sleep!
>   Sleep for eternity!
>   Ha ha ha, ha ha! (*Cradles the child in her arms.*)
>   Your father was an evil man,
>   He made your mother a whore; . . .
> Ha! A drop of blood! I must kiss it away – another one! – that too!
> (*Kisses the child on the wound.*) What is this? – sweet! very sweet! But
> a bitter aftertaste – ha, now I recognize it – the blood of my own
> child! – and I'm drinking it? – (*Throws the child on the bed.*) Sleep
> there, Gröningseck! Sleep! Sleep eternally! . . . (*Kinder*, 6)

Critics who find this scene affecting mention neither the drinking of
blood nor the inadvertently comical effect of throwing the child on the
bed.[73] This episode provoked intense audience reactions, sarcastically
described in 1778 by Johann Georg Schlosser, Goethe's brother-in-law.

> Then there appeared I don't know what sort of enervated critics
> and dilettantes and the opera-buffa-audience and screamed – like
> the benevolent women of Toulouse, who torture a Calas to death
> on the rack but who can't bear to watch a Beverley suffer on the
> stage – they screamed: Oh, away! Away! Who can watch that?
> Who can stand it? We're dreaming about the child; we're sick from
> fear; we're haunted all night when we see something like that; we

get headaches, palpitations, hot flashes — please don't send us sick
from the theater![74]

Schlosser makes a valid point about privileged audiences who revel in
atrocities in real life but who want their theatrical entertainment
properly sanitized, yet the revulsion they showed toward Wagner's
"realism" may have at least some justification. Unlike Gerstenberg's
dramatization of Ugolino's Tower of Hunger, Wagner's representation
of infanticide is sensationalistic. Its unexpectedly lurid details colonize
the spectator's imagination; their shock effect preempts one's attention
on character and action. In a manner of speaking, sensationalism casts
an obstruction into the stream of aesthetic perception. The viewer more
readily recalls a disproportionately lurid feature than the complexity of
the aesthetic whole. By introducing gratuitous detail strictly to amplify
affective impact, sensationalism reifies an event, trivializing both the
action and its agent. In Aristotelian theater, violence is normally mediated through narrative, allowing the spectator the freedom to imagine
a frightful act and thereby — at least in theory — intensify its impact.
Graphic violence onstage can indeed be highly manipulative, because
through their reactions, actors dictate to spectators its "correct" reception. An all-too-obvious co-optation of emotional response defeats itself, because excess is apt to convert unintentionally into its opposite —
as I indicated above, a reader/spectator may find Evchen's actions
inappropriately comical. This is not to deny that standards concerning
the representation of violence, sex, and other human functions are culturally and historically variable. In this regard, Wagner's play is an en-
lightening sociological document: despite considerable audience resistance, Wagner could dare to stage a graphic infanticide, yet the act of
seduction — easily portrayable on a modern stage, in various degrees of
nudity — had to occur offstage.

The conclusion of The Child-Murderess is quite at odds with itself —
less so this time because of Wagner's weaknesses as a dramatist than
because of the lack of consensus in his time about solving the social
problem his play addresses. The authorities have come to arrest Evchen, and although "the law that condemns the child-murderer to
death is clear and has admitted no exception for many years" (Kinder,
6), von Gröningseck is determined to travel to Versailles to ask for a par-
don. When Evchen raises the crucial question about how such a fate
might have been avoided, von Gröningseck offers an Enlightenment

homily: "if you had trusted me, had succumbed less to melancholy, had believed somewhat more in virtue–or I somewhat less [namely, in Hasenpoth's presumed virtue]." The last words belong to Evchen's father, a vigorous character type cast in the mold of Lenz's Major von Berg. He symbolically tears open his vest:

> The whole world is becoming too narrow for me! (*Takes a deep breath.*) Puuh! (*Claps the lieutenant on the shoulder.*) If you need money, sir! Traveling expenses! You understand?–A thousand, two, three thousand guilders lie ready at my house!–And I'd give ten thousand if the ball with all its consequences were sent to the devil!

Wagner achieves a moderate degree of closure with von Gröningseck's didactic summation and a reference to the plot's starting point. Yet to its credit, the ending does not treat the play's social theme as something that has been overcome, about which one need no longer concern oneself. Even though von Gröningseck's moralizing, which places all blame on the individual, undermines the drama's sociocritical thrust somewhat, the resolution offers a glimpse of hope. In its imagination, the audience will ride off to Versailles with von Gröningseck and will cheer him from the sidelines as he attempts to influence the court. If it were to rule in Evchen's favor, the law itself might eventually become more humane. Thus the promise of restitution overcomes the sense of fatalism that lies so near at hand. Nevertheless, the stageworthiness of the play's conclusion from the murder onward was considered dubious–not least, ultimately, by the playwright himself.

Less than a year after the drama was published, Gotthold Ephraim Lessing's younger brother Karl adapted it for the Döbbelin troupe in Berlin (which had performed the premiere of *Ugolino*). The Lessing brothers believed it to be a play by Lenz–a plausible error, considering that *The Child-Murderess* is derivative of *The Tutor* in many ways. Karl Lessing's adaptation radically bowdlerized Wagner's work: the salacious events of act 1 were narrated rather than acted out; the villain was transformed from an aristocratic Iago to a well-meaning meddler; the vigorous Sturm und Drang dialogue was toned down. Lessing's declared purpose was to prepare a stageable text for "respectable people" by eliminating the original's portrayal of "the utterly vulgar Strassburger milieu" and by smoothing out the work's "uneven tone,"[75] thereby bringing it into greater conformance with prevailing generic categories. Although he altered the text sufficiently to produce a didactic sentimental comedy, his adaptation was banned in Berlin anyway, presumably because of its unfavorable depiction of the military. Two years later, Wagner countered with his own adaptation, now titled *Evchen Humbrecht Or: You Mothers, Pay Heed!* These events were described as follows by the colorful J. G. Schlosser.

> —the silken little men screamed too, and there quickly appeared a poet [Karl Lessing], who . . . poured rose water over the frightful portrait, perfuming it as best he could. . . . As if that weren't enough, the playwright, who wanted to see his drama performed, succumbed to temptation and poured several drops on it as well, and behold! Instead of the brave, noble girl, admirable despite her crime, there now stand a sweet bride and a dim-witted youth, who are so happy that they melt in ecstasy and can't stop talking. The benevolent spectators go home cheerfully, eat supper without grieving over the poor child and the rescued mother, chat about it for a quarter of an hour, and then fall asleep without palpitations or headaches, yawning as much as they did in the theater.[76]

In unsigned critique of Lessing's revision, Wagner had taken the adapter pedantically to task for his textual intrusions.[77] Wagner continued his attack in the preface to his own adaptation, in which he thanked the Berlin police for banning the unauthorized version.[78] He claimed that his original version was meant only to be read, not to be performed—an important distinction for eighteenth-century drama that I will not pursue here, however, because his assertion cannot otherwise be documented, and the original text was, in fact, performed several times before his adaptation was published.[79] He belittled the expectation that contemporary theater could have a positive social impact, because the theater-going public, he claimed, concerns itself only with superficial displays of virtue. Therefore, "having nothing better to do at the moment," he had set about modifying his text "so that even in this refined era, in which one babbles of virtue, [the play] might appear with honor in our so-called wholesome theaters." Since contemporary tragedy had in his view become wholly anemic so as not to offend the spectators' sensibilities, he had decided "to spare [his] audience a sleepless night" by giving the play "a different twist."[80]

Despite the polemics against Lessing, Wagner's new "twist" in fact resulted in a text generically similar to the one he was attacking. He too omitted the entire first act, the infanticide, and Frau Humbrecht's death. Evchen is interrupted by the sudden appearance of her father before she can commit the murder, and the play concludes with a family reconciliation. Von Gröningseck promises marriage and Humbrecht a dowry, while Evchen contemplates fate's arbitrary ways: "Thank heaven! . . . Yet it could have gone either way – in an instant. – " (An ironic reflection on the ease with which a playwright can twist a plot in a different direction?) Her father delivers the final moral, warning girls not to indulge in "parties de plaisir" with those of higher rank.[81] This is a manifestly conventional close to an eighteenth-century comedy of morals, conforming to popular expectations. Far from regarding the ending as satire, I would interpret Wagner's compromises as literary opportunism.[82] He capitulated to, rather than challenged, the affirmative function of the contemporary theater, which disseminated conservative middle-class values interspersed with light entertainment to suit its financial benefactors, the aristocracy.[83] Whatever his intent may have been, *Evchen Humbrecht* was effective Enlightenment drama with an ideological strategy distinctly contrary to that of *The Child-Murderess*.[84] The original ending had highlighted an unresolved social injustice; the hope for its amelioration lay in a social institution, namely the court. The revised text repeats the lesson of early Enlightenment didactic drama that social vices are to be overcome not by systemic change but by individual self-improvement. In other words, von Gröningseck's reprimand to Evchen near the end of *The Child-Murderess* advances from a secondary to the primary message in *Evchen Humbrecht*'s conclusion.[85] Worse yet, the latter version exonerates the seducer from all culpability, claiming that it is the woman's responsibility to steer clear of dubious liaisons. "You mothers" are the ones who must learn this lesson, as the subtitle implies. So, instead of standing by his principles – as he well might have, considering that his original text was being read, discussed, and performed – Wagner cynically rendered harmless much of *The Child-Murderess*'s provocative impact, displaying his rebellious disposition only in his caustic preface.

Chapter 3

The Impossibility of Ending:
J. M. R. Lenz

The poet's voice breaks when he speaks of it.
— Bertolt Brecht, "On Lenz's Middle-Class Tragedy *The Tutor*"

The dominant fictional persona of the Sturm und Drang dramas of Gerstenberg, Leisewitz, Klinger, Goethe, and Schiller was the Promethean hero. Embodying the spirit of rebellion, he was nonetheless cast in the classic mold of the Aristotelian tragic hero. "Larger than life" in his emotional vitality if not also in social standing, he was brought to fall through his flawed character and his hostile environment. His destabilizing influence was assimilated into the ritual of upheaval and purgation from which tragedy had originally developed. In most instances, the wildest storms of passion were caged within the Aristotelian unities and expiated by rituals of retribution. Sturm und Drang heroes thus had a lasting cultural impact partly because of their conventionality: they gave drama new voices but did not subvert its dominant forms.[1] Even a Shakespearean epic such as Goethe's *Götz von Berlichingen* commemorated the demise of its protagonist with a moralizing lament. Schiller's *The Robbers*, *Fiesko*, and *Intrigue and Love*, the afterburners of the Sturm und Drang, ended in protoclassical reconciliation. As a whole, the era's dramatic resolutions performed, more or less convincingly, their age-old function of mediating between fictional rebellion and the spectator's regulated social order. Although theatergoers were on occasion shocked and repelled by a play's intemperances, they were not challenged to reevaluate their habits of cultural consumption.

   Paradoxically, the Sturm und Drang, which envisioned a more radically emancipated individual than did any other literary movement of the century, tended to produce fictional heroes who were anything

but exemplars of democratic principles. By general consensus, the
quintessence of unbridled Sturm und Drang longing, frustration, and
alienation is Guelfo in Klinger's *The Twins*, who happens to be an aristocrat and a tyrant. The yearning among younger intellectuals for a "great
man" who could inspire spiritual and national rejuvenation within a
fragmented Germany conflicted with their egalitarian ideals. In their
works, frustrated ambition was normally traced to individual rather
than systemic injustices: Guelfo, Julius of Tarent, and Karl Moor are
victimized by arbitrary parental dictates; Ugolino, Götz, Clavigo, and
Fiesko are brought to fall by personal ambition and political rivals.
When the causes of misfortune grow indistinct, blame turns inward:
"Our misfortune comes from our own temperaments; the world has
contributed but not so much as we," maintains Wild in Klinger's drama,
Sturm und Drang.[2] In their explorations of inner conflict, the dramas
echoed the melancholic introspection of Shakespearean and baroque
tragedy.[3] Yet this was but one strand of the literary movement; one of
its adherents employed the techniques of Enlightenment drama to seek
out the environmental determinants of the alienated subjectivity that
characterized the Sturm und Drang. Significantly, this innovator,
Jakob Michael Reinhold Lenz, was a translator of Roman and
Shakespearean *comedy*.

As a moralist and social reformer, Lenz was a product of the Enlightenment; as the creator of a tradition of anti-Aristotelian social
drama, he is in the small category of "modernists" such as Kleist, Büchner, and Kafka whose artistic perceptions have never been eclipsed,
who seem to have written for an audience that does not yet exist. For
numerous reasons, it is exceptionally difficult to analyze the mechanisms of closure in Lenz's major dramas. A conventional denouement
is a singular event that grows logically out of a series of other occurrences; Lenz's endings tend to be multiple, simultaneous, and arbitrary. To an unprecedented degree, his art was intertwined with his
unstable personal situation, his frustrations and ideals. His aesthetic
goals were inconsistent and contradictory. Searching for structure in
Lenz's life and art, critics usually pinpoint several major currents in his
oeuvre and examine their interrelationships; Klaus R. Scherpe's con-
trastive study of Lenz's "project-making" versus his artistic reproduction of social reality is a particularly useful example.[4] The only way I
have found to cope with the dilemma of writing about Lenz's drama

endings is to imitate his characteristic nonlinearity by juxtaposing con-
stellations of dramaturgical themes and methods.

The Aesthetics of Servitude

"My dearest friend! I'm standing on one leg, like a crane ready for
travel, and am scrawling my farewell to you on this paper with the
other," wrote Lenz to his mentor Salzmann in August, 1772.[5] From
1771–74 he was employed as a manservant to two young noblemen
who planned to become officers in the French army. He lived with them
in various garrisons, where he served at their beck and call, often in humiliating circumstances. He had little free time, little privacy; his employers read his mail. "I've hardly had one minute when I could say to
myself: now I'm resting. I'm split apart by my own and others' troubles,
by rational and emotional, philosophical and poetic concerns" (*Werke*
3:259). He slept poorly and was often ill. He had chosen this way of life
in order to pursue his literary interests, contrary to his father's wishes
that his son would follow in his footsteps as a pastor in their native Lat-
via. Even after Lenz left his demeaning employment, he led a financially insecure existence, dependent on the income from tutoring, literary endeavors, and support from his friends. In 1776, he was still
complaining that he "lacked the poet's leisure, warm air, and blissful
spirit" (*Werke* 3:406). More than any other eighteenth-century German
writer, he embodied the antithesis to the affluent, self-assured Enlightenment author for whom literature was an avocation of one's "idle
hours."[6] The disjointed texture of Lenz's social dramas, *The Tutor or The
Advantages of Private Education, The Soldiers,* and *The New Menoza or The
Story of Prince Tandi from Cumba,*[7] suggests numerous analogies to the
circumstances of his writing-on-the-run. Having experienced in his
own flesh the fragmentation of labor, he created an open, multifaceted
realism that could be called protoproletarian. He perceived his attempts to mediate reality through drama as never being *finished,* even
though they had in some cases already been published.

> When I have time to rest, I'll dramatize [all of my plays].
> All . . . are deep mines of ore that must be excavated, melted
> down, and finally transformed into *dramas*, so that all of their plots
> will merge into a unified portrait. (*Werke* 1:750–51)

My dramatic portraits are still without any style, scribbled down
wildly and sloppily. (*Werke* 3:406)

His dramas arose out of spontaneous perceptions that defied preestablished concepts of totality. The social reality he experienced contradicted the Enlightenment's faith in humankind's progressive per-
fectibility; the only accurate aesthetic mediator of such a disordered
world was, therefore, the fragment, the "snapshot" of the present
seemingly detached from historical continuities.[8] His viewpoint is that
of the servant, who, not being master of all he surveys, has only a piece-
meal conception of his environment—yet he is so close to what he sees
that no room remains for illusions. From this perspective, Lenz obses-
sively unmasks pretension, somewhat like Gulliver in Brobdingnag,
revealing the all-too-human failings of his subjects. Breaking with the
prudish conventions of eighteenth-century character portrayal, Lenz
emphasizes his figures' physicality in order to demystify the roles they
have assumed for themselves. In the manuscript version of *The Tutor*,
for instance, Läuffer tells Gustchen, after kissing her, to rinse out her
mouth because her breath smells, and later her father, an aristocratic
military officer, is shown in his nightshirt with uncombed hair.[9]

Lenz's anti-illusionistic strategy has, of course, a weightier intent
than mere ridicule. His servant perspective exposes social injustice and
economic dependency; his protagonists are German drama's first anti-
heroes, for whom the exercise of free will is not a philosophical issue
but a matter of money and gender. He dramatizes sexual exploitation,
the arrogance of wealth and false learning, and the limited horizons of
the underprivileged, recounting the humiliations rather than the glory
of the struggle for the betterment of one's social position. A recurrent
theme is the naked self-interest that lies beneath the rites of social behavior. *The New Menoza* contains a classic unmasking of such motivations that family decorum normally manages to conceal. Professing
their parental respect for their child's freedom to choose a spouse, Herr
and Frau von Biederling importune their daughter Wilhelmine, who is
being wooed by Prince Tandi and Count Chameleon.

FRAU VON BIEDERLING: We gave the Prince our word neither
to persuade nor dissuade you, but you must know beforehand
that the Count has formally asked for your hand and wants to
make you the inheritor of all his estates.

> HERR VON BIEDERLING: And you also must know beforehand
> that the Prince offers you an entire kingdom and to oblige me
> will remain here in this country for another seven years with
> you. . . . I'm telling you, my daughter, we're absolving you of
> all obedience toward us, now you yourself are father and
> mother; what does your heart say?

Her heart says that she wishes to remain single, but *this* alternative is unacceptable to her father, who wishes both to "possess" and "sell" her.

> HERR VON BIEDERLING (*tears himself away from her*): Damn it all,
> no (*stamps with his foot*) I don't want that. (*Werke* 2:7)

Here the patterns of servitude prevail even at a rather high social
level;[10] whoever grovels in order to attain wealth and recognition will
become entangled in self-destructive contradictions. With this insight,
Lenz transcends the primary level of political drama that simply divides
society into oppressors and victims: he portrays the often grotesquely
comical deformations of human nature arising from repressed drives,
from accommodation and ambition. The first scene of *The Tutor* ends
with Läuffer bowing repeatedly before the aristocrats he has just pri-
vately maligned, and the impact of the following scene is devastating
not just because he evokes pity as a victim but because he has internalized the social conventions that debase him. Marie Wesener of *The Soldiers* becomes a virtuoso in the language of flirtation as she ventures
into the amoral realm of aristocratic military officers. Unlike any of his
contemporaries, Lenz dramatizes the *process* of victimization that occurs when the self-interest of exploiters converges with the unarticu-
lated needs and false illusions of the oppressed.

A noteworthy aspect of Lenz's aesthetics of servitude is its intended audience. Goethe's famous complaint during the writing of
Iphigenie: "Here [in Apolda near Weimar] the drama won't develop, it's
cursed, the King of Tauris must speak as if no stocking weavers in
Apolda were starving,"[11] was not an issue for Lenz. He who called himself "the stinking breath of the people" (*Werke* 3:333) wrote "comedies
[that were] not merely a performance to evoke laughter but a performance for everyone" (*Werke* 2:703). His "portrait[s] of society" fused
comic and tragic elements, for "the *Volk* for whom one writes or ought
to write is such a mish-mash [*sic*] of culture and barbarity, morality and

savagery" (*Werke* 2:703).[12] A pedagogic function of his plays was to "show social classes as they are, not as persons from a higher sphere imagine them to be," in order to confront "the common man" with the consequences of his vices (*Werke* 3:325–26). His theater audience model resembles that of his idol, Shakespeare, whose audiences indeed spanned the social spectrum. Lenz's ideal did not, however, conform to the cultural realities of his day. As he himself points out in *The Soldiers*, the contemporary German theater was not so much a moral institution as a playground for aristocratic officers. Theater directors were contractually obligated not to offend public taste; the artistic level of productions was generally low, and as much as middle-class reformers attempted to revitalize the theater as an autonomous cultural entity, financial support remained in the hands of the nobility.[13] Since Lenz was, in effect, writing for a theater of the future based on the theater of the past, it is unsurprising that none of his plays was performed in his lifetime.[14]

Eighteenth-century German drama typically ended by acknowledging a social or moral collective – how then could an aesthetics of servitude emphasizing social alienation and disjunction, directed at an audience that did not yet exist, achieve closure?

"Casuistic" Scenes

In his "Review of *The New Menoza*, Drafted by the Playwright Himself," Lenz insists that his portrayals derive not out of thin air but from the "half-authenticity *of a historian*" (*Werke* 2:701). *The Soldiers* is based on an incident in which Lenz was involved; characters in the original manuscript of *The Tutor* are named after real acquaintances. Initially, his dramas were to function as a "record of what [he] heard and saw everywhere, when [he] went among the people" (*Werke* 2:807). This primary mimetic level corresponds to what he calls in his "Notes on the Theater" the first source of poetry: the imitation of divine Creation. After the creative act, however, follows the unsettling Leibnizian recognition that "the world has no bridges" and that the desire to comprehend totality cannot be fulfilled (*Werke* 2:642, 646). Faced with a multiplicity of fragments, one tends to simplify and generalize, yet one is equally impelled to preserve the immediacy of the detail. The writer's "everlasting struggle to unravel once again our collected concepts, to make them transparent, vivid, and relevant" thus becomes, for Lenz, the second

source of poetry (*Werke* 2:647). Correspondingly in his dramas, each
scene seems to evolve autonomously according to its own logic rather
than from a central plan. The scene's momentum is centrifugal rather
than centripetal, as in Aristotelian drama. Plots unfold side-by-side,
with few obvious "bridges." The teeming verbosity of the first version
of *The Tutor* reveals more clearly than the published version an aesthetic
of self-indulgence; that is, Lenz's characters display seemingly irrelevant aspects of their personalities, as they would if they were alive.
They thereby attain far greater autonomy than figures in classical
drama that are hierarchically categorized according to function. Lenz
employs, instead, unpredictable distractions and detours, banalities of
everyday life as agents of dramatic action and characterization.[15] His
figures' passions are as intense as those of any Sturm und Drang hero,
but they are not monomaniacally focused; they shift with comic sud-
denness from one obsession to another.[16]

The characters thus appear to generate the scenes, creating "a circumstantial portrait of things as they are" (*Werke* 2:675). Wenzeslaus —
who with his unquenchable pedantry hijacks every scene in which he
appears — speaks at one point (*Tutor*, 5, 9) of a "casuistic" sermon he has
just delivered — that is, a homily tailored to a particular situation,
namely Läuffer's. Although Lenz's use of *casuistic* here is not entirely
unironic, the term captures the formal principle underlying his scene
construction: each scene addresses a particular mode of behavior in a
specific situation. It is as long or short as it needs to be — which in most
cases means longer or shorter than one would normally expect. Lenz's
scenes often seem either breathless (4, 4–8 of *The Soldiers* consist of five
scenes on little more than one page; 3, 7 of *The New Menoza* takes place
on horseback) or too full of breath (cf. any appearance of Wenzeslaus;
the debate between Läuffer's father and the Councillor von Berg in *Tutor*, 2, 1; the lengthy philosophical debates in *The New Menoza*). They
are cinematic rather than theatrical units; the action progresses in unmediated "cuts" from location to location. Lenz implies at the outset of
The New Menoza that its structure will offend Aristotelians: "The location," he writes after listing the characters, "is here and there." Synchronic and diachronic links among his episodes often seem to happen
by accident. By his own admission he was a dramatist who hated telling
stories on stage (*Werke* 2:703) — a dramatist, in other words, who hated
exposition. This antipathy clearly hindered him from creating works
that would appear finished, free of incongruities.[17]

His scenes, of course, are not wholly discrete; the multiple plots of *The Tutor* and *The Soldiers* indeed (eventually) complement each other. The Pätus/Miss Rehaar episode recapitulates the Läuffer-Gustchen seduction, and the mischief of the soldiers with the Jew, Aaron, and Mrs. Bishop are variants of their persecution of Stolzius. Lenz thereby undermines the uniqueness of a particular action, emphasizing the typicality of certain forms of behavior. In this way, closely observed reality converts into generalizable perceptions of social relations. But can numerous instances of a particular injustice be resolved by a single "solution"? How can an aesthetics based on disjunction achieve closure?

Melodrama Plus

The beginning of *The New Menoza* is utterly commonplace: at home in Naumburg, Herr von Biederling introduces an honored guest, Prince Tandi, to his wife and to Wilhelmine, his daughter. Before the short scene is over, the drama will veer toward Gerstenberg's *Ugolino*, and Wilhelmine will lie unconscious on the floor. Called upon to describe his past, the Prince tells of his unjust imprisonment in a "pyramid tower." Finding himself in a coffin-sized enclosure, he decided to jump out into an abyss, in which he saw "nothing but myself and the movement I made to leap out. I sprang—" at which point Wilhelmine, who has not yet said a word, faints, and the Prince's story remains literally up in the air, never to be resumed.

Fainting is endemic in *The Tutor*: Gustchen, Läuffer, Major von Berg, his wife, and Fritz become incapacitated at various points in the play. The recognition of father and daughter in the penultimate scene of *The Soldiers* culminates in the startling stage direction: "*Both roll half-dead on the ground.*" These sudden shocks have been described as the explosion of an intense feeling at a moment of low resistance that propels the figure from one emotional extreme to another.[18] As a rule, Lenz's protagonists are inhibited by social decorum, and they lack the Promethean hero's safety valve of hyperbolic rhetoric. Excessive stress thus causes an abrupt breakdown. Unlike the proverbial Kleistian swoon—a dramatic climax occurring when a character is overcome by conflicting desires or pressures—the Lenzian faint seems like an *over-reaction*, a psychological breakdown of such melodramatic extravagance that it appears comically inappropriate. In *The New Menoza*,

fainting is, in fact, subjected to an inspired parody by Herr von Biederling, after Prince Tandi has recovered from a swoon.

> HERR VON BIEDERLING: . . . (*Places both hands on his forehead.*)
> Prince! I'm feeling the same way you did, I'm losing my voice,
> devil take it, and soon I'll lose my senses, blast it . . . (*With a
> weak voice.*) Wife, will you wake me?
> FRAU VON BIEDERLING: God, what is . . . (*Goes to him.*)
> HERR VON BIEDERLING (*Jumps up.*): Nothing, I just wanted to
> make a joke. Ha ha ha, you women can be fooled anytime.

The joke is also on the spectator, who can never be certain about the
genre in which Lenz is operating. After all, he originally subtitled *The
Tutor* "Comedy and Tragedy," which was changed to "A Comedy" by
another hand (*Hofmeister*, 10)—although Lenz repeatedly referred to it
as "my tragedy" (*Werke* 3:259, 287, 290). An often-cited example of
Lenz's conviction that dramatists must write comically and tragically at
the same time is Major von Berg's rescue of his daughter from drowning
in a pond (*Tutor* 4, 4–5). After his heroic leap ("This is the way to Gustchen or to hell!"), there is much cursing and fumbling with a pole. The
episode concludes:

> MAJOR VON BERG: . . . (*He takes her in his arms.*) There, girl—I
> really ought to take you back to the pond (*Swings her toward the
> pond.*)—but we don't want to go swimming until we've learned
> how to swim, I think.— (*Presses her against his heart.*) Oh, my
> only dearest treasure! That I can carry you in my arms again,
> you wicked scoundrel! (*Carries her off.*)

Such simultaneity of conflicting moods is one of Lenz's most significant
dramatic innovations. The situations he creates resist generic classifica-
tion because he wants to overcome the traditional elitism of these categories. He claims in his "Review of *The New Menoza*" that comedy, the
genre of the *Volk*, was devalued to "the comic" by post-Shakespearean
aestheticians. As a portrait of society, contemporary comedy must
reflect both its serious and comic visages (*Werke* 2:703). By not placing
a great deal of importance on the circumstances he portrays—that is, by
not incorporating signals indicating their "correct" interpretation according to a hierarchy of aesthetic response linked to social status—he

presents dramatic events as "open concepts" that do not correspond to conventional generic expectations and, therefore, cannot be passively "consumed." Robbed of predictable stereotypes and vicarious emotions, spectators are compelled to reconstitute themselves as critical observers if they wish to understand Lenz's art.[19]

In a sense, Lenz dramatizes reality from inside and outside; that is, intense emotion is shown to be subjectively real but at the same time—depending on its context—objectively ridiculous. To call this dramaturgy tragicomic is inadequate, because Lenz does not simply combine the genres;[20] he allows them to coexist, compelling the spectator to ponder the tragic and comic implications of a single action as if it were a hologram that changes appearance when viewed from a different perspective. In terms of characterization, Lenz emphasizes the frailty of the subject, who appears as an indeterminate composite of free will and attitudinal conditioning. The individual's environment offers no consolation: it causes suffering, but it does not reflect it. Lenz heightens and clarifies conflict through caricature and melodrama,[21] but at the same time he complicates the interpretation of conflict by stripping tragedy of pathos, comedy of liberating laughter. His dramas somehow manage to stage *themselves* against the grain, leaving their audiences with vacillating judgments.

If dramatic actions cannot be generically differentiated, and if they, like their characters, tend toward melodramatic collapse, can traditional categories of closure apply to them?

Shifting Ideologemes

In his *Theory of the Middle-Class Tragedy in the Eighteenth Century*, Peter Szondi analyzes three paradigms of middle-class existence in eighteenth-century European drama: the merchant, the paterfamilias, and the victim. The latter is symbolized by the tutor Läuffer, who is driven to self-mutilation by a society "whose citizens prefer to kill the revolutionary rather than the dictator."[22] As a historical and aesthetic signifier of oppression, the image of the castrated menial is indeed powerfully evocative, yet Lenz's dramaturgy tends to undercut such a conceptualization of reality. He relativizes potential ideologemes, or units of an ideological structure, as if to strip them of their artificial aura, presenting them instead as everyday chance happenings that must somehow be taken in stride.[23] Employing an estrangement technique contrary to that described in the previous segment, Lenz de-melodramatizes events that conventionally generate high emotional intensity. After Läuffer admits to Wenzeslaus that he has castrated himself, he immediately regrets the act (*Tutor* 5,3). Instead of offering his sympathy, Wenzeslaus—who in a sense castrated himself long before—praises Läuffer extravagantly. The latter tentatively accepts this expression of solidarity, hoping to be "reborn as Wenzeslaus," but a few scenes later he has fallen in love with Lise and has no greater wish than to undo his present condition. To his amazement, he discovers her to be a willing bride, and so his final status as a social casualty remains ambivalent. From the moment he announced the castration, he has been deprived of the martyr's consistency and grandeur that would ennoble his victimization.

The New Menoza offers a similar example: no sooner have the recently married Prince Tandi and Wilhelmine discovered to their horror that they are brother and sister than the pedantic Magister Beza appears, claiming that the incest taboo does not violate Holy Scripture. Instead of joining the general lamentation, he and Herr von Biederling ride off to Leipzig to get an expert opinion on the matter. The tragic weight of the dramatic crisis is siphoned off by arguments and counter-arguments until the dilemma is abruptly resolved by Babet's melodramatic revelation of Wilhelmine's noble birth. In both plays, Lenz debunks entrenched theological/philosophical conceptions about castration and incest through comic twists. What would normally be viewed as a blow of fate, to be accepted with resignation, is shown to be circumstantial, open to constant reinterpretation. Those who nonetheless hold firmly to conventional beliefs, as do Prince Tandi and Wilhelmine, suffer the most.

Certain character types in Lenz's dramas also undergo surprising metamorphoses. In particular, his blustering, authoritarian father figures are subjected—perhaps for autobiographical reasons—to humiliating personality changes that transcend the convention of these roles. Major von Berg is the outstanding example; his comic breakdown ends up parodying not only the self-indulgent sentimentalism of the affluent classes but Sturm und Drang melancholia itself. When his daughter's health deteriorates, his gloom drives him first to manic farming: "I must work, I must scratch out a living to get my daughter a place in the hospital" (*Tutor* 2,6); "I'm going to . . . take my shovel and become a peasant" (3,1). Once his daughter has run off, he yearns for a more potent diversion: "They say the Russians are fighting the Turks; . . . I'm going to leave my wife and die in Turkey" (4,1). These "excesses," as his brother calls them, signify a loss of control beyond the normal parameters of the character. Yet his behavior, though ludicrous, is not unrealistic; Lenz exposes an aspect of the social type that decorum ordinarily conceals.

If conventional signifiers shift so readily, how can a dramatic structure be sturdy enough to sustain the weight of closure? The subsequent sections of this chapter will attempt to measure some of the components of Lenz's denouements.

Happy Endings

With its three semiautonomous plots, *The Tutor* comes to multiple conclusions. They all result from implausible coincidences, and their mood seems unnaturally cheerful compared to the injustice and misery that precede them. The generic and stylistic shift from "black" to sentimental comedy is indeed formidable; as Girard writes, "Gellert is substituted for Lenz."[24] Critics frequently interpret the resolutions as parodistic, satiric, or absurdist commentary on Lenz's middle-class milieu.[25] Scherpe's and Winter's contentions that Lenz was unable to resolve the contradictions he discerns between human nature and social reality are persuasive,[26] yet I would question the apparent consensus among critics that by the end of *The Tutor*, its figures are, in Winter's words, "hopelessly discredited when they arrive in the legitimate harbor of marriage," inhibiting audience identification or empathy.[27] The logic and momentum of Lenz's resolutions, I think, run a different course.

The first denouement is Läuffer's and Lise's engagement in the penultimate scene. This finale is not quite so bizarre as it might seem when one considers the alternatives open to Lenz at this point in the play. The generic options during the eighteenth century were clear-cut: every major character either dies, exits society (into a convent, jail, etc.), or, if single, gets married. Not even a dramatist of such modernist sensibilities as Lenz considered, as far as we know, leaving characters to face a wholly open, ambivalent future. For Läuffer, the convent option would have meant becoming like Wenzeslaus, yet he already knew that the schoolmaster's way of life would be intolerable for him. Having him be killed (as he almost was) or killing himself would have been "horrible" in Lessing's sense (see chap. 2); unlike his counterpart Stolzius, who becomes a murderer, Läuffer is largely unresponsible for his condition. Beyond being partly culpable for Gustchen's pregnancy, he has caused no harm to others. For Lenz's liberal contemporaries (if not for the religious orthodoxy), Läuffer's otherwise unmotivated death surely would have been perceived as unearned suffering, exceeding the limits of what could be shown as the effects of an unjust society.[28] A tragic death for Läuffer – in remorse, perhaps – would have been simply out of character, because this half-comic figure could not possibly assume the role of possessor of a tragic flaw.[29] He is not even adept at the discourse of pathos; his most sustained attempt – a conventional apostrophe to the audience – rings false to modern ears: "O Innocence, what a pearl you are! Ever since I lost you, I've taken step after step in passion and ended in despair. If this last step does not bring me death, perhaps I can begin a new life and be reborn as Wenzeslaus" (Tutor 5,3).[30] One other alternative is hinted at by Major von Berg: after fishing his daughter out of the pond, he says to her: "If you had said just one word earlier, I would have bought the rogue a patent of nobility, and then you could have crawled in the sack together" (Tutor 4,5).[31] Here Lenz's skepticism-realism seems to prevail: he apparently thought *this* possibility to be even less likely than Läuffer's finding a beautiful young girl who is so ingenuous as to argue her way into a marriage with a eunuch.

Though naive and infatuated with superficialities, Lise is a surprisingly strong character. Utterly convinced of her incipient good fortune, she counters every remonstrance from Wenzeslaus and, as the scene ends, she raises Läuffer's hopes to ecstasy: "Let's go to your father, Lise! His consent will make me the happiest man on earth!" Although her logic is bizarre, the momentum of her sincerity overcomes any devaluation of her outlook; unlike *Stella*'s conclusion, this ending seems free of skepticism. That is, although the couple's happiness may seem extremely tenuous, it is valid for the moment, like the ending of a fairy tale that offers at least a glimpse of a utopian future before reasonable doubts arise concerning unrealistic solutions, gender stereotyping, and so forth. The ending may well be relativized by other currents in the play, but it is not *negated* by them. Lenz's dramaturgy, we recall, does not permit the term *context* to stand for a monolithic or totalizing principle.

For Läuffer, Lise's unqualified acceptance of him is like winning a lottery (which is precisely how Pätus achieves his good fortune). Although a one-in-a-million chance, it is nonetheless what Büchner was to call "a possibility of existence." In Läuffer's case, there is even historical precedent: during the eighteenth century, some castrati did marry. Considering Lenz's commitment to and self-identification with the oppressed, he would certainly have believed that a handicapped tutor, like everyone else, is entitled to happiness. (Does a critic's stridency about Läuffer's and Lise's supposedly grotesque or absurd union perhaps testify to a subconscious bias against the handicapped?) A passage in his tract *On Soldiers' Marriages* concisely expresses Lenz's sensibility toward the sufferings of the exploited.

> Oh, a person never dreads the unavoidable hardships of a situation when happy and alluring prospects are before him on the opposite shore. —But no human creature, not even a beast, can endure for long being tormented or even just harassed *without interruption*. (*Werke* 2:811)[32]

He sympathizes because the exploited embody aspects of his own situation, and the comic genre allows him to give them their deserved "humane" rewards.[33] The highest goal a drama can strive for, he in fact maintains, is to "reveal a prospect that delights our entire being, creating a feeling of bliss such as we have never experienced before." If a play fulfills this emotional need for an ending, it deserves being called "excellent" (*Werke* 2:673). Such statements, it should be noted, are very much in conformance with the aesthetic expectations of his time.

Gustchen, like Läuffer, is weak rather than heroic or malevolent. Despite an unnaturally long pregnancy and considerable hardship,[34] her child is quite robust, so Gustchen too has no crimes on her conscience and is hence disqualified for tragedy.[35] Pätus is a rather appealing bungler, and, as a seducer, he is, in Fritz von Berg's imagery, "a teakettle that can't control itself" rather than a "villain" (*Tutor* 6,6). He pays his moral dues and wins the lottery, an incredible solution to a hopeless family dilemma, but nonetheless once again a "possibility of existence." Not only is Old Pätus miraculously reformed, but he is reunited with *his* mother. This metamorphosis in particular seems autobiographically motivated, considering Lenz's vain attempts throughout his life to win the respect of his own father.[36] Despite the accumulating improbabilities, a fairy-tale rather than parodistic mood prevails in these reconciliations, because, as with Läuffer and Lise, the playwright does not undermine the sincerity of his figures through debasing caricature or cynical commentary. The happy endings are wish realizations for them, himself, and his audience. The sons reform the fathers, and the bourgeoisie achieves (momentary) symbiosis with the enlightened aristocracy.[37]

Prince Tandi and Wilhelmine are joyfully reunited as well in a conventional comic denouement that promises them a lifetime of middle-class respectability. Yet Lenz's most unusual, intense, and narcissistic happy ending is that of his play, *Friends Make the Philosopher*, begun in late 1775, the same year Goethe wrote *Stella*. Like *Stella*, it is a short, five-act drama, in fact almost of identical length. The original title of this curious mixture of philosophical play and drama of intrigue apparently was to be "The Poet, Path to a Husband." In *Friends Make the Philosopher*, Goethe's configuration is reversed: two men vie for the same woman. In the final act, the protagonist Strephon seems to have misplayed his opportunities to win his Seraphine, who has just married Don Prado. On their wedding night, Seraphine tells Don Prado that she will always love Strephon. Strephon enters through the window, intent on shooting himself in the couple's presence. But Don Prado has already agreed to step aside for Strephon's sake, calling himself "Heaven's agent for your happiness" and claiming that "delight in a great deed compensates for delight in great pleasure" (*Friends* 5,2–3). He announces that they will live according to a "plan, which will remain an eternal secret among the three of us." Significantly, the drama ends with Strephon embracing not his bride but Don Prado's knees, exclaiming: "O what a delight it is to worship a human being!" (*Friends* 5,3).[38] It seems likely that Lenz, a congenital second fiddle in affairs of the heart, idealized himself in both men—the philosopher/hero who finally gets the woman he deserves, and the admirable abdicator whose sacrifice makes him an exemplar of humanity.

Of course, none of these utopian solutions change the structure of the society in which they occur.[39] As long as Lenz maintains his focus on individuals rather than on social relations, happy endings are still possible.

Silenced Women

The complex reconciliations of the von Berg and Pätus families at the conclusion of *The Tutor* are negotiated by five men. Gustchen and Miss Rehaar are mere props and speak not a word; the Major's wife is absent.[40] No women appear in the last scenes of *The New Menoza*; *Friends Make the Philosopher*, as we have just seen, ends with a man embracing another man. The entire Sturm und Drang movement, for that matter, counts no women among its authors, and its dramatic repertoire of women figures is limited to a handful of character types, such as the innocent daughter, marked for seduction; the "comic" mother, often with social ambitions; the liberal, well-educated aristocrat; the vengeful aristocrat; or the "old crone." Some of the most differentiated representations of women in eighteenth-century German literature derive, in fact, from Enlightenment authors rather than from those of the Sturm und Drang period, since the latter had been influenced by Rousseau to define gender inequality as an unalterable phenomenon of nature.[41] Moreover, their preoccupation with the psyche tended to translate into male self-absorption, but in their defense one could claim that they accurately reproduced the passive, subservient role of women in the patriarchal society of eighteenth-century Germany. The stereotypes, in other words, may have been essentially correct. What is vital to ascertain, however, is to what degree the Sturm und Drang playwright assumed that women must fatalistically accept their status, or whether his insights into oppressive social mechanisms also generated potential forms of resistance against them.

As I indicated in chapter 2, the Sturm und Drang's social conscience was focused particularly on the plight of the seduced virgin and the unwed mother. Their ostracism and the unmerciful punishment they faced if harm came to an illegitimate child outraged many enlightened citizens. The topic had dramatic potential as well, for it conveyed with exceptional vividness the exploitation of the weak by the strong, and much pathos could be wrung from the tribulations of an abandoned and defenseless woman. Lenz's dominant concern, however, was to document rather than to emotionalize a social injustice. His three-page fragment, "Magisters Lieschen," is a textbook study of sexual harassment: having been cast out by her employers, Lieschen seeks shelter and money from the Magister, who will help her only if she agrees to sleep with him. A scene in the unfinished "The Lowly Ones" highlights male fickleness, and the unjustifiably neglected novella "Zerbin or The New Philosophy" presents an idealized yet deeply affecting portrait of a woman who is to be executed for a concealed pregnancy that resulted in a stillborn child. To the last, she refuses to name her cowardly seducer. However, Lenz's exceptional achievement in this regard, as I mentioned earlier, is to have demonstrated how the exploited collaborate in their victimization and internalize the ideology that oppresses them. Here, gender is of secondary concern: Gustchen enters into a self-destructive liaison because she is isolated and repressed, but so too is Läuffer—like Zerbin, they "had to love something" (*Werke*, 2:367). Gender distinctions do arise, however, in the *quality* of the characterizations in *The Tutor*—Läuffer, Major von Berg, and Wenzeslaus are more complex figures than the rather bland women. Since *The Tutor*, overtly a "message" play, focuses on the hardships of an occupation that Lenz himself had endured, Gustchen's pregnancy and Miss Rehaar's seduction are presented as significant yet ancillary results of a male dilemma. *The Soldiers*, on the other hand, achieves a greater thematic equality of the sexes: the remarkably multifaceted Marie Wesener and the forceful, well-intentioned Countess de la Roche balance if not overshadow the many male roles. In this instance, the play had germinated out of his concern about the injustice done to a woman by one of his employers. Unlike *The Tutor*, *The Soldiers*—despite its title—could be said to have a "female center."

Lenz tended to worship women from afar, pouring his feelings into his letters. His psychological instability alienated him from those with whom he might have had more lasting relationships. His favorable representations of women tended to be idealized, and his portrait, in *The Soldiers*, of the Countess Sophie de la Roche, whose name he used without alteration, was a wish fulfillment of a more than personal dimension. As he wrote to her in 1775, he saw in her kind a potential savior for the oppressed.

> If only persons of your rank, your insights, your sensibility could lower yourselves wholly into the lives of these poor people, perceiving like God what causes them grief and joy, and how they cope in their own way with their grief, which often could be simply pushed away by an enlightened person's hand, like the stone before Christ's grave. (*Werke* 3:325)

In his play, she becomes Marie Wesener's benevolent patron, who, typical for an Enlightened aristocratic reformer, goes beyond merely perceiving Marie's grief and joy and tries to alter her behavior.[42] At the drama's conclusion, she initiates the suggestion that certain women be "sacrificed" to soldiers in order to protect "the remaining wives and daughters" (*Soldiers* 5,5). The Colonel concurs, and gender distinctions disappear as they alternately present their ideas. Soon thereafter Lenz revised the ending, indicating that his reformist zeal had given way to an awareness of the plan's injustice toward women (*Werke* 1:733–34). The Countess now contradicts the Colonel, and her objections culminate in: "How little you men know the heart and desires of a woman." The consensus is destroyed and the plan seems invalidated because it could only be carried out by imposing it on women against their will. Lenz appears to have been of two minds on this issue: by ignoring the Countess, the Colonel converts into an insensitive, authoritarian figure, but he is nonetheless granted the last word. The scene as a whole becomes an illustration of gender antagonism rather than a conduit for a reformist message.

    The discrepancy highlights Lenz's persistent attempts to understand the difference between male and female perceptions and expectations of each other. "If I have studied myself correctly," he wrote to Sophie de la Roche, "the greatest wish of our sex is to be loved by yours in a *flattering* way; perhaps the greatest wish of your sex is to be respected by ours in an impeccably gallant way" (*Werke* 3:330). At times naive, at times sagacious, he endeavored to diagnose the effects of intellect, sentiment, sexuality, and prevailing codes of behavior on male-female relationships. His methodology seems inconsistent: whereas the enlightened Countess de la Roche emerges as the equal of the highest ranking male figure in *The Soldiers*, women are relegated to the margins until they become virtually invisible by the end of *The Tutor*. Moreover, Lenz allows Fritz von Berg to say about "his" Gustchen: "She need only look in the mirror to be assured that she is the source of all my happiness, and yet she always trembles at what she calls her unbearable thought that she will make me unhappy. Oh, can I expect anything else from such a woman besides heaven?" Modern sensibilities will find this disconcerting, yet it remains unclear whether Lenz admired or was parodying such timid dependency. The uncertain status of women at the conclusions of his dramas are symptomatic not only of his personal insecurities but of the changing conception of femininity during his era. The emergence of the passive, sentimentalized help-mate as a feminine ideal was displacing the more progressive role model of the learned woman—who in turn persistently found herself at odds with the male-directed impulse toward enlightened social im-provement. In late eighteenth-century drama, this impulse tended to degenerate into didactic blustering before the curtain falls, and it is con-ceivable that Lenz was trying to spare women this indignity. When a woman does speak up—like the Countess in the revised ending of *The Soldiers*—she explodes the reformist dream.

Self-reflexivity

No eighteenth-century German writer tore the veil of discretion from the process of thinking and writing as violently as did Lenz. In his "Notes on the Theater," a hybrid of several lectures converted into a published introduction for his translation of Shakespeare's *Love's Labour's Lost*, he transforms his irresolute, self-questioning method of conceptualization into a theme of the play. He goes to extreme lengths to undermine the authoritarian gestus of theoretical discourse: he ad-mits not having finished reading something, he forgets what he was go-ing to say, he prepares to stop because he is getting tired, and he fails to end his last sentence. The effect is, of course, quite modern, inciting skepticism of closed philosophical systems and self-reflexivity concern-ing one's mode of discourse. It is impossible to determine exactly how premeditated or spontaneous was his disjunctive style that attempted to mediate without closure between metaphysics and empiricism.[43] Not only was Lenz skeptical about adequately formulating an idea, but he was startlingly frank about the difficulty of getting it across in writing.

> In the midst of the most brilliant perception of [a writer's] magical powers, of their impact on [a reader's] heart, a million unwelcome thoughts—your page of criticism—your unfinished novel—your letter—often down to your underwear—gone are the sweet illu-sions, there you wriggle on the sand again after swimming for a moment in a sea of passion. (*Werke* 2:657)

Lenz's anticipation of the language crisis, the literary epidemic of the twentieth century, surfaces in his dramas as well.[44] Distrust of

inherited patterns of discourse coincided with doubts about established generic forms. His experimentation in this regard reached its climax in *The New Menoza*, Germany's first postmodern drama.

The play is alternately a social comedy verging on tragedy, a fairy
tale, a didactic critique of Western civilization, and a drama of violent
passion and feudal intrigue with an ending that has nothing to do with
any of this.[45] On numerous occasions, Lenz apologized with good
cause for its inconsistencies and fragmentary state. Of interest to us
here are its final scenes, which constitute what is surely one of the most
surprising endings in the history of European drama. After Prince
Tandi and Wilhelmine are rejoined, and the Count Chameleon has got-
ten his just deserts, the last two scenes are given over to a minor character (Zierau) and his father (the Mayor, who appears for the first time).
Contrary to the precepts of classical aesthetics, the ending introduces
not only a new character but an entirely new theme, which is *the play
itself*. The drama becomes self-reflexive;[46] the first words of the Mayor,
"Nice stories! Nice stories!" can be read as a reference to that which the
audience has just seen. He now, however, wants "recreation": the puppet show. His lower-class preference for Punch-and-Judy comedy is
countered by his jaded son's disquisitions on good taste and the
Aristotelian unities. Lenz recapitulates here (on another level of self-
reflexivity) his disputes with the Aristotelian drama theorists of his
day. The Mayor grudgingly promises to pay heed to the unities and to
"the imitation of nature" during his evening's entertainment. But upon
his return, the Mayor (Lenz?) beats his son (Lenz's critics?) for having
destroyed his pleasure by making him too conscious of himself as a
fault-finding spectator. This literally slapstick finish itself resembles a
puppet play,[47] which proves its point not primarily by its arguments
but by its comic effect. In retrospect, the aesthetic of the puppet play
clarifies the rather amorphous structure of the entire drama:
comic/melodramatic stylization counterbalances the play's centrifugal
tendency toward extreme individuation. The work defines itself as an
uninhibited, convention-flouting entertainment for the masses, with
intense passions, broad comedy, and doses of useful wisdom. For
Lenz, the arbiters of culture had become so elitist in distinguishing
"higher" from "lower" forms of art that hitting them over the head was
probably the only way to draw their attention to the neglected dramatic
potential of a venerable folk tradition. Through the puppet play, Lenz
moves toward the theater of the future.

There is (as usual) an alternate ending: Lenz wrote a more definitive conclusion for the Count Chameleon-Donna Diana subplot (*Werke* 1:723–24). I know of no scene in Sturm und Drang drama that portrays aristocratic depravity and violence – to which Lessing could only allude in *Emilia Galotti* – so graphically. While recovering from the stab wound Donna Diana inflicted on him, the Count begs her forgiveness and proclaims his love, but only to manipulate her into procuring Wilhelmine for him, who is, of course, not only married but his own relative. The enraged Donna tears off his bandage, "*scratches his wound with her nails*," calls him a sodomite, muffles his screams with a handkerchief, and leaves him to die as the curtain falls. Lenz insisted in his "Review of *The New Menoza*" that far from exaggerating his portraits of the aristocracy, he was toning them down to avoid offending his audience (*Werke* 2:702). What appears to be conventional fire-and-brimstone dramaturgy turns out to be yet another form of behavioral documentation: for Lenz, the real life of the dissipated upper classes resembled a bad melodrama. They may be as ruthless as the aristocracy of *Macbeth* and *King Lear*, but they lack its grandeur. Lenz did not shut his eyes to the contradiction that this was the class from whom he expected enlightened leadership in social reform.

A final ambiguity: it is impossible to determine unequivocally whether this scene was written before or after the published ending.

Reformism

For Lenz, drama was never an end unto itself. Like Creation, which art was to imitate, it was governed by a purpose. "With every newly published play, let our question be the great, divine *Cui bono?* . . . what is its impact?" he wrote in his essay on Goethe's *Götz von Berlichingen* (*Werke* 2:639). His emphasis on art's usefulness and value links him to the Enlightenment, but what distances him somewhat from the tradition of didactic drama ranging from Gottsched to Brecht is his Sturm und Drang conception of theatrical impact as a chiefly affective rather than cognitive stimulus. He counterposed his ideal against the ephemeral effects of French theater.

We take home with us a lovely, delightful, sweet feeling, as if we had drunk a bottle of champagne – but that's all. One good night's sleep and it's all gone. Where is the *living* impression that later

intrudes into one's sentiments, deeds, and *actions*—where the
Promethean spark, which having crept unawares into our inmost
soul, . . . inspires our entire existence? (*Werke*, 2:639)

His art was a response to the question he poses at the outset of "Zerbin
or The New Philosophy": "We live in a century in which the love of
mankind and Sentimentalism are no longer rare: why is it then that one
encounters so many unfortunate people among us?" Most "humanitar-
ians," he claims, love mankind only in the abstract, being too callous
and self-centered to love individuals (*Werke* 2:354). Through his writing
he hoped to arouse sympathy for the disadvantaged and to "counteract
moral decay" (*Werke*, 3:326). In his "Letters on the Morality of *The Sufferings of Young Werther*," he maintains that literary works must be judged
by "their moral effect . . . on the hearts of the public," yet he denies
that his works have a moral *intention*, "for then [the poet] ceases to be
a poet." The Councillor's criticism of private tutoring, he insists, derives not from the playwright's Weltanschauung but from the character's personality (*Werke* 2:675–76). That is, the play's sententiousness allegedly originates from Lenz's objectifying, "casuistic" dramaturgy
rather than from a preconceived ideological standpoint. Apodictic
statements are to be understood as having a situational but no absolute
validity. This contradiction between trying to reproduce individual experience realistically and to extrapolate intersubjective generalizations
from it remains unresolved in his aesthetics, letters, and his social
dramas. Thus, on the one hand, he strives to heighten the impact of the
real by erasing his presence as its mediator; on the other, he shapes his
characters' rhetoric to move his audience to pity and indignation. He
wants art to be as shocking as nature, although he knows that his audience accepts in life what it will not accept in art. He "opens" his scenes
to make room for the boundless complexity of a single being while ar-
ranging his plots and incorporating lengthy debates to convey his opin-
ions about social inequities. He articulates reformist ideals from both
the believer's and the skeptic's perspective.

These warring impulses undermine the basis for unified endings.
In the midst of the multiple reconciliations in *The Tutor*, the play's social
theme suddenly—and awkwardly— resurfaces. Fritz von Berg, who
has become stiffly didactic, as if he were warming up to deliver the final
moral, picks up Gustchen's child and says: "This child is now mine as

well – a sad testimony to the weakness of your sex and the folly of ours; but most of all to the advantages of educating young girls by tutors" (*Tutor* 5,12). Another long argument threatens, but the Councillor squelches it with: "But we shall talk of this another time." When a line like this occurs in the denouement of a Shakespearean play, it means to spare the spectators the retelling of events they, but not all the characters, are familiar with. In Lenz's drama, it signifies what the play has already illustrated: the problem remains unresolved. A public school education under the likes of Wenzeslaus is no alternative to the ills of private tutoring. Besides, as Lenz implies in his "*Werther* Letters," no individual is sufficiently capable of rising above self-interest to make a definitive, generally valid statement about such a matter. Debate, therefore, does not conclude, it simply stops. Undeterred, Fritz speaks the last line as if he were ending a conventional Enlightenment comedy, symbolically transmitting the play's lesson to future generations: "In any case, my dear boy, I shall never let you be educated by tutors." What is utopian about this ending is not its message but its *form*. Like the happy endings described previously, the enlightened solution is an essential ingredient of Lenz's aesthetics of affect. It symbolizes a prospect of happiness necessary for human survival because it interrupts the torment of life's injustices. As before, social reality does not negate but coexists with the utopian ending, which is worthy of being celebrated, however briefly.

In *The Soldiers*, the tension between regulative morality and explosive violence is heightened by jealousy. At an early stage of the play's genesis, Lenz contemplated a different outcome for Stolzius: he encounters his rival and "tears out his guts after plunging his sword in his heart." Later he happens upon Marie and being drunk, tries to rape her, but upon recognizing her, "he dies in her arms" (*Werke* 1:732–33). His poisoning of Desportes and himself in the published version seems quite benign in comparison. The murder scene, however, shifts uncharacteristically from intense drama to moralizing; Lenz allows Stolzius to spell out the plot's didactic intent in the explicit style of the early Enlightenment.

DESPORTES: I'm poisoned.
STOLZIUS: Yes, traitor, you are. . . . If the likes of you can't live
   without ruining women, why do you pick on those who can't

resist you, who believe every word you say? You are avenged, my Marie! God cannot condemn me. (*Sinks to the floor.*)

(*Soldiers* 5,3)

To show a cloth merchant murdering an aristocrat was, in Lenz's day, a daring act that evidently required unambiguous moral legitimation.

The Soldiers' final scene confirms that the play is even more of a thesis piece than is *The Tutor*. After the Colonel promises to use his wealth and influence to rehabilitate the Weseners, the rest of the scene addresses the problem of soldiers' immorality, which for Lenz was a personal crusade on two distinct levels. First, he hoped that his play might prevent the possible dishonor-through-abandonment of Cleophe Fibich, betrothed to Lenz's employer, the Baron Friedrich Georg von Kleist. As Lenz explained to Herder:

> The girl upon whom the main figure of my *Soldiers* is modeled is now happily expecting her fiancé, an officer, to return to her in good faith. Whether he'll do it or deceive her, God knows. *If he deceives her*, then *The Soldiers* couldn't become known quickly enough, to destroy the man or perhaps to whip him into doing his duty. *If he doesn't deceive her*, then the play might possibly destroy all her happiness and her honor. . . . (*Werke* 3:416)

Lenz had, in fact, helped draw up the marriage contract. His outrage about wrongdoing was clearly as intense in the private as in the public sphere, and he used his most potent weapon, playwriting, to effect a resolution.

The drama, moreover, was a component of his plan to eliminate once and for all the danger posed by unmarried soldiers to vulnerable but respectable middle-class girls. In both versions of the final scene, the hope is expressed that "someone could be found to implement these ideas at the court." Here Lenz rather brazenly refers to himself or to a highly placed person influenced by his endeavors, which culminated in the tract, *On Soldiers' Marriages*. He planned to submit it to the courts of Weimar and of France. *The Soldiers'* final scene and its revision represent early stages of his ideas on the subject, and Girard is correct in viewing the essay essentially as the "third ending" to the drama.[48] Lenz's willingness to revise his dramatic text or to suppress it entirely, depending on his assessment of its function (see *Werke* 3:353–54), underscores its unfinished, provisional quality. Having to "freeze" a text in print clashed with his apparent desire to communicate uninterruptedly with his audience. No drama of its time, in fact, reflected its origins so openly—that is, none contrasted as radically with the classical ideal of transforming spontaneous, quotidian experience into "timeless," immutable art. Lenz was constantly "inside" the problems he dramatized. Perceptual distortions were therefore conspicuous and unavoidable—yet nonetheless preferable to the *disguised* perceptual distortions of the so-called objective observer, viewing from a depersonalized distance.

Critics have neglected to comment on the hyperbolic conclusion to the final scene. In language most peculiar for a colonel, he expresses his conviction that state-supported prostitutes for soldiers would cause a "disrupted society to bloom anew and there would be peace and well-being for all, kissing each other in serenity and joy."[49] His final utterance is rather childlike—is Lenz emphasizing that all utopias are naive, that only childlike faith can sustain them? This final vision, including the image of "kissing each other," survives in the revision despite the many other alterations; Lenz was apparently convinced of its appropriateness, continuing to believe in the validity of the optimistic, inspirational conclusion of Enlightenment comedy. To maintain that the social conditions he dramatized refute Lenz's reformist idealism is to reduce their multilayered endings to expressions of cynicism or despair.[50] As an eighteenth-century writer, Lenz was perhaps losing his faith in positive resolutions—his hyperbolic rhetoric may be a symptom of the strain of sustaining such a belief—but, unlike many modern writers, he had not yet lost it entirely. His reformism was at once farsighted, unrealistic, and obsessive—and I hasten to emphasize that I consider all three to be positive qualities. The exploitation and moral corruption he described were epidemic and called for systemic remedies that were gradually applied only in the course of the next century.[51] "Realistic" reformism, however, was that espoused by Goethe in Weimar, which represented for Lenz too much of a compromise and for Goethe eventual disillusionment. Lenz did not go so far as to envision class warfare; for him the enlightened aristocracy was still the only truly *potent* source for social change, since he seemed to have no hopes of revolution from the submissive, fragmented middle classes. Not being a social theorist, his point of origin was inevitably the individual's suffering and hopes. As detrimental as it surely was to his mental health, his obsessiveness sustained his optimism and his creativity. He disregarded, for instance, Goethe's advice to burn his drafts of *On Soldiers' Marriages* and continued to work on the project (*Werke* 2:946). Although his activism was ineffective during his lifetime, he appeared to be driven by the perception that those who merely demand the possible achieve nothing, whereas those who demand the impossible at least achieve the possible.

Anticlosure

No one among Lenz's contemporaries believed more firmly that he was a prophet than he did himself, and in his typically maladroit fashion, he made no secret about it. In his literary satire *Pandämonium Germanicum* (1775), a gold mine for psychoanalytic critics, he has Klopstock, Herder, and Lessing announce in chorus: "Even if [Lenz] accomplishes nothing, his perceptions were grand" (*Werke* 1:270). While Goethe "accomplishes" in the present, Lenz calls out to the next century (1:270–71). He who found so little support and confirmation during his lifetime might have been consoled to hear how certain catchphrases of the 1960s and 1970s evoke aspects of his legacy: "the medium is the message"; "the personal is the political." The manifold, open structure of much of his writing transmits a raw, uncensored subjectivity that perpetually evolves, questioning and contradicting itself, rebelling against finality. His "hologrammatic" dramaturgy, which erases bias through constant shifts in focus, renders problematic concepts of class and gender, as well as genre, plot, characterization, and conclusion. The social dramas give the impression that they could be endlessly rewritten, with different scenes and changed endings. In this they conform more to Brecht's theory of the learning play than do Brecht's own models. Rooted as he is in eighteenth-century dramaturgy, Lenz does not deny his audience cathartic relief as radically as does Büchner, yet Lenzian catharsis is always partial, always accompanied by a sense of impermanence. His endings are an accumulation of contradictory moods that fail to resolve into a uniformly positive or negative stance. Yet his denial of closure never coalesced into an *ideology* of open-endedness (which would, in fact, be self-contradictory). Lenz's methodology was more spontaneous than intentional, more a necessary expression of his nature than a self-conscious program of enlightenment. His insecurities and obsessions prevented him from making the compromises necessary for a stable existence; they freed him to pursue and articulate "unacceptable" insights. His nature predisposed him to resist closure whenever it signified complacency.

It would be false, however, to view Lenz's philosophy and art as fundamentally relativistic and, hence, to depoliticize it. His "aesthetics of servitude" had a profoundly moral basis, and his location of the subject between autonomy and determinism was rooted in the social reality of his time.[52] Unresolved controversies persistently intrude into the fairy-tale-like atmosphere of his plays. While affirming idealism, Lenz repudiated fixed concepts and ideological stasis, implying that no matter what may have been achieved, there is always a need to "talk of this another time," as the Councillor says. In this sense, Lenz was a post-revolutionary dramatist writing in a prerevolutionary time, for, in Brecht's terminology, his dialectic perspective is as applicable to the "challenges of the plain" as to the "challenges of the mountains" (i.e., the revolution) that precede them.[53] Lenz might well have been "a connoisseur of the deeper frustration suffered by collectivities without the requisite identity even to begin consequential revolutionary thinking," as Leidner maintains,[54] but precisely this sensibility can be seen as a vital complement to systematic theorizing. A disjunct rather than synthetic methodology such as Lenz's is receptive to the unintegrated detail, to the unanticipated circumstance that no theory, however elaborate, can predict.

"It is undoubtedly unusual that plays teach when they are themselves only learning," wrote Ernst Bloch in *The Principle of Hope*, "that their people and their actions are turned in a questioning-examining way and also transformed."[55] He classifies "dramas with several possible versions, evaluations of their course, their outcome" as models of the theater that "puts to the test," that continually seeks new alternatives to conventional perceptions and actions. He mentions Goethe's *Stella*, with its two endings, in this context. Lenz's social dramas likewise "play out the ways of behaving"[56] that put established assumptions to the test of their validity, yet, in contrast to other such plays, Lenz's experiments appear to be out of control. Dominants are shattered by emergents, wounds open up that deny closure, and there is never a guarantee of a meaningful or even comprehensible ending.

Chapter 4

Women, Death, and Revolution: Büchner's *Danton's Death*

At the end of the third act of *Danton's Death*, the dramatic action has played itself out. Danton and his faction have been arrested, his self-defense before the National Convention has failed, and the masses have shifted their allegiance from him to Robespierre. Robespierre himself has disappeared from view; after displaying a trace of humanity in act 1, he has reverted to being nothing more than a speech-making functionary derided behind his back by his own supporters. The epoch-making events of the Revolution – the fall of the Bastille, the arrest and execution of King Louis XVI, the September massacres, the purge of the Girondists – exist only as memories. The leaders have failed to serve the needs of the masses, who continue to call for bread although the aristocrats have been deposed. The downfall of Danton presages the downfall of Robespierre, signaling the Thermidorian reaction and the end of the Revolution. Both figures have no further historical function than to wait for death. History appears to have come to a stop; act 4 of *Danton's Death* justifiably begins with the words, "It's all over,"[1] and what follows is stasis.

The analogy to Büchner's situation is apparent. The revolutions of 1830 in France, Belgium, and Poland had failed; attempts to foment revolt in Hesse through agitational pamphlets such as the *Hessian Messenger* were unsuccessful; and the disparity between the trivial political reforms granted by the aristocracy and the necessity for fundamental social change was enormous. In his letters, Büchner often deplored how unsuitable the times were for revolution.

> . . . I have recently learned that only the essential needs of the masses can bring about change, that all activity and shouting by *individuals* is vain folly. (*CWL*, 252 [June, 1833])

I wouldn't tell you this if I could believe in the slightest possibility
of a political upheaval at this time. For the last six months I've been
utterly convinced that nothing is to be done and that anyone who
sacrifices himself *right now* is foolishly risking his neck. . . . Let's
hope for times to come! (*CWL*, 273 [1835])

Danton's Death is a product of the post-1830 malaise of a clear-sighted
social activist who considered impromptu rebellion to be "vain folly."
His drama is a critique of the shortcomings of the Jacobin hegemony;
his choice of the year 1794 rather than 1789 was motivated by his conviction that the ideals of the French Revolution had remained unrealized
and that the excesses of the Reign of Terror were an attempt to conceal
the failures of the ruling factions. Büchner's dilemma as a student of
history and as an artist was: how does one go on when historical progress appears to stagnate? How does one fill the void? The play's final
act takes place during such a historical hiatus; understanding how
Büchner resolves this formal and ideological problem can help us map
the intersections between his personal, political, and literary concerns.

In classical drama, the cessation of action is followed by ritual, such
as an execution, which in turn evokes a concluding lament bewailing
the tragic fall of the protagonist. Although *Danton's Death* can be considered, on one level, to be a requiem for the Dantonists and their ideals,
the play does not sustain the traditional hierarchical focus on one or
more primary figures. As the drama concludes, a significant gender
shift takes place: the last act is framed by women, who dominate the
dramatic action even though the bulk of the dialogue occurs in the
prison scenes, during which the Dantonists sit passively, waiting to be
executed. The mood of the play changes as well, as the historical
models for his female characters are displaced by literary ones. Büchner
allows Julie Danton and Lucile Desmoulins, who begin and end act 4,
to deviate considerably from reality: Julie Danton (actually named
Louise) did not precede her husband in death but married a baron in
1797 and eventually outlived even Büchner; Lucile Desmoulins did not
become deranged and sacrifice herself to the authorities but was arrested at the same time as her husband and went to her death fully in
control of her mental faculties. In the course of the last act, Büchner's
primary sources for these figures, Thiers's *History of the French Revolution* and Strahlheim's *Our Times*, give way to Shakespeare;[2] the

women's French-Revolutionary identities seem to blend into an amalgam of Shakespearean heroines. Why Büchner focuses on women and allows literary figures to overshadow historical ones in the final scenes of a drama about the French Revolution deserves exploration.

In act 1, scene 2, Portia and Hamlet are mentioned nearly in the same breath by the prompter Simon. Unwittingly, Simon has found a highly appropriate analogy for Danton and Julie; in his introspection and doubt, Danton is surely a Hamlet in extremis, and Julie imitates Portia's actions down to the detail of sending a servant to inquire after her husband's well-being.[3] Beyond the surface image of the loyal wife performing the ultimate sacrifice, however, the similarities end. Portia has, as she herself says, "a man's mind" (2, 4). She attempts to transcend the proverbial weaknesses of her sex in a drastic manner: she makes "strong proof of [her] constancy" by inflicting a "voluntary wound" on her thigh (2, 1) — the equivalent of a dueling scar as a proof of manliness. Her eventual suicide, prompted by her husband Brutus's misfortunes, is gruesome: Brutus reports that she "swallow'd fire" (4, 3). (That is, she "tooke hote burning coles and cast them into her mouth, and kept her mouth so close that she choked herselfe.")[4] Julie, on the other hand, drinks a vial of poison and pronounces her death "pleasant." Obviously, she is meant to project an image of femininity closer to that of her near namesake, Juliet, for whom poison is "a restorative."[5] Julie's description of the dying earth: "She's becoming ever paler; she's sinking like a corpse into the flood of the ether. Will no arm catch her by her golden locks and pull her from the stream and bury her?" (4, 6) recalls yet another Shakespearean woman, namely Ophelia, who also materializes in Lucile's apparent insanity and self-sacrifice. The lyrical tranquillity of Julie's and Lucile's final monologues expresses a peaceful acceptance of mortal endings. However, within the larger context of male-female relationships in *Danton's Death*, Büchner's portrayal of such uncompromising wifely devotion is quite problematic.

Dorothy James has recently pointed out that male Büchner commentators have tended to idealize Julie and Lucile uncritically.[6] These characterizations, she maintains, are "obviously to many an appealing fantasy."[7] Büchner's women are, indeed, often lauded for what is perceived to be their incorporeal purity, their naive innocence, and their emotional nature untainted by rational contemplation. Until the final act, Julie is nothing more than Danton's nurturing wife, and Lucile, worse yet, adores Camille so mindlessly that she cheerfully admits to not understanding a bit of the intellectual conversation that goes on around her (2, 3).[8] Julie's and Lucile's self-chosen deaths, James maintains, "are depicted totally without cynicism, as acts of beauty, of poignancy, something to shed unsophisticated tears over." "Büchner is very good at this,"[9] she writes, which is true. There is no distancing at work here, at least not *within* the scenes devoted to the women. In a woman's death, some critics sense classical grandeur: Danton and Camille, after all, *have* to die, but Julie and Lucile may choose to live if they wish; their demise thus glorifies free will.[10] Yet to a certain extent, Julie's death in particular is simply a fulfillment of Danton's unambiguous wish: "Oh, Julie! If I had to go *alone*! If she were to abandon me! (3, 7). And after he receives her assurance that she will accompany him in death, he even thanks her in absentia: "I won't go alone—thank you, Julie" (4, 3). She dies, in fact, not only *with* him but *for* him; that is, she dies the aesthetic death unavailable to him: "DANTON: . . . And yet I'd have liked to die in another way, as effortlessly as a falling star, as an expiring tone kissing itself dead with its own lips, as a ray of light burying itself in clear waters" (4, 3)—a close anticipation of the imagery Julie employs before ending her life three scenes later. Her surrogate death-as-a-work-of-art restores substance to his life and his death, both of which have lost their meaning within the political sphere. Her death offers him satisfying closure, in keeping with his epicurean philosophy, which extends to the pleasurable anticipation of one's own death as drama.[11]

What prevents audiences from viewing this as an act of supreme selfishness on Danton's part and supreme stupidity on Julie's is the ageless perception of woman as victim, whose fulfillment lies in renouncing herself and serving the needs of others. Analogous to this is the literary convention that decrees: a good man dies for his ideals, which is tragic, whereas a good woman dies for her man, which is beautiful. A male's ending is traditionally endowed with sociopolitical resonances, whereas the female's is restricted to its aesthetic effect. When a man's political effectiveness has been neutralized, as has Danton's, he is merely displaying established patriarchal reflexes when he attempts to create for himself a vicariously experienced "feminine" ending.

Although Büchner was indisputably far ahead of his contemporaries in his depiction of women, he was nonetheless capable of creating such male fantasies as Danton's. One need only take cues from *Leonce and Lena* (1, 4; 2, 3; 3, 1) to justify, for example, the reduction of women to flowers and other forms of vegetation.[12] Some of his female figures retain traces of the Madonna stereotype inherited from romanticism and its forebears; in his eclectic readings, Büchner surely encountered a host of female "beautiful souls" who influenced his perceptions of women. In the characterizations of Julie and Lucile, biographical as well as literary models become discernible. An obvious source is Büchner's relationship with Minna Jaeglé, to whom he became engaged in 1834. Most of what we know about their romantic attachment is based on letters he wrote to her from Giessen in February and March 1834, and from Zürich in January, 1837, in which he confides to his fiancée the agonies of his loneliness and political disillusionment. His expressions of love for this pastor's daughter, however, never transcend much beyond nineteenth-century middle-class propriety, leaving us at a loss to know whether or not his extraordinary insights into the psyche of a Marion or of *Woyzeck*'s Marie derive from personal experience.

The letter to Minna Jaeglé containing the famous passage about the "terrible fatalism of history" is rarely overlooked in analyses of *Danton's Death*. However, citations of it usually end with the lines: "What is it within us that lies, murders, steals? I no longer care to pursue the thought," thereby suppressing Büchner's emotional yearning for a resolution of the crisis: "If only I could lay this cold and martyred heart on your breast!" (*CWL*, 260 [after March 10, 1834]). He desires from Minna what Julie offers Danton during his self-recriminations about the September massacres (2, 5): the emotional closure of loving consolation. Büchner's letter is, after all, not exclusively a disquisition on fatalism, because only one-third of it deals with the consequences of studying "the history of the Revolution." It is therefore misleading to metonymize this letter as a "fatalism *letter*,"[13] for it also contains complaints about the mediocre environment in Giessen, his difficulty writing, his recent illness, his decline into an automatonlike existence, inquiries about Strassburg, declarations of his plans for travel, his longing for Minna, and a final ironic disclaimer: "This letter is a hodgepodge: I'll console you with another." As a whole, his letters to her are soul barings to an idealized recipient, who is alternately mother, child,

and nurse.[14] His image making, born out of loneliness, is hardly
surprising: during the less than five-and-a-half years they knew each
other, they were apart approximately as much as they were together.
The most telling evidence for Büchner's predilection for romantic
fantasies is to be found in the diary of his friend Alexis Muston, who
reports that, in Darmstadt in the summer of 1833, Büchner was seized
by "a kind of mystical adoration for a fallen girl, whom he dreamed
of restoring to the ranks of the angels. . . ."[15] Were it not for the reference to "a fallen girl," one would assume that Büchner was speaking
of Minna Jaeglé. Lacking substantial testimony from Minna herself or
from third parties, we cannot fairly assess the reality behind the
ideal.[16] In the stereotypical aspects of Julie and Lucile in *Danton's
Death*, the conventionality of such qualities that men habitually attrib-
ute to women emerges: women are products of male self-absorption,
which generates "mystical adoration" that "saves" women by making
them into angels. Such objectification occurs even during Marion's extraordinary monologue: Danton remains outside as the voyeur, unable to internalize her identity in any way but sexually. Büchner emu-
lates his protagonist's wife/prostitute categorizations to the extent of
not allowing, for instance, *Julie* to utter such emancipated thoughts
as Marion does.[17]

My purpose here is not to *blame* Büchner, a nineteenth-century
male author, for occasional lapses into what we now declare to be female stereotyping. Without doubt his works display an eroticism of
revolutionary potential; not until the "middle" Heinrich Heine does
one find a comparable provocation of bourgeois prudery.[18] But the
"regressive" aspects of Büchner's female characters cannot be overlooked as long as his interpreters persist in dematerializing them into
a kind of Rilkean "tranquil heart of the stars." In order to determine to
what extent Büchner internalized conventional images without reflecting upon them and to what extent he challenged them, a comprehensive assessment of his concept of women, including as well a sociological analysis of women's status within the nineteenth-century German
family and society, would be necessary.[19] One would need to inves-
tigate whether Büchner's social environment indeed contained "only
married women and prostitutes, only sentimental feeling and un-
adulterated eroticism," without "intermediate levels" that could serve
as models for a more independent, more differentiated womanhood.[20]
Yet even a thorough investigation of this sort might still not be able to

resolve the ambiguity between "regressive" stereotyping and "progressive" insight in such passages as the following.

> DANTON: No, Julie, I love you like the grave.
> JULIE (*Turning away.*): Oh!
>
> (1, 1)

> LEONCE: *Addio, addio* my love, I shall love your dead body. (*Rosetta approaches him again.*) Tears, Rosetta?
>
> (*Leonce and Lena*, 1, 3)

> LEONCE: Dear corpse, you rest so beautifully on the black pall of night that nature begins to hate life and falls in love with death.
> LENA: No, let me be. (*She jumps up and rushes off.*)
>
> (*Leonce and Lena*, 2, 4)

One might fault Julie, Rosetta, and Lena for becoming inarticulate when their men's love-death fantasies grow too explicit; or one might commend them, with latent condescension, for being "creatures of nature" with spontaneous nonverbal responses; or one might argue, as does Christa Wolf, that such reactions are the *only* appropriate means to counter what she calls "man's strenuous intellectual activity" that compensates for his "fear of contact . . . [when] he withdraws from reality's abundance. . . ."[21] Gestures of rejection or grief as quoted here would thereby signify the undesirability of further entanglements in male discourse—an insight that would serve to confirm anew Büchner's modernity.

Such ambiguous passages can sometimes be clarified by placing them in context. For example, Büchner juxtaposes Marion's utopian sexuality against the unromantic life of starving prostitutes,[22] and in such contrasts lies a complex realism that breaks down stereotypes. Büchner's dramatic language has a similar effect: Julie's final lyrical, "atmospheric" monologue (4, 6) cannot be called specifically feminine, for her evocation of the dying earth is stylistically very similar to Danton's musings on death a few scenes earlier. Moreover, Hérault speaks almost exactly in her idiom in the lines immediately preceding her death scene: "The clouds hang in the quiet evening sky like a dying Olympus with fading, sinking, godlike forms" (4, 5). If Julie's language is to be thought of as feminine, romantic, even sentimental, then that of Danton's faction must be adjudged so as well. Linguistic categorizations according to gender or political conviction do not exist in Büchner's plays; the Danton and Robespierre factions often share the same cynical idiom, and in his monologues at the end of act 1, Robespierre himself uses language that would be wholly appropriate in the mouths of Danton, Leonce, or even Lena. Büchner destroys stereotypes through a kind of stylistic democracy that obliterates conventional distinctions between "higher" and "lower" characters.[23]

Deviating both from the ennobling verse of classical historical drama and the class-specific prose of the Sturm und Drang tradition, Büchner's dramatic dialogue mixes poetic and political rhetoric, cynicism, obscenities, and artless simplicity without regard for conventional distinctions between public and private spheres. A drama that presents "common folk" who speak like politicians who speak like prostitutes who speak like philosophers who speak like "common folk" without subjecting them all to a uniform verse or prose form is subversively egalitarian even today, since such a perspective anticipates a reordering of social structures. Henri Poschmann correctly notes that, in *Danton's Death*, the democratic idealism of the constitution of 1793 "becomes formative as an aesthetic principle for the creation of a new type of drama."[24] The classical concept of character as a "bearer of ideas," which implies a trickle-down process of enlightenment, is supplanted by a dramaturgy that highlights the limitless diversity of the subject. Since any representational medium can only hint at such diversity, this aesthetic strategy must remain extremely open-ended by definition.

However, despite Büchner's numerous quotations from historical sources, little of the dramatic dialogue in *Danton's Death* can be called realistic. Artistic intensification—rather than naturalistic reproduction—of human experience dominates, especially toward the end of the play. Significantly, Büchner's emphasis on lyrical expression arises not arbitrarily but organically out of the dramatic situation. His figures resort to poetic flights and musical prose as a form of self-aestheticization intended to counter their inability to affect their environment. As in numerous dramas of the Sturm und Drang, lyricism in *Danton's Death* represents a means of sublimating alienation and political impotence. Words rush in to fill the void or, to paraphrase Goethe's Werther, to decorate the walls that imprison one.[25] Both the poetic imagery in *Danton's Death* and the drama as a whole can be viewed as cultural responses to the zeitgeist of disillusionment in 1794 and 1835. Both Danton contemplating the guillotine and Büchner the playwright produce lasting meaning for themselves by converting language into art. As death approaches them in act 4, the Dantonists, Julie, and Lucile indulge in a lyricism that sustains the spirit of revolt in an increasingly mechanized society.[26] Lyricism's relativizing, anarchistic impact—like that of sexuality and other pleasures throughout the play—provides at least the illusion of defying one's mortality. By poeticizing death, one compensates for its horror—unlike *rationalizing* death, which increases its horror, as St. Just unintentionally demonstrates. Behind the postromantic epigrams, the ceaseless questions without answers, there is no longer any definable belief system. The characters construct rhetorical circles around metaphysical concepts, undermining simplistic concepts of linear historical progress. Their idiom restores dialectical openness to what they perceive as an oppressively controlled existence.[27]

Death is the theme of the play's lyrical prose; in fact, the title, *Danton's Death*, is itself an ending. Death is not merely the final stage of a natural cycle ("The Life and Death of . . ."); in Büchner's genitive formulation, death is a personal possession, a nearly material entity that can be yearned for or rejected. Death is already present at the outset of the play; Danton's comment to Julie: "You sweet grave—your lips are funeral bells, your voice my death knell, your breasts my burial mound, and your heart my coffin" anticipates the structural premise of the last act, namely a theme and variations on death. To alter a phrase from *Leonce and Lena*: "how many scenes does one need to sing up and down the scale of death?"—Büchner achieves extraordinary variety in nine scenes filling less than twelve pages.

1. Julie prepares to die with Danton.
2. Dumas announces to a shocked citizen that he is anticipating without any remorse whatsoever the guillotining of his wife.
3. Lacroix and Hérault contemplate their physical deterioration in jail; Danton meditates over his imminent demise; Camille fears that Lucile might be harmed and, after a brief nightmare, fears losing his reason.
4. A jailor and two cart-drivers who transport prisoners to the guillotine joke about their trade;[28] Lucile searches for Camille and tries to grasp the concept of "to die."

5. Prisoners are dying; Danton predicts Robespierre's downfall; Camille ponders his separation from the "deranged" Lucile; the Dantonists philosophize about mortality.
6. Watching the sun set, Julie takes poison and dies.
7. A woman distracts her children from their hunger by letting them see the executions; jeered by the crowd, the Dantonists ascend the scaffold one after another.
8. Lucile tries to cope with death by attempting to bring time to a halt; three women comment approvingly about public executions.
9. Two executioners finish their work at the guillotine; Lucile sings of Death the Reaper, shouts "Long live the king!" and is led off by the watch.[29]

These final scenes constitute both a lament and its negation — tragedy accompanied by irony, as in a Heine poem. They are suffused by death imagery: night, sleep, decay, the grave, Charon, and so forth. Death is individual and collective; we hear of the death of the self, the death of ideals, the death of love, the death of the revolution. Death and birth come together in Lucile's contemplation of the guillotine as a "dear cradle."[30] Death is both extraordinary and ordinary; the agony of the condemned individual contrasts with the all-in-a-day's-work attitudes of the carters and executioners, who are as human as their victims. Laughter in the face of death is a recognition of mortality, the destruction of heroic illusion. Death becomes theater, savored both by spectators and participants. Those sentenced to die sustain themselves, like the incarcerated protagonists of Sturm und Drang dramas, with dreams and visions. Yet Danton believes that death is no solution because it is distressingly conventional and predictable: "There's no hope in death; it's only a simpler — and life a more complicated, organized — form of decay; that's the only difference!" (3, 7). Danton wishes to die a noninstrumentalized death, dissolving Ophelialike rather than becoming a monument, but he knows he cannot evade the public appropriation of his demise.[31]

The emphasis on love and death in the final scenes of *Danton's Death* has prompted critics such as Peter Michelsen to maintain that the theme of ongoing revolution has become secondary — or has vanished entirely: "*Danton's Death* is a drama about the end of history, a play not so much about the Revolution as about how humans prepare for death."[32] I would counter that Büchner had no intention of writing about the *end* of history, which would indeed be fatalistic if not nihilistic, but about its seeming *pauses*, when the present appears to be a rupture between the past and the future. *Danton's Death* is an open-ended analysis of the ideals and failures of the French Revolution;[33] Danton's question in the drama's first scene: "Who's going to accomplish all these beautiful things?" — as well as "how?" — remains unanswered, because the 1830s offered Büchner no models for the possible synthesis of revolutionary idealism and human needs. Then, as during the 1790s, political reform was centered in the middle classes, who feared that a broadly based social revolution would turn against them. But Büchner's drama does not lose sight of the French Revolution's "categorical imperative," as articulated by Hérault: "The Revolution must stop and the Republic must begin" (1, 1). *Danton's Death* depicts both the actual and the ideal transition from Revolution to Republic, real versus fundamental change. By piling such contrasts upon each other, he penetrates ever more deeply into the details of French-Revolutionary reality. Instead of deviating into revolutionary agitation that, according to Lenin, allows "no orgiastic occurrences,"[34] Büchner highlights these "occurrences" in order to explore their origins and contradictions. Such complexity creates a pessimism that is, as Herbert Marcuse writes, not leveled against the idea of revolution itself but against "the trivialization of change."[35] Pessimism and utopian visions coexist within the realistic framework of conflicting perspectives. Rather than cancelling each other out, they mutually illuminate each other. Formally, the drama's comedy contextualizes and heightens its tragedy, and vice versa; thematically, the people's hunger and the pleasure of the more affluent in "beautiful things" do not negate each other.[36] Rather than a "neither/nor," Büchner's aesthetics produces a "both/and." Instead of allowing history to appear first as tragedy, then as farce,[37] Büchner reveals their *simultaneity*.

As *Danton's Death* progresses toward the inevitable reductionism of an ending, which of the thematic "balls in the air" will drop? Which note, which gestus will dominate, silencing the others? What will be the ideological and aesthetic consequences of formal closure? That the question can have political ramifications is demonstrated by the efforts of East German critics and directors during the 1950s and 1960s to subvert what they perceived to be the drama's excessively ambivalent, pessimistic, "bourgeois" conclusion. Renate Zuchardt, for example,

suggested (in 1959) that the ending be altered in performance so that
the spectator would accept Danton's fall as political necessity and welcome the victory of the "uncompromising revolutionaries" over the
moderates, instead of becoming overly involved in "pity with those to
be executed." Her solution: placing speeches by Robespierre or St. Just
at the end, in order to elevate the conclusion from "the private sphere
once again to the level of political drama," insuring that the final voice
be one of "all-controlling rationality."[38]

Significantly, the drama ends after four rather than five acts, recalling the Baroque tradition where, according to Walter Benjamin, the
plot (if not the drama) ended after the fourth act, evoking the idea of
repeatable actions.[39] To what extent is *Danton's Death*'s ending cyclical?
Had Büchner ended his play with the words Danton speaks to the ex-
ecutioner: "Do you want to be crueler than death? Can you prevent our
heads from kissing at the bottom of the basket?" (4, 7), the moment of
closure would be powerfully symmetrical: the lines strongly echo the
love-death dialogue that opens the play, and the title's message would
be reinforced (that is, after Danton's death, all else is insignificant). The
play's self-referentiality as historical drama would be emphasized, because Danton's lines derive nearly verbatim from Büchner's sources.
The final spotlight would frame the fallen hero, a self-serving aphoristic
lament on his lips—a potent generator of emotional identification. Left
to the spectator's imagination would be the historical aftermath as a
largely undefined "terrible confusion" (4, 5)—Danton's "après moi le
déluge" testament. If Büchner ever considered this alternative, he
presumably would have rejected it because of its counterrevolutionary
implications.[40]

Instead, Lucile, a woman not even related to Danton, is granted
a second and third appearance in the drama before it ends. Alone on
the street after the executions, she is the "last rebel," challenging the
insensitivity of nature and the very passage of time with her scream.
Christa Wolf calls this dramaturgy of the scream "an absurdity for the
theater of more or less resolvable contradictions";[41] it counterposes an
individual's pain against man-made systems of social control. Lucile's
insight after the failure of her scream experiment: "I suppose we must
bear it," turns out in retrospect to be not just passive resignation but
acceptance of present and future suffering. After her separation from
Camille, her blunt, disjointed discourse invokes the image of "poor

Ophelia / Divided from herself and her fair judgment."[42] But we cannot, therefore, simply pronounce her "insane," even though Camille says so ("Insanity lurked behind her eyes" [4, 5]). To stigmatize her as such would create yet another condescending stereotype and would reduce *Danton's Death*'s conclusion to a modernist cliché: the insane have the last word, ergo the world is absurd, quod erat demonstrandum. Büchner's nonjudgmental portrayal of her can be best understood by comparing it to his fictionalization of Jakob Michael Reinhold Lenz: for Büchner, Lenz's mental imbalance is a "possibility of existence" (*CWL*, 146) worthy of investigation because it breaks through conventional perceptions of reality, heightening the creative potential of the human imagination. Like Lenz, Lucile opens herself up to her environment totally and voices her uncensored reactions. An instinct within her transforms the unspeakable into familiar memories, prompted by what Raymond Williams calls "the nostalgia for ballad experience"[43]—the guillotine becomes an angel of death, and her song of Death the Reaper is interrupted by: "You dear cradle, who lulled my Camille to sleep, who smothered him under your roses. You death knell, who sang him to the grave with your sweet tongue." Like Danton and Julie, she succeeds in aestheticizing death by placing her unique linguistic stamp upon the experience. She externalizes and confronts death with poetry and song in an act of self-assertion that cannot save the body from the "logic" of death but that manages to rescue a bit of immortality through art.

Lucile's language, if not its context, derives from romanticism. Although her utterances are relativized by the cynical comments of "several women" about the executions and by the earthy songs of the executioners, a curtain falling immediately after her verse, "A hundred thousand, big and small, / His sickle always makes them fall" would nonetheless generate such an emotional impact that the play's tensions between the individual and the Revolution would be obliterated by sentimentality.[44] *Danton's Death* actually ends with lines wholly free of romantic overtones:

A CITIZEN: Hey—who's there?
LUCILE: Long live the king!
CITIZEN: In the name of the Republic! (*She is surrounded by the watch and is led off.*)

The conclusion is so laconic that it prompted Büchner's first editor, Karl Gutzkow, to preface Lucile's "Long live the king!" with the stage direction, *"pensively and as if making a decision, suddenly."* The stage direction is not in Büchner's manuscript, yet for unknown reasons he did not delete it from the "Darmstadt" and "Hamburg" copies of the play's first edition, in which he made many other corrections. Consequently, Franzos, Bergemann, and several recent editors have retained Gutzkow's stage direction, apparently believing it to be, as Bergemann insisted, indispensible for the motivation.[45] To retain it seems wholly inappropriate, however, because it introduces a note of calculated rationality into Lucile's spontaneity, resulting in a didactic tableau similar to the conclusion of Schiller's *Wallensteins Tod*: after receiving a letter of promotion for his betrayal of Wallenstein, Octavio Piccolomini *"is startled and looks mournfully heavenward."* Schiller achieves closure here by anticipating divine retribution. Gutzkow's editorializing stage direction enjoins Lucile to carry out a deliberate, logical, even heroic action that brings the play to a close. The drama's aesthetic, however, would seem to preclude such Schillerian explicitness and measured ethical balance.

Lucile's "Long live the king!" is an age-old cliché, but it becomes deadly because it is a "misquotation" of the obligatory slogan, "Long live the Republic!"[46] Her phrase is the language of the counterrevolution, recalling the monarchy and anticipating the Thermidorian Reaction, the Napoleonic Restoration, and Büchner's Germany, when "Long live the king!" once again became obligatory. She utters a sentence she does not believe because she knows it will destroy her. Heretofore one of the drama's most powerless figures, she manipulates political language in order to fulfill private desires. She achieves a *Liebestod* without the pathos of suicide, without the sentimentality of bourgeois resignation. Instead of compromising with the forces of reaction, she involuntarily compels her oppressors to reveal their inhumanity, which Büchner evokes but does not sensationalize. With muted, spontaneous irony, she exits in a burst of "meaning."[47] Yet her unadorned exclamation lacks the rhetorical flourish, the self-stylized theatrical posing that often characterizes the speech of the male figures. The spareness of her statement prevents art from silencing history, which reemerges in this final moment in the form of a quotation from one of Büchner's sources. Lucile's action is documented more than once in *Our Times*.

I saw more than ten women who, not having the heart to take poison, shouted "Long live the king!" and through this dreadful device they left the task of ending their lives to the Tribunal—some wished not to survive a husband, others a lover, . . . none because of passionate love of royalty.[48]

The wife [of the Commandant of Longwy] had tried every means to save her husband, but in vain; when his sentence was announced, she cried out, in order to die with him, in a strong voice: "Long live the king!"[49]

In fact, Lucile's "Long live the king!" is both historical *and* fictional. Whereas other women went to their deaths in precisely this fashion, her historical namesake did not—although it would have been in character for her to do so, as Thiers reported.[50] However, Büchner's highlighting of Lucile's self-sacrifice at the drama's close, reinforcing Julie's prior death, results in a kind of gender imbalance: men love women and men die, but they do not die *because* they love women, whereas the reverse is true. Although Büchner did not distort history simply to suit a fantasy, the drama's ending conforms, at least in part, to the conventions of male wish-fulfillment.

The drama's last spoken word is not "love" nor "death" but "Republic." The juxtaposition of the two final lines creates an absurd yet illuminating effect: "Long live the king / in the name of the Republic!" The authoritarian regimentation of the monarchy has, in fact, been resurrected in the police state atmosphere of the Jacobin reign. Lucile's imminent death is grotesque—her compatriots consider the words "Long live the king!" to be a capital crime.[51] Here Büchner emphasizes the discrepancy between the policies of the Jacobin state and the Dantonists' vision of what a republic ought to be (1, 1), analogous to his diatribes against sham constitutional reforms in Germany.[52] Yet at the final curtain he does not explicitly denounce the Revolution of 1789, nor does he allow Jacobin barbarity to reign absolute. Lucile is indeed led off to prison, which recalls how the "motors of history" were throttled in Danton's and Büchner's time, and she, like Danton and Julie, articulates the desire to "dissolve" passively out of an intolerable environment. Through her instinctive self-assertion, however, she single-handedly prevents the play from lapsing into fatalistic resignation. As

Büchner indicated to the last in his letters, one must persist, even in stagnant times, to combat the absurdities of history. The potential of what will yet happen "in the name of the Republic" is counterposed against Lucile's spontaneity, lyricism, and the multilayered irony of her situation—a contrast that anticipates impending defeats as well as inextinguishable resistance.

Chapter 5

Naturalism and Melodrama: Hauptmann's *The Weavers*

On May 3, 1891, a festival celebrating the international workers' movement took place at the Freie Volksbühne in Berlin. The main event was titled *Through Strife to Freedom: Historical Melodrama in 3 Acts with 3 "Living Pictures."* Beginning with the rebellion in 1844 of the Silesian weavers against the factory owners, the melodrama followed the fortunes of a single impoverished family past the storming of the barricades in Berlin in 1848 up to the present May Celebration of 1891. The performance concluded with the allegorical figure of Tyranny confronting the united workers and falling prostrate at the feet of Freedom, whereupon the enthusiastic audience joined in singing the Marseillaise.[1]

Such inspirational political theater, usually including music, declamatory recitations, and tableaux vivantes, was a common form of cultural activity among German workers' organizations in the late nineteenth century. Despite the obvious similarity of theme to Gerhart Hauptmann's *The Weavers*, the "historical melodrama" *Through Strife to Freedom* would appear to be antithetical to the naturalist social drama that Hauptmann was attempting to create. German naturalism's meticulous reproduction of realistic detail, its complex web of causality, and its fatalistic Weltanschauung would seem to have nothing in common with the simple abstractions and upbeat emotionalism of festival melodramas. Yet *The Weavers'* phenomenal international impact, lasting several decades after its premiere, can only be fully understood, I believe, if one looks beyond the drama's familiar naturalistic components to its undeniably melodramatic character. Hauptmann's play demonstrates that the qualities of melodrama are not merely sensationalistic but political. Nevertheless, would not *any* tendency toward melodrama in *The Weavers* magnify what Bertolt Brecht was to call the work's "monumental weakness"?[2] I will begin by attempting to argue Brecht's case.

In theory, a naturalistic depiction of character would call for extreme individuation. Hauptmann's weavers, however, are largely character *types*, predefined figures that do not deviate from their original classifications. The lengthy stage directions at the drama's outset create a genre painting of generalized suffering.

> . . . *Most of the waiting weavers resemble people standing behind the bars of a courtroom where they await decisions of life and death with tortured anxiety. . . . In addition, there is an inflexible feature of harassed irresolute brooding in their expressions. The men, who have much in common with each other, half dwarfish, half schoolmasterly, are predominantly sunken-chested, coughing, poverty-stricken people with dirty, pale complexions. . . . Their women look less typical at first glance. . . . The young girls are nonetheless not unattractive; waxen pallor, tender shapes and large, protruding melancholy eyes are typical of them.*[3]

Hauptmann's stage directions routinely go beyond scene setting into editorializing: the weavers are presented as a collective concept, as mass victims of oppression to be viewed as objects of pity. He shows not only their physical deprivation, but throughout the play he persistently diminishes their stature by emphasizing their childishness, naïveté, and emotional intemperance, be it in their anger, joy, revolutionary idealism, or destructiveness. Similarly, Dreissiger is cast as the conventional villain, from his "quivering nostrils" down to his tasteless furniture. Yet to absolutize oppression in this way means to obscure its origins and make it appear unalterable. Except for the factory owner and his minions, the victimizing forces—heredity, environment, the state—are anonymous and, hence, unreachable. As Brecht wrote about *The Weavers*: "environment appeared as fate; it was not presented as having been created by human beings, nor could they alter it."[4] Hauptmann's play is fatalistic because it highlights a historical *situation* rather than a historical *process*; class struggle is viewed as a Manichean rather than a dialectical phenomenon. *The Weavers* is therefore necessarily ambivalent about its central theme: rebellion.

The ebb and flow of rebellion determine the structure of *The Weavers* from the outset. In acts 1 and 2, an instigator (Bäcker and Jäger

respectively) brings the notion of revolt to the weavers. Their enthusiasm is quenched by opposition (Dreissiger in act 1) or by incapac-
ity (Baumert's excitement "to the point of frenzy" in act 2), followed in
turn by renewed signs of unrest. In act 3 the rebellion, fueled by the leit-
motivic "Weavers' Song," becomes reality and culminates in the destruction of Dreissiger's house in act 4. Act 5 concludes with simultaneous victory and defeat. As Hauptmann describes it, the weavers'
insurgency of 1844 was motivated by an unspecific yearning for release.
The often-quoted justifications for revolt appear at dramatically powerful moments: Hornig brings down the third act curtain with "Well, every man must have a dream" (*Weavers*, 52), and during the final peripeteia of act 5, Baumert leaves Hilse to join the rebels, saying "a man must
breathe fresh air just once in his life" (85). In fact, Hauptmann consistently presents rebellion in terms of emotional excess, warning against
its innate irrationality. When the rebels enter Dreissiger's private
rooms, the first to speak is an old weaver who distances himself from
the break-in: "it'll come to a bad end. No one with any sense would do
a thing like this" (67). Although Bäcker lays plans to extend the rebellion to neighboring towns, act 4 ends with Ansorge's proclamation of
his derangement: "I've gone crazy! I don't know what's going on, I'm
not right in the head," finally exiting *"with a cry . . . into the salon"*
(68). Luise, who defends the rebellion in act 5, is allowed to degenerate
into a frenzy, and Hornig describes the self-mutilating excesses of the
rebels in Bielau (79). Hauptmann's depiction of the insurgent weavers
tends to confirm Pastor Kittelhaus's apocalyptic judgment that "sheep
[have been turned] into wolves overnight" (62). While the details may
well have been historically accurate, and the insurgency was certainly
fated to collapse, Hauptmann's portrayal ultimately serves to denounce spontaneous revolt, which he considered to be as beyond the
control of its participants as the rise and fall of a fountain.[5]

The introduction of Old Hilse in act 5 and the ensuing "privatiza-
tion" of the weavers' revolt have disconcerted critics from Theodor Fontane to the present.[6] But, in fact, the grounding of the revolt in the private sphere is already evident in Hauptmann's dedication of the drama
to his father. His awareness of the weavers' plight, he states, originated
in family history: his grandfather was a weaver, and Hauptmann intended to commemorate this legacy. By equating the rebellion throughout the drama with "impermissible" excess, Hauptmann does not
drastically change course in act 5 but only brings to the foreground his

dualistic view of the uprising: ambivalence between desire for social reform and fear of anarchy. No weavers had openly opposed the revolt
prior to the last act, but now the rebels Luise and Baumert are pitted
like classical antagonists against Gottlieb and Hilse. Revolutionary
idealism is confronted with fatalistic resignation; for this reason, act 5
is the most *analytical* portion of the play, since it problematizes the revolt in a way that the more linear previous acts do not.

It is highly significant that, after the tumult at the end of act 4, act
5 begins with a prayer. Hauptmann stated on various occasions that his
drama had germinated out of the spirit of Christian charity.[7] The
weavers themselves were conceived as models of obedient piety, childlike in their loyalty to their God and their king.[8] The weaver-versus-
factory owner confrontation rests on a moral foundation; lamenting a
lost Golden Age of religious communality, Ansorge complains that the
factory owners are not "better men."

> In the old days things were different. The factory owners allowed
> the weavers to live too. Today they keep it all to themselves. And
> what I say is that it's because the upper class doesn't believe any-
> more, neither in God nor the Devil. They don't know about Com-
> mandments and punishments. (*Weavers*, 30)

Old Hilse trusts in divine justice to punish those who "wallow in lux-
ury" (79). His spirituality, counterposed against the materialism of the
rebels, functions as a means to undermine the rebellion's moral
legitimacy and to defuse the latent explosiveness of poverty itself.[9] His
theology of suffering and faith in business-as-usual makes poverty
bearable and rationalizable for a bourgeois audience by implying that
charitable reform is the medicine of choice for social ills. The relative
weight of Hilse's Weltanschauung increases the instant a stray shot
converts him into a tragic figure. As much as his death appears to be
blind coincidence, it is not unrealistic—during the actual uprising in
1844, innocent bystanders were killed when soldiers fired upon the
crowd.[10] Yet in drama, coincidence is never coincidental; Hilse's death
is a dramatic statement—although the bullet that kills him is, to be sure,
an ambivalent signifier. Coming from the barrel of a soldier's gun, it
represents the deadly power of the state against the ultimately defenseless weavers. More generally, it emanates from the violence of the rebellion and can be interpreted as Hauptmann's denunciation of such

violence, whatever its origins. In metaphysical terms, the bullet is a tool of the uncontrollable power of fate that blurs all distinction between revolt and passivity.

Hauptmann's drama about collective rebellion thus concludes with a lament not for the weavers as a whole but for the play's most reactionary figure. The revolt literally loses its dramatic immediacy: *"The uninterrupted cheering gradually fades into the distance"* (*Weavers*, 88). The final tableau highlights little Mielchen (with a finger in her mouth) and her disabled grandmother, who have not yet comprehended what has happened.

> MIELCHEN: Grandpa, Grandpa! They're chasing the soldiers out of the village! They've stormed Dietrich's house, the same way they did over at Dreissiger's. Grandpa!?
> *She is suddenly frightened, becoming aware of what has happened. She sticks her finger in her mouth and carefully approaches the dead man.* Grandpa!?
> MUTTER HILSE: Why don't you say something, Father? You're frightening me.

This dramatic irony clearly means to arouse pity: a tragic defeat in the private sphere undercuts (momentary) victory in the public sphere. *The Weavers'* ending anticipates Hauptmann's "transcendence" of poverty in *Hannele's Flight to Heaven* (1894), which seems to refute intentionally the political legacy of Heine's *Germany: A Winter's Tale* by building to a climax of angels, harps, a divine messenger, and a chorus of "We bear thee away to the Heavenly Rest / Lullaby into the Land of the Blest."[11] Intense sentimentality was, in fact, present in naturalism from the start: Holz and Schlaf's *A Death* (whose ending may have influenced Hauptmann to conclude his play with the death of an old man) and *The Selicke Family* are as steeped in emotionalism as eighteenth-century sentimental literature. For the naturalists, sentimentality was a means to make the tedium of lower-class existence appear more dramatic. Whereas it is relatively easy to depict discrete events realistically, the extended action of a full-length work is difficult to sustain without emotional intensification and dramatic conflict. More important, sentimentality lessens the impact of poverty's severity on a middle-class audience, smothering the origins and effects of the class struggle in bathos. Concluding with a sentimental-private moment, *The Weavers* allows its audience to savor vicariously the emotions of family tragedy and to luxuriate in nonspecific angst.[12]

The text's critical stance toward lower-class rebellion would seem, however, to be very much at odds with the drama's actual impact after its publication and first performances. The attempt to ban public stagings of *The Weavers* in Berlin led to what Manfred Brauneck calls the most spectacular political censorship trial in the history of German literature.[13] To avoid similar bans elsewhere, theaters raised ticket prices 200 to 300 percent and performed only on weekdays, in order to prevent workers from attending. The government in Berlin feared that the play's "one-sided tendentious characterization" would incite demonstrations among Social Democrats;[14] after its premiere, conservative newspapers warned that the play "creates . . . *the mood for the great Day of Revenge.*"[15] The first performances met with vociferous approval; a particularly vivid report appeared in *Der Reichsbote*.

> The excited spectators and their raucous cheers gave one the impression that the theater was about to be demolished. The drama of the revolution has been found! On the day it begins (if God in His grace fails to protect us!) this play will be performed, and the masses will know what to do.[16]

Another critic claimed that Hauptmann's work contained "more revolutionary dynamite than all the writings of Marx."[17] Ruling authorities were obviously concerned that the play might provoke analogies to current social injustices. Among leftists, Hauptmann's popularity soared, and he later acquired the nickname, "Labor Union Goethe."[18] The liberal bourgeoisie, characteristically relishing the opportunity to applaud its own demise within the safety of the theater, praised the drama's artistry and its social reformism. In the United States, *The Weavers* was the most-performed and best-known play among German socialist theater groups during the late nineteenth century. It was the only one of such plays ever to be banned for performance—in Newark, New Jersey, because the Newark police chief feared that it would inflame an already protracted labor strike.[19]

The extraordinary impact of the drama appears to be at odds as well with Hauptmann's manifest intentions. Claiming to have been inspired in equal measure by pity and social justice, he admitted that the theme's primary attraction for him was its potential as *drama*: "social drama was in the air, even if only as an empty concept. How to bring it to life was at that time a prize question, and whoever solved it would be considered the initiator of a new epoch."[20] Therefore, his main concern was not the imminent alleviation of poverty but its aestheticization: "As deeply as I may have been moved by the weavers' sufferings when I planned my play, as soon as I set to work I only saw the wonderful material they offered for creating a great, heartrending human drama. In the joy of constructing my scenes I forgot everything else."[21] At the outset of act 2, for example, the impoverished weavers blend once again into a highly atmospheric genre painting.

> The weak, rose-colored evening light forces its way through two small windows. . . . It falls onto the loose, light blonde hair of the girls. . . . The warm glow falls fully upon the face, neck and chest of the old woman. . . . Amongst this is the deep constant whirring of the spooling wheels, which sounds like the humming of bumblebees. (Weavers, 19–20)

Such poeticizing of the proletarian milieu seems to have been anticipated by Hauptmann's famous description of poverty in the Eulengebirge as "poverty in its classical form."[22] By isolating, in classicist fashion, real suffering from the "material . . . for . . . a great, heartrending human drama," Hauptmann could insist, as he often did, that his work was free of tendentiousness and political bias.[23] "Political bias" signified, of course, the material interests of the contemporary proletariat, whereas "political independence" connoted the presumed objectivity and neutrality of bourgeois humanism. The fundamental irony of The Weavers may be, however, that precisely this focus on dramatic technique, seemingly working at cross-purposes with political content, was responsible for the play's enormous political impact. In fact, several critics at the drama's premiere bluntly warned that the drama was "dangerous" particularly because of its artistry.[24] Assessing its potential impact on both sides of the class struggle, Max Baginski, editor of the Proletarian from the Eulengebirge and Hauptmann's guide through the historical locales of his dramatic subject, conceded that The Weavers was capable of arousing sufficient pity among the middle classes to bring about certain material reforms, but, in the last analysis, "it's hard to make an impression on well-fed virtue. On the other hand I imagined that the play must have a powerfully stirring effect on the oppressed masses themselves."[25] The authorities' persistent attempts

to ban the play confirms this reading of its inspirational potential—
which Hauptmann just as persistently denied. To clarify these dis-
crepancies between artistic intent, interpretation, and actual impact,
we must reexamine the play's melodramatic aspects.

Since the nineteenth century, "melodrama" has had pejorative
connotations: sensationalism, artificial posing, excessive pathos, lack
of subtlety, simplistic solutions. Its detractors have claimed that its
reductionism manipulates emotions and erases individuality by reinforcing a collective ideology. But an adequate discussion of the genre
must take into account its positive effects as well. Originally designat-
ing a mixture of music and dialogue, melodrama juxtaposed nonverbal
against verbal expression. It defined and heightened a drama's emotional content by articulating it simultaneously on a connotative as well
as a denotative level. Of course, such clarification and intensification
can occur in drama without the addition of music, for example by sim-
plifying and exaggerating character and dialogue. Effects produced by
these nonrealistic techniques have come to be called melodramatic;
when they violate an observer's aesthetic, melodramatic becomes
pejorative. Since the term is now largely a value judgment and is, therefore, governed by cultural bias, it is impossible to determine precisely
where dramatic ends and melodramatic begins—which accounts for
the profound disagreements among critics as to what segments of
drama history constitute "the melodramatic tradition."[26]

The stereotyped characters of melodrama serve to define virtue
and vice as clearly identifiable moral absolutes locked in eternal combat. Stripped of complexity and ambivalence, the opposing positions
are immediately recognizable as embodiments of abstract principles,
transposed from a specific historical context to a more generalized
sphere of human experience.[27] The audience can thereby "take sides"
and vicariously enter into an unproblematical good-versus-evil conflict. Such ethical simplification makes dramatic action predictable and
reassuring, especially when antagonists appear in familiar guises.
Hauptmann's stereotyped portrayal of poor and rich in The Weavers, for
example, is based on easily recognizable models: Dreissiger appears as
a variant of the evil lord of the manor, the minions of church and state
are apologists of oppression, and the weavers embody the heroic
peasants.[28] The conflict is, of course, not totally abstract, because the
dramatic figures are sufficiently individualized (in performance, less so
in the written text) to permit audience identification, sympathy, under-

standing, or rejection. Even Old Hilse's melodramatic presence contains a strongly positive aspect: he personifies the ethos of faith and labor. It is significant that, just before he is shot, he sits down to resume his work at the loom. His action attempts to bring about an "ethical recentering,"[29] a utopian intact universe in the face of disorder. The powerful emotional impact of his sudden death (intensified by Mielchen's and Mother Hilse's naïveté at the conclusion) heightens the expression of an unrealized wish for a morally secure world.

Melodrama is a medium of moral and emotional rebellion; the pathos of melodrama gives voice to the unfulfillable desire to impose one's feelings upon reality.[30] As an affirmative or subversive cultural force, melodrama is always political; when it confronts repressive social mechanisms with images of suffering and visions of a liberated humanity, its impulse becomes reformist. Despite its reliance upon artistic convention and ideological consensus, it tends to be antihegemonic when it defends individualism and condemns injustice.[31] Since the discrepancy between wish and reality, between individual well-being and external constraint was particularly agonizing in the milieu the German naturalists chose to portray, it is not surprising that they employed melodramatic techniques to call attention to abhorrent social conditions. *The Weavers's* ability to arouse public indignation (and conversely, the desire for its suppression) can be traced to the play's melodramatic tendencies: typification of the masses through stereotype; genre paintings that convert the mundanity of the naturalist milieu into an allegorical denunciation of oppression; collective singing (of the "Weavers' Song") as a stimulus for solidarity; and the visceral impact of the destruction of Dreissiger's house—a dramatic effect far more powerful than Hauptmann's attempts to neutralize it through dialogue.[32]

Hauptmann applied this dramaturgy to a theme that was ultimately explosive not only in the cultural sphere, as he had hoped, but in the political sphere as well. Employing a bourgeois medium, the theater, he appealed to bourgeois values in order to make a statement about a group of impoverished weavers who were in the public eye during the 1890s, because their continuing indigence had again become a matter of public discussion and an object of reformist activities. On the surface, his drama had an informational function, but on a deeper level it subverted entrenched bourgeois perceptions of the Silesian weavers. The weavers were viewed as pious and loyal subjects of a patriarchal society, who practiced an age-old craft in an unspoiled, preindustrial rural environment.[33] Through images of this sort, poverty had been tamed and aestheticized for centuries in order to legitimate its existence within the divine order of things. But in Hauptmann's drama, those who were expected to remain passive and grateful when the hand of charity was extended to them were suddenly reincarnated as rebels. Had Hauptmann chosen the modern urban proletariat as his subject, a rebellion could have been rationalized away by his critics as socialist agitation. But the weavers' revolt symbolically threatened the illusion of beneficent capitalism, converting nostalgic reassurance into the anxiety of class warfare. Employing the myth-making power of melodrama, Hauptmann, a relentlessly middle-class writer who could not be conveniently relegated to the sidelines, had created a proletarian counter-myth to replace the bourgeois myth he was destroying.[34]

Significantly, he chose not to end his play with the historical fact of the weavers' defeat. At the conclusion, naive Mielchen reports that the revolt goes on – an inspirational victory that only hindsight is able to relativize. Had Hauptmann written a final scene showing weavers being killed and arrested, it might have either culminated in cathartic lament and restoration of (repressive) order, fatalistically negating the idea of rebellion per se – or, less likely, it might have ended on a defiant note like Friedrich Wolf's *The Sailors of Cattaro* (the arrested ringleader stands *"eye-to-eye"* with his captor, saying: "This isn't the end, it's only the beginning!"), implying that *defeat*, not victory, is merely a transitory phase of revolution. In *The Weavers'* actual ending, Old Hilse's death lends a private tone to the conflict, inviting emotional identification with the counterrevolutionary side. Yet the temporarily successful revolt stands in ironic counterpoint to his death, sustaining the delicate balance between conservative and progressive tendencies so typical of bourgeois art.[35]

Predictably, the ambiguous ending disconcerted critics of various persuasions. Conservatives feared that the lack of a properly didactic and conciliatory denouement would allow the proletariat to jump to its own conclusions, and that Old Hilse's death might be interpreted as poetic justice against those who fail to join a revolution – which is exactly how certain Marxist critics did view it.[36] As often happens, attempts were made to have the drama's ending conform to a particular political philosophy. In 1943, Hauptmann was offered the opportunity to have his play filmed if he would agree to write a final scene showing how the weavers were currently thriving under Nazism; he refused.[37] In East Germany, stagings have omitted Hilse's death, ending with Mielchen's report of the weavers' victory over the military.[38]

Whereas the drama's final tableau anticipates the sentimentality of *Hannele's Flight to Heaven* and *The Sunken Bell*, it also anticipates the continuation of the naturalist tradition in *The Beaver Coat, Rose Bernd, The Rats*, and others. Hauptmann's dualistic development is, in a sense, analogous to the subversion-versus-escapism tension in melodrama. Since its inception, melodrama has been a form of popular entertainment, and with the advent of film and television, spectatorship has increased exponentially. Although mass entertainment, primarily for economic reasons, tends to affirm prevailing values and trivialize social issues, its impact is not *uniformly* regressive nor manipulative. The personalizing, emotion-oriented techniques of melodrama can evoke the historic reality of suffering with powerful immediacy,[39] affording the opportunity to detect victims and oppressors within an unexpected context and to project one's feelings into their conflict. For artistic and political reasons, Brecht was obliged to reject Hauptmann's naturalism, but the literary critic seeking a comprehensive theory of political theater must be able to account for the enormous impact of such "flawed" works as *The Weavers* – or more recent examples such as Rolf Hochhuth's *The Deputy* and the U.S. television drama, "Holocaust," both of which prompted discussions about Nazism in West Germany on a vastly greater scale than that achieved by artistically and politically more sophisticated works. The often-expressed "dilemma" of the critic who rejects morally or politically unacceptable content but nonetheless feels deeply moved by the presentation needs to be more closely examined. Well-educated audiences may indeed be irritated by melodrama's reductionism, its polarization of values, and its lack of self-reflexivity. But to ridicule every positive response to melodrama as being naively uncritical may, in fact, be attributable to unreflected cultural bias and/or class prejudice. Is there really a *qualitative* difference between, for example, the impact of Marquis Posa's "Grant us freedom of thought" upon a bourgeois audience, especially under a repressive regime, and Luise's incendiary speeches in act 5 of *The Weavers* upon a proletarian audience, facing similar inflexibility in its confrontation with power? Posa speaks with the measured restraint of an idealized aristocrat while Luise rages in a lower-class dialect, but the melodramatic gestus and its potentially subversive effect is essentially the same. Both document the aspirations

of a disenfranchised class. To idealize one while belittling the other
would seem to have no objective basis, and it is precisely such perceptual limitations that the sledgehammer techniques of melodrama are
designed to overcome. After all, since truth *never* shines through reality
as clearly as we would like it to, the essence and value of melodrama
might ultimately lie in Flannery O'Connor's simple insight: "to the hard
of hearing you shout, and for the almost blind you draw large and startling figures."[40]

Chapter 6

Female and Male Endings?
Fleisser's (and Brecht's)
Soldiers in Ingolstadt

> I forced my way into the theater like a cheeky brat. I didn't belong there, I
> didn't count. I slipped in compulsively and had an aching thirst, but their cups
> held nothing to quench it. I sat there in dismay.
> —Marieluise Fleisser, "Those in the Dark"

In 1929, having recently completed her two most successful plays,
Marieluise Fleisser wrote a brief essay called "Women's Sensibility for
Drama," in which she asserted:

> If a mere fight were a drama, many women would have already
> written dramas. But a woman has no affinity for the so-called well-
> made play. Only very indistinctly does she feel that a play must
> rise to a climax; she doesn't see the single, clear line. For this rea-
> son, women's dramas are constantly criticized for lacking a struc-
> ture. When a woman thinks about a drama she wants to write, she
> visualizes individual scenes, masterful in their compressed dic-
> tion, effective in saying things of general concern so vividly that
> they get under one's skin. Yet she can combine the scenes into a
> whole only subconsciously through the increasing impact of their
> atmospheric qualities. This is the point where she needs further
> training, everything else is already there. We have the language,
> we have scenes, above all we have the characters, the woman's
> speciality, because she has a sense for exact detail, for seeing a per-
> son whole and finding the characteristic features with a perception
> lacking in a man. Our next achievement must be—the play.[1]

During her subsequent "inner emigration" under Nazi rule, she followed her own advice by studying Gustav Freytag's hoary *The Technique of Drama* (see chap. 1), and after years of work, she completed
Charles Stuart, an undistinguished historical drama "with rising action,
climax, peripeteia, falling action"[2] quite unlike her earlier epic style; it
has never been performed. In her essay, her assertions about gender-
specific aptitude for drama are ambivalent: on the one hand, she appears to accept, however reluctantly, the traditional preference for the
well-made play over less structured forms; on the other, she claims that
the female playwright has a greater aptitude than her male counterpart
for psychological detail, for "atmospheric qualities." Like most of her
writing, her rare theoretical statements on drama were a form of self-
analysis. She was convinced that her writing was intuitive and, hence,
typically "female." How such preconceptions affected her dramatic
treatment of a "male theme" (soldiers) with a male collaborator is the
subject of this chapter.

Looking back on her literary production shortly before her death
in 1974, she maintained that she was "not very intellectual"[3] and that
her writing was spontaneous, arising from the subconscious as a force
that took possession of her (*GW*, 4:623). She called her "instinctive"
style "feminine,"[4] implying that premeditated creativity was somehow
characteristically masculine. Male critics have seized on this polarity
and made it explicit: Walter Dimter claims, for example, that whereas
Ödön von Horváth's dramas reflect what the playwright "*observes* ana-
lytically," Fleisser's show what she "*experiences* emotionally/physi-
cally,"[5] and Günther Rühle asserts that "all her works are free of theory" in contrast to those of Brecht,[6] thereby reducing the concept of
theory to a particular form of explicitly rationalistic discourse. Rühle
and others impose an additional dichotomy on female authorship
when they contrast feminine and feminist writing, representing the
former as naive (hence acceptable to the critical mainstream) and the
latter as ideological and doctrinaire.[7] Such categorical distinctions are
obviously patronizing, yet to a certain extent Fleisser herself endorsed
what feminists would identify as sexist value judgments concerning female authorship. Since Fleisser's life and works were so strongly
branded by her conflicting longings for autonomy and male support,
defining her "female voice" without resorting to psychological or
belletristic clichés is indeed difficult. Besides, certain aspects of drama
do appear to be inimical to the strategies of many women writers.

Of the major genres, drama is the least intimate and most abstract. Thematic material is wholly objectified, requiring total subordination of the authorial self to character and action. Fictional personae are compelled to interact without a mediator (i.e., a narrator with an "epic," subjective viewpoint). Women writers who search for a long-suppressed female literary voice, who explore through literature what it means when a woman says "I," might therefore incline to consider drama unsuitable for their purposes. Moreover, dramas that depict realistically the social oppression of women tend to resemble a "prison-house of art," since it is difficult to counteract their aura of defeatism with a subversive female consciousness.[8]

In her essay quoted here, Fleisser perceives an additional form of subordination inherent in drama: the manipulation of scenic material into "structure." Dramatic structure traditionally demands a hierarchy rather than a coexistence of elements. Character and action are weighted according to relative significance. The more prescriptive one imagines the rules of drama to be—and we recall that Fleisser was soon to turn to Gustav Freytag—the more the genre appears to be the product of force, the assertion of authority.[9] Because women tend to experience subordination differently than men, women writers may well be more reluctant than their male counterparts to impose prioritizing techniques upon their literary inspirations. Furthermore, contemporary women authors often attempt to counter the abstractions of patriarchal society with the materiality of the (female) body, which emerges as the source and the subject of writing. Yet the dramatic text is reductionist in precisely the opposite direction: it distills a character's corporeality into a mere voice with a name.

Corporeality returns, of course, when drama becomes theater. The bodies in question, however, are inevitably distant from the writer's original concept, for theater alters the notion of authorship far more radically than a publisher's mediation of a literary text to its readers. Both are cultural institutions that commercialize a literary product according to standards governed by audience expectations. When a dramatic text is converted into a theatrical text, the author is normally absent. Even if he or she is present, the project is no longer individual but collaborative, subject to existing institutional (in most cases, patriarchal) hierarchies. The intimacy and wholeness of authorship is "violated" by other artists—behind whom stand agents of financial interests.

   The tensions between a feminine aesthetic and drama are determined, I believe, by sociocultural factors rather than by an essential
concept of gender-bound artistic expression and form.[10] With respect
to Fleisser, one must take into account the intersecting contexts, discourses, or paradigms that shaped her perspective, such as provincial
environment, literary influence, Berlin intellectual and theatrical life,
women's status in cultural and private life, and Germany from the Weimar Republic to the 1970s. Her initiation into Berlin's leftist theatrical
scene during the mid-1920s was a downright melodramatic enactment
of private authorship engulfed by the public cultural sphere. Schooled
in a convent, the shy young woman from the provinces discovered that
she was to be the instrument with which the up-and-coming playwright Bertolt Brecht planned to stage a theatrical scandal. Her first
play, *Purgatory in Ingolstadt*, had been a critical success, and her second,
Soldiers in Ingolstadt, premiered to mixed reviews in Dresden, but for the
production in Berlin's Theater am Schiffbauerdamm (following on the
heels of the enormously successful *Threepenny Opera*), Fleisser's text
was reworked during rehearsals by Brecht and his collaborators as if it
had been one of his own plays. Fleisser reported:

> As always, [Brecht's] active mind viewed the work in question as
> a kind of raw material, in which no stone was left standing. I had
> to rewrite and rewrite, there was no end to it. . . . (*GW*, 4:476)

> Learning was the method here, there was no divine inspiration,
> things were tried out. . . . A text was never finished, that was its
> finest quality . . . and the author was least important, every ac-
> tor was worth more in the theater. (*GW*, 3:152)[11]

A slow writer, she could not tolerate the pressure; she could not conform to Brecht's "favorite image" of "a hard nut in a rough shell" (*GW*,
2:308). She stayed away from the final rehearsals, bore the brunt of the
ensuing right-wing protests and fell sick—a rebellion of the body,
paralleling her original "aching thirst" for the theater (see this chapter's
epigraph). Throughout her life she continued to feel like an interloper
in the theater, bearing her play's notoriety like an albatross ("that
damned play" [*GW*, 3:161]) and insisting that her literary talent lay in
narrative prose rather than in drama. Yet the daring plan to market a
woman as a controversial playwright had been a success; it might well

have been the only way to achieve it, considering the prevailing bias against female dramatists.[12] In Berlin's turbulent cultural scene "one had to be conspicuous, that was important" (*GW*, 2:310). To gain access to male-dominated cultural institutions, a woman needed male mentors, and Fleisser's other-directedness caused her to acquiesce to experienced advice as well as to public relations efforts not unlike those of Hollywood or Madison Avenue. For example:

  —her name. Born Luise Marie, called "Lu" by her first boyfriend, she became Marieluise at the urging of Lion Feuchtwanger, who introduced her to Brecht.
  —her earliest prose writings. During an "angry afternoon" (*GW*, 2:309) she burned everything that Feuchtwanger had criticized.
  —her first play, which she called "The Foot-Washing." Its producer, Moriz Seeler, informed the press before writing her that its title (according to advisers including Feuchtwanger, Brecht, and critic Herbert Ihering) would be "Purgatory in Ingolstadt."
  —her second play. The idea, form, style, plot details, numerous characters, and methods of gathering materials for *Soldiers in Ingolstadt* were all suggested by Brecht, who, with his collaborators, helped rewrite the first version. The title was invented by Heinrich Fischer, the head dramaturge of the Theater am Schiffbauerdamm. Brecht also initiated the staging of her last play, *Of Sturdy Stock*, in 1950.
  —the revision of *Purgatory in Ingolstadt* in 1970–71. The Wuppertaler director Günter Ballhausen and dramaturge Horst Laube "overcame [her] shyness" and went through the play line by line with her, proposing alterations (*GW*, 1:439). Their production was the first of numerous postwar stagings of the work in German-speaking countries.

In a late interview, she declared that she "always falls for violent men; I don't mean that physically, but men with great assertiveness."[13] Her story "Avantgarde" recalls her fascination for Brecht; to free herself from his influence she entered into a self-destructive affair with the reactionary, egomaniacal minor writer Hellmut Draws-Tychsen. After immortalizing this failed relationship in a drama, *The Deep-Sea Fish*, she returned to Ingolstadt and married her persistent hometown admirer Josef Haindl, sportsman and tobacconist. Contrary to a premarital agreement, he immediately employed her full-time in his shop; even after her nervous breakdown in 1938 he showed no sympathy for her avocation: "'Writing you can do at night' " (*GW*, 4:533). Hitler's ascension to power was the death blow for her writing career, and during the Nazi years she lived "chained up like a dog" (*GW*, 4:503). Shortly before Brecht's death in 1956 she sought his help, intending to leave her husband and Ingolstadt. Brecht's advice was ambivalent, and she endured her marriage until Haindl's death in 1958. After recovering from a heart attack, she slowly expanded and revised her literary efforts until her "rediscovery" in the late 1960s, a mere half-decade before her own death in 1974.

Each segment of her literary career was affected by traumatic experiences. Particularly, her drama *Soldiers in Ingolstadt* reflects what might be called her insecurity of authorship, considering that she felt unqualified to handle the topic, inadequate to revise it according to Brecht's procedures, unwilling to call it her own after she had abandoned it to Brecht's circle and after it had been viciously criticized by the right-wing press as well as by fellow citizens of Ingolstadt. Like her Sturm und Drang predecessors, she finally "tamed" the drama by altering its genre. Yet despite self-doubts and patterns of dependence, she created a work that ranks among the best of her era. I intend now to explore in detail the play's metamorphosis from Fleisser's original version written in 1926–28 (V1) through the collaborative effort of 1929 (V2) to her revision of 1968–70 (V3). By assessing the qualities of the various drafts I will work toward a conception of *"Soldiers in Ingolstadt"* that deserves a place in world literature as well as on contemporary stages because of its originality and theatricality.

Version 1

The genesis of *Soldiers in Ingolstadt*[14] coincides approximately with the premiere, in 1926, of *Purgatory in Ingolstadt*, a wholly original work that, like its successor, deals with the repressed desires of young people in Fleisser's Bavarian home town.[15] *Purgatory in Ingolstadt* shows the suffering caused by the gang mentality of teenagers who have internalized the authoritarian controls of a provincial, deeply religious environment. The play's language is intense, at times enigmatic; its characters are generally introverted, obliquely and openly hostile to one another, relatively inaccessible to a spectator's empathy. The drama's blend of

psychological realism, symbolism, and mysticism recalls the dramas of
Ernst Barlach more than those of the early Brecht, whom Fleisser identified as the primary influence on her dramatic style. The central figure,
Roelle, is a would-be savior who, despite drastic and bizarre efforts, can
do nothing to alleviate the "purgatory" in which he and his school-
mates find themselves.

The performance text for *Purgatory*'s premiere in Berlin already
bore the imprint of Brecht's intervention: during the final rehearsals he
"radically cut the atmospheric passages, and I helped him. . . . I had
accepted him as a kind of norm" (*GW* 4:474). The single performance
earned the praise of the leading (rival) critics Herbert Ihering and Alfred
Kerr; Fleisser remarked to her surprise that "without knowing anything about drama I had created lots of character parts" (475). When she
told Brecht about an "invasion" of Prussian soldiers (called "Pioneers")
who had come to Ingolstadt in peacetime to build a bridge for the town,
he immediately urged her to observe the event on the spot and write
a play about it. (He was working on his own soldier play, *Man is Man*,
at the time.) According to her, he suggested furthermore:

> . . . the play shouldn't have a real plot, it should be rigged up like
> the cars one sees in Paris, made out of parts the do-it-yourselfer
> just happened to find, but it drives, it drives! (Exactly these
> words.) A father and a son belong in it, a servant girl belongs in
> it, a car belongs in it that a traveler tries to palm off on the son be-
> cause it won't run anymore. The soldiers have to go walking with
> the girls, a sergeant has to bully them. At the end the son blows
> up the bridge because the Pioneer cuts him out with the servant
> girl. (*GW*, 1:442)

Fleisser dutifully followed instructions, even going for walks herself
with the soldiers in Ingolstadt and noting their dialogue. Brecht's off-
the-cuff synopsis essentially describes the plot of her first version—
which is a symptom of her alienated relationship to the topic. As she
insisted time and again in later interviews and letters, she would not
have written the play without Brecht's urging, for she considered herself unqualified to write about soldiers—"hardly a topic for a girl
brought up in the Institute of Mary in Regensburg."[16] In her uncertain
self-judgment she clung to the social cliché that sheltered women cannot write accurately about the military (which misogynist theater critics

were only too glad to confirm, as we shall see). As a critic of her own work, she deplored its allegedly unrealistic depiction of soldiers. But the drama belies her, even in its loosely anecdotal first version. It is not a documentation of military life; it centers instead on what Fleisser was later to identify as the dominant theme of all her works: "something between men and women."[17] The artistic sensibility that created the play is more complex than the amorphous, nonanalytical "feminine experience" alluded to by certain critics and by Fleisser herself. Once, while under Brecht's influence, she described her approach as "naive seeing" (GW, 4:421), the ability to observe the general within the particular and bring it to light in new, vivid ways. Employing a gestic style deriving from Brecht's epic theater, she devised unique representations of male-female relationships within a provincial setting, exposing patterns of domination, frustrated needs, and self-destructive behavior.

The subversive moment in what at first glance appears to have been a rote assignment carried out by a star-struck disciple is Fleisser's determination to focus her "naive seeing" on her own mentor. She had learned from experience and observation that leftist intellectuals such as Brecht bore certain similarities to the unsophisticated soldiers in Ingolstadt when it came to demeaning women. Consequently, phrases that she heard from Brecht are spoken by the male protagonist of *Soldiers in Ingolstadt*. Unlike the committed members of Brecht's circle who would have suppressed such insights for reasons of solidarity, Fleisser remained detached, soon to escape his influence and satirize him openly in her next play, *The Deep-Sea Fish*. The validity of her "untimely" observations has since been confirmed by the publication of Brecht's diary and by numerous critical studies.[18]

Considering that the milieu, certain themes, and character types are common to both *Purgatory* and *Soldiers*, the contrast between the two is startling: the former sustains a mood of wrenching despair, whereas the latter is a comedy. The first scenes of each underscore their differing paths. "I'd like to know why we have nothing to say to each other," asks Berotter of his feuding children after he has already once collapsed in anger (*Purgatory*, 1, 67). "I'd like to get to know a man," says the servant girl Berta innocently to her more experienced friend Alma (*Soldiers* V1, 4). Alma welcomes the arrival of the soldiers as a source of income, while Berta promptly finds true love in the Pioneer Karl.[19] He wants an affair, but not one of the heart, and he repels Berta's ardor without pity. Meanwhile her employer's son, Fabian (whom his father calls "a washrag"), courts her unsuccessfully. Interspersed with songs, the plot follows Brecht's outline, except that Fabian fails to obtain the explosives to blow up the bridge. Karl has his way with Berta and lightheartedly promises to become engaged to her. Fabian stands triumphant, having won the hand of Alma. The four pose before a photographer.[20] Version 1 ends as the soldiers march off to the next town – a cyclical ending. As the curtain falls, a Pioneer named Paleface "(*raises his hands to his mouth like a megaphone and imitates the bugle call*): To bed, to bed, if you've got a girl, if you ain't got one, go off to bed, to bed – to bed – to bed" (V1, 62).[21] The final lines – possibly from an off-color soldiers' song – reinforce the sexual tension pervading the play from the very start, when Berta inquires why the arriving Pioneers fail to sing "Be good, yes, good to the girls" (V1, 3). The play's trajectory thus begins with a plea for kindness and understanding only to culminate in male competitiveness, defensive boastfulness, and objectification of the female. The playful irony of the concluding song nevertheless sustains the drama's comic tone.

Soldiers in Ingolstadt was first performed in Dresden in March, 1928.[22] Having traveled down from Berlin to see it, Herbert Ihering declared it to be "a merry work with a hundred comical touches. Weak only in the depiction of events" (*Materialien*, 53). Fleisser herself called it "too soft" (*GW*, 4:477). Its scenes indeed often lack economy, losing their focus on significant themes and characterizations. Particularly, Fabian's purchase of the car is a lengthy process with little relevance. The songs are largely entertaining interludes, lacking the immediacy and irony of the songs in Brecht's contemporaneous early plays. Yet, as we turn to the far superior second version, a product of numerous hands, we must recall that nearly all of its dramatic qualities derive – in most cases directly – from the first version.

Version 2

Fleisser remarked about Brecht: "[He] never stuck doggedly to something after he had done it. He was always ready to change things, he obviously felt that everything was open, in flux – he favored process over product" (*GW*, 1:297–98).[23] To keep pace with him required flexibility and a quick imagination; for Fleisser, however, artistic creativity was gradual and private. During rehearsals in Berlin she helped

reshape roughly the first half of her play for performance, but eventually her "feverish . . . confused . . . desperate condition"[24] caused
her to absent herself before the final scenes had been worked out. Without a protocol of the rehearsals it is impossible to determine who was
responsible for which alterations. Not only Brecht contributed; Fleisser
reported that several passages were improvised by actors, and it is fair
to assume that she neither influenced nor authorized the altered conclusion.[25] Version 2 is far more streamlined and gestic than V1, emphasizing characteristic relationships rather than milieu. Brecht
deserves credit for deploying his experienced theatrical collective to
produce a better text, yet at the same time he confronted Fleisser with
"bewildering problems, giving no moral support" (*GW*, 4:502). In nar-
ratives such as "Early Encounter," "Avantgarde," "Two Premieres,"
and "I Had No Idea How Explosive It Was," she indicates how he, as
her formative artistic inspiration, tried to recast her in his image and
make her his "instrument" (502). Without him she may well never have
emerged from relative obscurity, yet her play's final version reveals, as
we shall see, that there is some truth to her contention that "Brecht destroyed something within me" (*Materialien*, 359).

The components of characterization in V1/V2 of *Soldiers in Ingolstadt* can be traced, I think, to the intersecting paradigms noted earlier
in Fleisser's biography. That is, historically specific forms of social relations and ways of constituting identity converged into certain character
types. To demonstrate the figures' (occasionally shifting) dramatic
function, I will employ three categories that appear to determine
characterization in Fleisser's texts.

1. "Role" – a character defined primarily by class standing and
   profession, typified by qualities referring to particular social
   conventions and reflecting their underlying ideologies.
2. "Gender" – a character defined primarily by his or her relationships with women and men apart from role but equally inscribed by conventions and ideologies.
3. "Temperament" – qualities that deviate from conventional images of role and gender; individualization that differentiates a
   character from stereotypes by evoking *unexpected* discourses
   and models. (Also a unique enhancement of a part by an actor
   in performance.)

Role and gender are a product of a character's self-image as well as the image projected on him or her by others; for example, they signify, respectively, what is conveyed by "soldier" and "masculinity" within the context of the play. The boundaries between these categories are, of course, quite fluid, yet the terms are nonetheless useful in ascertaining Fleisser's dramatic intent. They also provide a basis for comparing dramatic and performance texts (as well as the audience expectation horizons that influence them), since the proportions of the various components are often significantly altered when drama becomes theater.

The protagonist of Soldiers in Ingolstadt, who travels the path of experience to an enlightenment of sorts, is Berta. Her role is that of a young domestic servant in the German provinces in 1926. The forms of exploitation to which her counterparts in reality were exposed encompass both role and gender: victimized materially and psychologically, they labored in an environment of sanctioned prostitution that often left the victim no alternative but to convert the experience of victimization into a "public" profession.[26] Berta represents the naive, uncorrupted beginnings of domestic servanthood, whereas Alma embodies its endpoint. How vulnerable they are is revealed at the outset by the magnitude of the conspiracy against them: the town in which they live has contracted with the pioneers for free labor. As Alma explains, "the town provides the wood, and the Pioneers build [the bridge]. For that the town doesn't have to pay" (GW, 1:190). Yet it is already clear that the town is willing to offer not only wood but its young women to the soldiers—prostitution on a municipal scale.[27] Alma utilizes the situation as a means of earning a living. Berta innocently comments that "the big ones [presumably the capitalists] are losing out," but in fact it is "the little ones" such as she who are destined to suffer.

Her main tormenter is her employer, Old Benke. His exercise of power is anything but subtle: "Here at home I call the shots and not you. . . . I'll bring you to your knees yet, you wretch. I'll plague you, for sure. You'll feel how we have you in our power" (GW, 1:201). He strives for total control of her activities and inclinations; he objectifies her with breathtaking frankness as a sexual proving ground for his maladroit son, Fabian.

Berta's character, however, is by no means wholly defined by her social role. Her situation establishes, to be sure, a particular sociopsy-

chological context (similar to that of Lenz's protagonists) — confinement, isolation, inexperience, frustration — that affects her personal relations. Although I do not mean to overemphasize these distinctions,
the proportions of V1/V2 indicate that Fleisser was more interested in
Berta as "young woman" rather than "domestic servant"; that is, in the
aspect of gender rather than role. She once said about Berta and Alma
that they represented opposite poles of girlhood, with obvious reference to their attitudes toward men.[28] Yet the play begins with the depiction of a relationship that points beyond the gender of character to the
gender of authorship.

When two women converse in male-authored drama, chances are
they are talking about men. In *Soldiers in Ingolstadt*'s first scene, Berta
and Alma do indeed talk about ways of attracting soldiers, but an aspect
of their relationship is highlighted that might well not occur to a male
playwright.

> ALMA: If you'd come along, you would've known. I can't ever tell
>   you anything. . . .
> BERTA: Alma, I don't want to fight with you. . . . I'd like to
>   know what's going to happen to you.
> ALMA: It's not your problem.
> BERTA: You can't tell if it is or not.
> ALMA: I've never said one bad thing about you.
> BERTA: How can you say that? You'd be the first one to let me
>   down if the others knew something about me.
> ALMA: Berta, never! 'Cause I'd never do that.
> BERTA: Alma, we'll work that out. The friendship, that's got to
>   last.
> ALMA: Berta! I won't desert you. (*Extends her hand.*)
>   (*GW*, 1:189)

In the following scene, they sing a folk song together as they wait for
Pioneers to walk by, but as soon as Alma runs after one, Berta feels
betrayed, and Fleisser never brings the two together again. This lack of
autonomy and solidarity among women in her works have prompted
some critics to disqualify her as a feminist (see note 7), and it is true that
her views on the subject were rooted to a considerable extent in prevailing petit bourgeois convictions. In her only essay on women's rights
(1932), she wrote forcefully about male resistance to women's struggle

for personal dignity within the altered socioeconomic conditions after World War I. Her article ended, however, by extolling motherhood in terms similar to Nazi rhetoric on the subject ("one of the vital assets of a nation" [*GW*, 4:429]). Considering her provincial origins, her male-oriented life history, and her apparent lack of contact with women's movements of her day, it is not surprising that her works offer few emancipatory solutions for women's oppression. The theme of friendship among women nonetheless remains an undeveloped utopian moment in *Soldiers in Ingolstadt*, as it did in her life.

A gender-reversed symptom of her longing for such friendship appears, I believe, in her colorless historical drama *Charles Stuart*, written during the bleakest period of her personal life. She claimed to have been attracted by his sorrowful visage (*GW*, 1:460), and she interpreted the image of an isolated, dignified individual brought down by ruthless violence as a parallel to her own situation in Nazi Germany.[29] Yet the play's most striking motif is King Charles's unwavering friendship for the Earl of Strafford, for whom he is willing to sacrifice his family, kingdom, and life.[30] Fleisser fails to motivate or justify this bond; despite Strafford's lack of redeeming qualities, the King's friendship remains unequivocal. The drama thus absolutizes feeling, reducing overtly political conflict and historical accuracy (e.g., Oliver Cromwell as a protofascist tyrant) to insignificance. One can only speculate to what degree *Charles Stuart* embodies its author's wish projections. It appears to confirm Fleisser's unfulfilled yearning for a friendship that offers an escape from constraint and exploitation rather than merely a different form of submission.

In *Soldiers in Ingolstadt*, women compete with rather than support each other, since social advancement is perceived to depend on a man's favors. Alma's and Berta's handshake is supplanted by the insults Alma and three nameless girls hurl at each other later in the play (*GW*, 1:208–9). The drama's crux is thus "something between men and women"; the drama's merit lies in the extent to which it transcends the banality of this statement. In her best dialogues, Fleisser distills character and conflict with great precision and formal control. Although her dramatic idiom is that of the Bavarian hinterland, her characters are capable of the dialectical stichomythia of classical drama. As I attempted to show at the end of chapter 5, the affective impact of any dramatic language is culturally variable, irrespective of the social standing of the individuals being portrayed and of the traditional "nobility" of a particular form of discourse. In *Purgatory in Ingolstadt*, Fleisser relied on Biblical syntax and startling imagery (among other techniques) to raise her characters above the mundane; in *Soldiers*, comic exaggeration distances and clarifies suffering, similar to the multiperspectivism of Lenz and Büchner. Despite their generic dissimilarities, both *Purgatory* and *Soldiers* consist of characters who are, as Kurt Pinthus wrote, "a mixture of tragedy and absurdity" (*Materialien*, 368); only the proportions differ. Heiner Müller's criterion of emotional impact and distance (see chap. 1) is expertly fulfilled in Fleisser's dialogues, which build to climaxes that capture the comic/tragic clash of self-interest versus necessity in a few masochistic or sadistic words. Two examples from V2 of *Soldiers*:

> KARL: Don't fall in love with me, little girl.
> BERTA: I won't fall in love.
> KARL: A lot of women've said that and they fell in love anyway.
> BERTA: We're kidding around, Karl, right?
> KARL: I'm not kidding around. You've gotta be able to let me go.
> BERTA: You're the one I want, stupid. I picked you out from all the others.
> KARL: Don't fall in love with me, or you'll suffer.
> BERTA: I want to suffer.
>
> (*GW*, 1:198)

> BERTA: . . . If you've got something to wash, let me know, I'll get up at night and go to the washhouse. What can I do for you?
> KARL: Leave me alone.
> BERTA: You can't keep sending your girlfriend away when she's giving you all kinds of chances.
> KARL: What are you giving me?
> BERTA: Chances.
> KARL: I'm used to that.
> BERTA: I'll just wait 'til you have time.
> KARL: You'll be waiting long.
> BERTA: You know what'll happen?
> KARL: What'll happen?
> BERTA: Then I'll run after him [Fabian].
> KARL: I don't care.
> BERTA: But you can't act that way, 'cause nobody acts that way.

> KARL: The likes of you gotta be ripped to shreds.
>
> $(GW, 1:206)^{31}$

Berta's character is delicately balanced between the pitiful victim who willingly tolerates indignities and the rebel who denounces them. Perhaps the most ego-deflating lines in the play are her comments before and after her brief sexual encounter with Karl.

> KARL: Sometimes you've gotta give in and sometimes I've gotta
>   give in.
> BERTA: But not here? I managed to get the night off.
> KARL: Too bad. I'm in the army. I can only get away for a moment.
> BERTA: I feel sick.
>   . . . (*Both exit.*) . . . (*BERTA and KARL enter.*)
> KARL: What's bothering you this time?
> BERTA: Was that all?
>
> $(GW, 1:219-20)$.

The shortcomings of an exploitative relationship are expressed in physical terms from the female viewpoint. In this way, Fleisser undermines the Baal paradigm of male self-gratification at the expense of the throwaway female by focusing on the victim's bodily response, which she regarded as the primary source of insight into the needs that govern one's own and others' behavior. As early as 1925 she wrote:

> I believe that [a young person] desires most of all from a drama typically human experiences, to which one brings nothing more than one's body, with its fears and drives. . . . One wants to see all the situations in which one has been or will be, yet enhanced to a higher magnitude, wherein each character is equally right and equally worthy, because one penetrates ever deeper into a character's nature, grows into the physical feelings through which one's body recognizes the world. (*GW, 4:419*)

After her defloration, Berta concludes: "I'm just saying we left out something important. Love is what we left out" (*GW*, 1:206). In opposition to the reality of soldiers seeking momentary satisfaction, she articulates the familiar utopian vision of a mutually fulfilling union. Her concise eloquence as well as her self-assertiveness before Karl, Old

Benke, and Fabian exemplify my category of temperament: she embodies the autonomous, rebellious character who transcends social determinants (like Fleisser herself, who was always more than just "the victim"), sustaining dramatic interest through unexpected originality of
expression. This is not to say that a dramatic typification of woman au-
tomatically implies passivity, but that Berta's pretension-destroying
naïveté is an intersecting paradigm, atypical of the sociohistorically
specific role/gender that she personifies. The paradigm originates in
Brecht's concept of naïveté as the unmasking of socially ingrained self-
delusions and affectations. Uncomplicated and spontaneous, the
childlike voice seems to articulate uncensored wishes and reactions.[32]
This "inappropriate" yet affecting simplicity creates critical distance,
turning against itself or others the weapon of satire.

Uncertain to the last about her ability to portray soldiers, Fleisser
would have been surprised to hear a theater director claim that Karl was
"a great, realistic portrait of a German man."[33] The last word is significant, because it contradicts Fleisser's fixation on whether she had
depicted Karl's role in the military accurately. The relevance of her
drama lies not in the historical situations it portrays but in their ideological subtexts, recognizable from one generation to the next.[34] After attending the Berlin premiere of *Soldiers*, Walter Benjamin commended
the drama for displaying the collective power of the masses in uniform
as well as its provincial roots.[35] This is correct, yet like Berta's social position, Karl's role as a soldier is secondary to his gender-specific postur-
ing. In Lenz's *The Soldiers*, antagonisms within the military are largely
based on class distinctions; in Fleisser's play, the sergeant and his Pioneers are kindred petit bourgeois tyrants, bullying their underlings or
those who willingly submit to them. Fleisser captures the clichéd right-
eousness of the dominant male in Karl's posing:

> If you want something from a man, you can't show him how far
> he can go with you. (*GW*, 1:205)

> Today a girl has to give in, because there're not many men around.
> We decide how things are going to go, thank God! (206)

> You women have to believe in us, and then you have to let us be-
> tray you. Then you can cry, if you like. Then you really have to be-
> lieve in us, until you're a wreck. (206)

A woman has to keep her mouth shut when she's being taken.
(219)

In a scene not published in V1 or V2 but performed at the Berlin
premiere, the ultimate consequence of the soldiers' irresponsible
sexuality is dramatized: venereal disease.[36] Their language
represents, in Theweleit's words, a "colonization of reality, . . .
imperialistic against any sort of independent, vital activity."[37] For such
behavior, Fleisser's petit bourgeois, provincial milieu offers a plausible
setting, but it is only one of many possible ones: in other works she
describes similar propensities among male intellectuals of the Left and
Right. To what degree her representation of the military in Ingolstadt
was historically accurate is thus of ancillary importance; more consequential are the social origins and ideological roots of her gender
portraits.

Karl's character seems to be absorbed almost wholly by role and
gender, leaving him essentially without temperament.[38] Fleisser
denies him the dimensionality she grants Berta, accentuating his
extremism in order to denounce his type unambiguously. To ridicule
his ideology of domination from another angle, Fleisser provided him
with a foil, Fabian Benke. By virtue of his role as the financially privileged employer's son, Fabian is "entitled" to Berta.[39] In V1, Fabian
dominates the play by the sheer length of his dialogue; in V2 his role
is trimmed, but he is no less central, for he motivates most of the
dramatic action. Once it is established, the thematically paramount
Berta-Karl relationship becomes static, as do the other characters'
activities. Fabian, however, obtains a car, sabotages the bridge, plots
to blow it up, is assaulted by the Pioneers, and falls into the seemingly
compassionate hands of Alma. Like Roelle in *Purgatory*, Fabian is a
would-be Baal,[40] but his enactment of gender ends in comic disasters.
When they lapse into expressionistic pathos, both he and Karl reveal
a kinship to Roelle, but Karl's threats are real whereas Fabian's degenerate into inspired parody.

> KARL [to BERTA]: You don't know me. I can be evil, it's a moral
> depression. Berta, there's a curse on me that I have to torture the
> woman who's in love with me. Understand? The woman gets
> tortured.
>
> (*GW*, 1:198)

FABIAN [to BERTA]: Come near me! Do you believe in me, woman?

BERTA: What's wrong with you?

FABIAN: Woman, once in my life I want to be a villain.

BERTA: Why do you keep saying "woman"?

FABIAN: You are "woman" to me.

BERTA: That's 'cause you're excited.

FABIAN: Berta, I'm a strangler of women, I have to control myself so I don't hurt you. Whenever I see a woman I have to hurt her.

BERTA: Don't hurt me, Fabian, and I won't hurt you.

FABIAN: I'm merciless, you're biting on granite. (*An explosion is heard.*) What was that? I almost pulled it off.

(212–13)

His scenes with his father, who showers him with sarcasm, his attempt to trick the sergeant into giving him dynamite, and his imprisonment in a sack by the Pioneers resemble the dialogues of Karl Valentin, whose persiflages of petit bourgeois rigidity influenced Brecht's earthy social satire. In one of the few episodes in V2 that are not prefigured nearly verbatim in V1, a set piece was created for Fabian that could serve as a model for Brecht's gestic language.

OLD BENKE: There's your car. Now I'll go get Berta for you.

FABIAN: My car. The German and his car. How does a German sit in it, how does an American sit in it? The German sits and compresses his ribcage. The American sits relaxed, because he's used to it. How does a German take a curve? All four wheels on the ground — with the American, at least three are in the air. (*Pioneers laugh.*) Mob! (*Exits.*)

(*GW*, 1:205)

Fabian may even have been modeled, in part, after Buster Keaton (about whom Fleisser published a short essay in 1930) and Charlie Chaplin (who influenced Brecht at this time). Without doubt, the development of the character in V2 was affected by Peter Lorre, who made his debut in Berlin in this role.[41] Fabian is thus primarily temperament, undercutting bathos through the distancing effect of comedy. Like the Captain and the Doctor in Büchner's *Woyzeck*, Fabian is, however, not a harmless clown. His grotesque temperament heightens the tragic impact of his "role"; despite his ineptness, his social standing enables him to tyrannize the likes of Berta.[42]

Less than one-sixth of V2 contains material not originating in V1. As Fleisser testified, she wrote portions of the new text, but she withdrew from the collaboration before the conclusion was worked out. The final two scenes are much abbreviated but nonetheless faithful revisions of their counterparts in V1, yet it is inconceivable that Fleisser would have written the sergeant's speech that ends V2.

> Fall in! Attention! Unfortunately the Pioneers have not always shown proper restraint toward the female citizens of the town. Therefore an order has been issued that all Pioneers' furloughs will be reduced considerably for the time being. Statistics have shown that when 300 soldiers are stationed in a town, approximately 33 illegitimate children are born, whose fathers cannot be determined. That's ten percent, you blockheads! The number is to be reduced through preventive measures. So pull yourselves together in Küstrin, you pigs, then you won't look so worn out. What messes we get into! Forward march! Column left! Break step! (*Music. Girls wave at the soldiers.*)

The dramaturgical strategy of this ending — presumably under Brecht's control — appears to have envisioned a final sociocritical appraisal of the situation, instead of Fleisser's ambiguous reference to sexual fulfillment at the end of V1. The sergeant's announcement, however, sounds more like a boast than a reprimand; one can imagine the Pioneers cheering when they hear the statistics. As an institutional solution to a complex social problem, the measure backfires, even more so than Lenz's proposal for a military whorehouse at the conclusion of *The Soldiers*. The Pioneers march off as their conquests are implicitly legitimated, at least in terms of "male honor."

The theatrical scandal that erupted after V2 premiered in Berlin was a political confrontation incited by both sides. After the phenomenal success of his *Threepenny Opera*, Brecht wanted to goad the Berlin authorities into revealing that their liberal pose toward free cultural expression was hypocritical. Censorship had been officially abolished in the Weimar Republic, yet his next project, Peter Martin Lampel's *Poison Gas Over Berlin*, was banned from performance. Fleisser's drama was chosen as a substitute; in the manipulated uproar, she was an innocent bystander. The "pepper" (Fleisser's word [*GW*, 1:445]) with which Brecht seasoned the play included the discussion of venereal disease between Karl and Frieda, staged in a cemetery; an episode in which male high school students discuss female anatomy;[43] a rocking box in which Berta's defloration takes place (an idea said to have been borrowed from Charlie Chaplin).[44] Rightist protestors brought noisemakers and distributed themselves throughout the theater. After the first performance, the Deputy Chief of Police announced: "I was a lieutenant with the Pioneers in Ingolstadt. I saw no such goings-on there" (*Materialien*, 67). The "offensive" scenes were cut to avoid a ban, and critics were invited back the next day to evaluate the benign version, which continued for forty-three performances. The liberal and leftist press was enthusiastic; Albert Zimmer expressed the wish that Fleisser "would soon achieve breadth and become a stream yearning to reach the sea, and [or?] a gigantic mountain range, that casts shadows on many valleys and sends new rivers into the land" (*Materialien*, 377). The rightist press attacked Fleisser particularly because she was a woman who had dared to write so openly about sexuality and so critically about the military. One reviewer rhetorically called upon the mayor of Ingolstadt to "marry the girl off — maybe then she will give up writing plays, which seems to be the result of unresolved complexes. Bind her hands so she cannot hold a pen in her hand anymore!" (*Materialien*, 95). Of the two reactions quoted, the second rather than the first turned out to be remarkably prophetic of Fleisser's imminent fate under Nazism, in a hostile hometown, and in wedlock with Josef Haindl.

Version 3[45]

After enduring extreme psychological and physical hardship, Fleisser discerned a change in her identity and outlook, which she described in 1971 as follows:

> When I was still very young, I was fascinated by a person's uniqueness, by the exception, the offbeat. Today I try more to comprehend the typical. At the beginning of my career, they called me a shrinking violet. In the meantime I've become much stronger. Brecht always said: you have to develop a thick skin, like an elephant. . . . (*Materialien*, 349)

In other contemporaneous statements, she distanced herself from her earlier literary efforts by evoking an analogous gender contrast: the "instinctive" (female) social criticism in her prewar writing, she maintained, had now become "conscious" (male).[46] This paradigm shift was linked to Brecht's legacy, which she believed she comprehended more clearly than before. Encouraged in 1967 by Brecht's widow Helene Weigel to rework *Soldiers in Ingolstadt* for possible performance at the Berliner Ensemble, she set about rewriting it "as it should have been done in the first place."

> . . . I only understood belatedly what Brecht had wanted from me in *Soldiers* and what I still owed him after my first version. I tried to offer him that later, even though he was already dead by this time. The influence of Brecht's social criticism on me is apparent only in my 1968 version. (*GW*, 1:447)

By expanding the sociocritical component of her works, she was convinced that she was enhancing their relevance for postwar audiences.[47] With respect to *Soldiers*, she now felt more confident in her representation of the Pioneers' role than she had earlier. She expanded the second version by approximately 40 percent by placing increased emphasis on social antagonisms—between soldiers and their officers, civilians and police, domestic servants and their employers. She added episodes based on actual incidents that she had learned about only years after the completion of the second version. Looking back on the final version, she summarized her intent:

> *Soldiers in Ingolstadt* is a play about ordinary people's hopelessness.
> The servant girls have no hope, they can't defend themselves against exploitation. Their hope for self-realization would be love, but that doesn't really have a chance to start. They meet soldiers, who are themselves under pressure all day long and who try to get rid of the pressure by passing it on. For the soldiers have no hope either.
> But when girls like Alma think they can escape exploitation, that's merely a delusion. Her supposed goal will deceive her, it only leads into the ditch. Today there are no such servant girls

anymore, to be sure. But exploitation will always exist, because
conditions of dependence will never disappear. (*GW*, 4:517)

Her statement is morally unassailable, but, as I will attempt to prove,
it does not guarantee effective drama.

An indication of her direction in V3 is evident in a seemingly minor
alteration during Fabian's man-to-man talk about success with women
(scene 2). In V2, the episode was hilariously humiliating for Fabian because his outspoken mentor was his own father. In V3, Old Benke is
replaced by Zeck, a man in his late twenties, which Fleisser considered
to be more realistic.[48] The change conforms to her intention of placing
greater value upon the "typical" than upon the "offbeat," but she
thereby misconstrued Brecht's dramaturgy, which clarified social
processes by making the commonplace seem unfamiliar. In order to
give her social message added verisimilitude, she drew from personal
experience—primarily that of her late husband rather than her own.
The new scenes in V3 dealing with the theft of wood by members of a
swimming club have merely documentary rather than artistic value, because Fleisser was no longer always able to distinguish the typical from
the banal.

This is not to say that V3 is inferior to V2 in all respects; Fleisser's
clarification of plot and motivation is at times indeed a significant
improvement. For example, after Alma and Berta have sung their
"kitchen maid song" in scene 2 of V2, a Pioneer walks past, Alma
follows, and Berta (presumably) exits after simply calling her name.
V3 elaborates:

> BERTA: What are you doing?
> ALMA: It's time to start.
> BERTA: You can't run away from me like this.
> ALMA (*Turns toward her.*): Yes, for you it means "jump when I say
> so."
> BERTA (*Calls after her.*): Alma!
> ALMA: Help yourself. I'm not going to serve you anyone on a
> platter.
> BERTA: That's about as nasty as you can get. (*Berta goes off in the
> opposite direction.*)
>
> (*GW*, 1:132)

As this exchange indicates, V3's tone is harsher and more cynical than V2. Alma is more conscious of her economic interests; in a powerful, wholly new episode she berates the sergeant for refusing to pay for her services (*GW*, 1:162–63). In a related scene not included in the published version of V3 (and echoing the scene that was performed in Berlin but not published in V2), Alma accuses the Pioneer Münsterer of having infected her with a venereal disease. Münsterer callously shrugs her off. Fleisser added the ominous note: "The later short scene between Alma and Fabian thereby acquires the implicit undertone that after all his hesitation, Fabian will get infected the very first time he has sex."[49]

The transformation of V3 is so extensive, in fact, that the revision's generic designation becomes a misnomer: there is hardly a trace of comedy left. Karl ("Korl" in V3 as in V1) rather than Fabian is responsible for the sabotage that humiliates the sergeant, eliminating Fabian's ineffable revenge scene with Berta. Fabian is trapped in a barrel rather than a sack and is sadistically mistreated. Fleisser's "comedy" climaxes with the sergeant's death by neglect, when an anchor rope yanks him into the Danube and the Pioneers leave him to his fate.

Critics are divided about the merit of V3's elaborations. Wend Kässens and Michael Töteberg praise V3's expanded "social dimension" and claim that the revision reveals the roots of Fascism in the "authoritarian social order of the Weimar Republic." They believe that V3 will remain relevant as long as modern society manifests structural similarities to the pre-Nazi era.[50] Taking a more intrinsic view, Donna L. Hoffmeister maintains: "The plot of the final version is more convincingly motivated than the second version, the dialogue reveals more subtleties of human communication, and the added stage directions give insight into undertones of thought and feeling."[51] Barbara Stritzke disagrees: "Marieluise Fleisser forms her statements about conditions in the military apparatus as if the characters were speaking from memory, as if the words had been tacked on. . . . The 1929 version of *Soldiers* has no such clichés. . . ."[52] Theater critics reacting to performances of V3 observed that the social criticism was outdated, artificially Brechtian, and excessively wordy.[53] Indeed, too much programmatic communication among characters can undermine their dramatic credibility if they embody types who are supposed to be relatively inarticulate and spontaneous. Nevertheless, determining the dramatic appropriateness of such self-reflective declarations as the sergeant's "Pressure is always directed downward" (*GW*, 1:148) or Karl's "All day long I get pushed around, so I take it out on women" (167) is a relative matter, depending on the audience's familiarity with the subject. Clarifying motivation can be useful, unless it underscores the obvious.

To complicate the issue further, Fleisser was not *consistently* pseudo-Brechtian when revising earlier work. While redrafting *Purgatory* in 1970–71, she noted that "the figures have something monstrous about them, they are constructions — therein lies their theatrical poetry. It must not become too realistic. . . . The figures must often be left unexplained."[54] Confronting her unfinished *The Deep-Sea Fish*, she ordered herself to "introduce brevity. (More condensed, as in *Purgatory*.)"[55] Herbert Ihering had said the same about *Soldiers* already in 1929: "*Soldiers in Ingolstadt* is a short play. It is a fragmentary comedy. That is its appeal. It can bear no completion" (*Materialien*, 75). Yet Fleisser's perception of *Soldiers* was different, perhaps because of her long-lived antipathy toward the play and its consequences, perhaps because of her lingering insecurities as a dramatist that expressed themselves as an unfulfilled obligation to Brecht. Her infusion of additional plot and structure into V2 suggests the residual influence of Gustav Freytag's precepts of good drama, mechanically applied.[56] By converting the play into a demonstration of what she had since learned about military and civilian life in Ingolstadt, she stripped it of some of its greatest assets. Version 3 is primarily denotative, lacking the connotative, gestic openness of V2 as well as its rich interplay of serious conflict and comic exaggeration. Although V3 retains the Berta-Karl relationship with minor alterations, it obscures its centrality with extraneous subplots. In addition, it reduces Fabian to a rather colorless secondary figure. The comic pretensions that make him as memorable as Roelle and that indirectly ridicule Karl have been cut. The apparent erosion of Fleisser's sense of humor after decades of unrelieved adversity is neither surprising nor blameworthy, but her altered perception of the play's function causes Fabian to be stripped of his historically specific literary identity as a Karl Valentin offspring and as a parody of the expressionist hero, which relates him to figures in the dramas of the young Brecht, Sternheim, and Toller (*Wotan Unbound*). Here and elsewhere in the play, Fleisser in effect eliminated the uniqueness of temperament in order to emphasize the typicality of role and gender.

That the result tends to be a thesis play with many unoriginal insights is confirmed by the triteness of V3's ending. A new sergeant appears ("merely a new edition of the drowned sergeant" [*GW*, 1:184]) and recites military regulations as the Pioneers march off, singing as they go. There is little reference to seduction, merely a confirmation of the commonplace that military discipline allows soldiers little independence.

"Soldiers in Ingolstadt"

Considering the collaborative text V2 to be qualitatively superior to the two versions wholly written by Fleisser is not meant to be a disparagement of her playwriting abilities. The reproach rarely surfaces with respect to a male playwright such as Brecht, whose (mostly female) collaborators were persistently subsumed under the corporate term *Brecht*. As a female writer, shy by nature, with little experience in the hostile environment of institutionalized theater, Fleisser could not possibly attain personal dominance over the authorship of *Soldiers* once it had been ingested by Brecht's production machine. Brecht and his coworkers had an excellent eye for the strengths of V1 and the skill to bring them into dramatic focus. By and large, their stageworthy additions to the text were in the spirit of Fleisser's original. Brecht, in fact, continued to hold the play in high regard, commending the epic technique of *Soldiers* as late as 1951.[57]

Like Lenz and Büchner, Fleisser conveys the physicality of suffering arising from "the brutality of everyday relationships."[58] In chapter 3, I defined Lenz's dramaturgy in terms of an "aesthetics of servitude," a necessarily fragmented view from below that draws attention to the margins rather than to totalities. Büchner's and Fleisser's aesthetic techniques and goals were similar, resulting in numerous formal and linguistic correspondences among Lenz's social dramas, Büchner's *Woyzeck*, and Fleisser's Ingolstadt plays: gestic dialogue, loose scenic structure, and other anticlosural tendencies, for example. Yet the dramas' origins in personal experience, in which gender difference does play a major role, are far less analogous. Unlike the two male dramatists, Fleisser viewed servitude more in terms of gender than class. This distinction becomes far more obvious in dramatic content than in form or language. All three playwrights offer electrifying insights into the condition of female role and gender, yet at crucial points in the plays of Lenz and Büchner, women are absent or metamorphosed into stereotypes. Fleisser's perspective remains consistently focused on women—which is not to say that it is undifferentiated. She presents both the reality and the critique of a character's convictions,[59] emphasizing the interplay between wish and ideology. By avoiding a false synthesis of the two, her perceptions become profoundly and enduringly sociocritical. They originate in remarkably candid, unsentimental introspection—a daring strategy in her day particularly for a female author, since it rendered her all the more vulnerable to attack. Fleisser demonstrated that by progressing from self-knowledge to comprehending the social structures and discourses in which she exists, a woman can resist being "devoured."[60]

Before Fleisser died, her life's gendered influence patterns reversed: in the late 1960s and early 1970s she became the acknowledged model for a new generation of male writers of sociocritical folk plays. Martin Sperr expressed his enthusiasm for *Of Sturdy Stock*; Rainer Werner Fassbinder proclaimed that he would not have begun writing had he not seen *Soldiers in Ingolstadt*; and Franz Xaver Kroetz published a trenchant essay on the play, in which he contrasted Fleisser's realism with Brecht's idealization of the working classes (*Materialien*, 403–4, 379–86). Fleisser acquired the status of a literary mother figure, which she emphasized by titling her essay on the three playwrights "All My Sons" (*GW*, 4:508–13). Fassbinder was unquestionably her problem child; although he dedicated *Katzelmacher* to her, his stage version of *Soldiers* was initially unauthorized and his subsequent film (televised in 1971) combined scenes from V2 and V3 with explicitly erotic and violent episodes of his own devising. Once again Fleisser was obliged to endure protest against the play, as viewers expressed their outrage to her in letters and phone calls.

Fassbinder's adaptation resembles *Katzelmacher* in its understatement and stylization. It ends not with Fleisser's cyclical exodus of the Pioneers but with Karl seducing and abandoning Berta in the woods. Berta (Hanna Schygulla) lies sobbing on the ground for a full two-and-a-half minutes as the credits scroll by and a male singer croons: "You've filled my heart / So that it no longer cries / So that it finally laughs again. . . ."[61] Fassbinder's cynical desentimentalizing of the victim might well have won the approval of Lenz.

Although it was unfortunate that some viewers held Fleisser responsible for Fassbinder's creative interventions, her play is not served by adhering reverently to her final authorized version. If even many of Goethe's revisions of his work—not to speak of Gerstenberg's or Wagner's—are relegated to the variant apparatus in modern editions, there is no reason to apply different standards to a twentieth-century author. Each of the versions of *Soldiers in Ingolstadt* are important documents of Fleisser's literary development, and a genuine historical-critical edition is needed to render them available to modern readers.[62] More important for a wide audience would be a low-priced edition similar to Suhrkamp Verlag's *Ingolstadt Plays*[63] that would emphasize the centrality of V2 over V3 while retaining the possibility of augmenting V2 with portions of V3, especially in theatrical performance. After all, Günther Rühle has claimed from his close acquaintanceship with Fleisser that "even after the third version, the play remained open for further reworking."[64]

In this vein, I would like to conclude with the attempt to construct an appropriate ending for a *Soldiers in Ingolstadt* reconstituted from V1–3. Most of V2's ending is usable only if it is thoroughly ironized. I would suggest combining and abbreviating the sergeant's final speeches before the Pioneers' exit in V2/V3, adding a gesture of female solidarity in the spirit of Fleisser's first scene, and concluding with Rühle's misreading of V1 (see n. 21).

> SERGEANT: Fall in! Attention! Unfortunately the Pioneers have not always shown proper restraint toward the female citizens of the town. As we all know, we're returning now to Küstrin. I expect exemplary behavior from my troops and no further complaints from civilians. Every violation will be punished by disciplinary measures. Prepare for departure! Column left, forward march!
>
> PIONEERS (*Marching across the stage.*): We're singing: left-right, left-right, hey hey hey! (*Meanwhile ALMA walks over to BERTA. They embrace. With an arm around each other, they wave after the departing soldiers.*)
>
> FABIAN (*Raises his hands to his mouth like a megaphone and jeers at the two women, imitating the rhythm of the marching soldiers.*): To bed, to bed, if you've got a girl, if you ain't got one, go off to bed, to bed—to bed—to bed. (*Curtain.*)

Chapter 7
Endings and Beginnings

The preceding analyses leave the impression that original endings tend to be more successful than revised ones. A work in its first preserved draft by no means represents its original *conception*, which is a nebulous accumulation of ideas and images without definable beginnings. Once a structured text emerges, its unity derives from a specific artistic strategy, and its ending appears to grow organically out of the body of the work. A conclusion altered according to a different, later agenda may well resemble instead an artificial limb.

Further tensions exist between the permanence of a dramatic text and the ephemerality of a performance text. In the parlance of reception theory, every performance of a drama is a historically situated concretization of it. Despite their weighty ring, concretizations perpetually dislodge each other, just as any individual reading of a text is a temporal occurrence that diverges in some respects from all others. As influential as they may be for a time, theatrical concretizations are, therefore, not canonizable – unless they acquire the permanence of a *filmic* text.[1] Conclusions of performances tend to articulate the motivations that inspired the production, be they nostalgia, idealism, provocation, or spectacle. Since the theatrical mediation of a dramatic text can be so variable, a way to anticipate change would be to inscribe the alterability of endings into the texts themselves, as Heiner Müller has done more than once. His aesthetic strategy is a comment on contemporary society and, as such, a political provocation.

"An ending," he said in an interview about Büchner's *Woyzeck*, "is a judgment."[2] An ending's propensity for categorical pronouncements, such as the guilt or innocence of a Woyzeck victimized by circumstances over which he has no control, is for Müller a structural anachronism, reminiscent of the nineteenth century's all-knowing storyteller. His play, *Cement* (1972), represents a phase in his attempt to diminish the authority of an ending: he indicates that its final scenes

147

are interchangeable, depending on whether a particular staging is to conclude on a note of idealism or disillusionment.[3] In keeping with Brecht's theory of learning plays, the dramatic text is to accommodate itself to specific circumstances. As Müller becomes less Brechtian and more postmodern, he contends that individual and collective history is no longer reducible to a single, linear narrative of Aristotelian dimensions. He points out, for example, that the three segments of his avant-garde *Decaying Shore Medea-Material Landscape with Argonauts* (1982) derive from different periods of his artistic development and are to be presented "however one chooses" as simultaneous rather than sequential episodes.[4] The text is composed of "materials" or elements whose eventual structuring is a matter of chance. Hence, this play about a collective subject collectivizes the notion of authorship by minimizing the distinction between author and director.[5] Müller's self-reflexive dramatic forms appear to function as insurance against the naïveté of self-confident endings, which offer "solutions" with an authoritative gestus. He implies that such certitudes—like those emanating from political institutions—are grossly inappropriate, since their rhetoric no longer matches social realities.

Indeed, even a superb dramatic lesson in political consciousness raising such as Brecht's *The Mother* can appear antediluvian if postrevolutionary disenchantment rather than prevolutionary fervor prevails among its spectators. In a 1988 East German production, in fact, its political polarities seemed to have reversed: the bourgeois teacher had become the subversive, earning laughter and applause when criticizing the revolutionaries with such lines as "Can't you make your newspaper more entertaining? Nobody reads it." The play's ending, which celebrates the power of revolutionary solidarity, may well have evoked little more than indifference, since its inspirational rhetoric has been appropriated long since in East Germany by omnipresent slogans. However, during the social unrest before and after the opening of the Berlin Wall in 1989, the final lines, "For yesterday's conquered are tomorrow's victors / And never becomes: today" may once again have acquired their original revolutionary force.

The point of this example[6] is that the impact of celebratory and didactic endings in particular is susceptible to extreme variation, since it depends on how their representations of social entities (the individual and the collective, the family and the state, the poor and the rich, blacks and whites, women and patriarchal structures, etc.) are perceived by specific groups of readers or spectators. Instead of measuring a drama's impact with respect to a multiplicity of audiences, cultural commentators tend to universalize their own context and ascribe dominance to a particular cultural trend. Thus, the current era is declared to be postmodern and Brecht's didactic dramas are pronounced outmoded – although this judgment might only, in fact, apply to those whose material status distances them from the urgency of his social critique. What may appear jaded to a coterie of white male intellectuals can be energizing and relevant to an audience of labor union members, Hispanic women, or children[7] – a truism meant to emphasize that contexts ought to be *particularized*, which means recognizing the different needs and expectations of social groupings defined by class, race, gender, and age. Perceiving the simultaneous validity of varying cultural forms such as classical tragedy, commedia dell'arte, melodrama, children's theater, or street theater democratizes the act of critical evaluation.

Drama endings take a stand. If a beginning, according to Said, "is the first step in the intentional production of meaning,"[8] then an ending is its last, asserting the importance of that which preceded it. By demonstratively ending a process, it challenges another to commence in its place. "Every situation," mused Gerhart Hauptmann, "as explosive as it might be, leaves behind enough fuel to ignite another, this one in turn ignites the next and so on, expanding into infinity."[9] Thus every ending makes room for a new beginning.

Notes

Chapter 1

1. *Aristotle's Poetics*, trans. S. H. Butcher, intro. Francis Fergusson (New York: Hill and Wang, 1961), 90.
2. J. Hillis Miller, "The Problematic of Ending in Narrative," in "Narrative Endings," *Nineteenth-Century Fiction* 33, 1 (June, 1978): 5.
3. Miller, "Ending in Narrative," 5.
4. Arthur Schopenhauer, *Die Welt als Wille und Vorstellung*, in *Arthur Schopenhauers Sämtliche Werke*, ed. Paul Deussen (Munich: Piper, 1911), 2:499.
5. *Aristotle's Poetics*, 91.
6. Sue-Ellen Case draws attention to the semiotic distinction between the written and published text, the director's and the rehearsal text, and the audience's reception (or "production text"), each of which are discrete interpretations of the original. "The importance of the author's intent gives way to the conditions of production and the composition of the audience in determining the meaning of the theatrical event. This implies that there is no aesthetic closure around the text, separating it from the conditions of its production" (Sue-Ellen Case, *Feminism and Theatre* [London: Macmillan, 1988], 115–16).
7. Gerald F. Else, *Aristotle's Poetics: The Argument* (Cambridge, Mass.: Harvard University Press, 1957), 439.
8. Georg Wilhelm Friedrich Hegel, *Vorlesungen über die Ästhetik. Dritter Teil: Die Poesie* (Stuttgart: Reclam, 1971), 265.
9. Hegel, *Vorlesungen*, 274; italics added.
10. Hegel, *Vorlesungen*, 279.
11. Hegel, *Vorlesungen*, 310.
12. Gustav Freytag, *Aufsätze zur Geschichte, Literatur und Kunst*, in *Gesammelte Werke von Gustav Freytag* (Leipzig: G. Hirzel, 1897), 16:189.
13. Gustav Freytag, *Die Technik des Dramas* (Darmstadt: Wissenschaftliche Buchgesellschaft, 1965), 121.
14. Freytag, *Die Technik*, 122.
15. John Gassner, "Catharsis and the Modern Theater," in *The Idea of Tragedy*, ed. Carl Benson and Taylor Littleton (Glenview, Ill.: Scott, Foresman, 1966), 62.
16. Gassner, "Catharsis," 62.
17. H. B. English and A. C. English, *A Comprehensive Dictionary of Psychological and Psychoanalytical Terms* (New York: Daniel McKay, 1965), 91. Cf. Barbara Herrnstein Smith, *Poetic Closure: A Study of How Poems End* (Chicago: University of Chicago

Press, 1968), 2: "a structure appears 'closed' when it is experienced as integral: coherent, complete, and stable."

18. Bernhard Beckerman, *Dynamics of Drama: Theory and Method of Analysis* (New York: Drama Book Specialists, 1979), 153–54.

19. Edward W. Said, *Beginnings: Intention and Method* (Baltimore: Johns Hopkins University Press, 1978), 41.

20. Said, *Beginnings*, 49–50.

21. Frank Kermode, *The Sense of an Ending: Studies in the Theory of Fiction* (New York: Oxford University Press, 1967), 89, 8.

22. Alexander Welsh, "Opening and Closing *Les Miserables*," in "Narrative Endings," *Nineteenth-Century Fiction* 33, no. 1 (June, 1978): 20.

23. Terry Eagleton, *Literary Theory: An Introduction* (Minneapolis: University of Minnesota Press, 1983), 185.

24. Eagleton, *Literary Theory*, 186.

25. See Kermode, *Sense of Ending*, 7.

26. Jean Duvignaud, "The Theatre in Society: Society in the Theatre," in *Sociology of Literature and Drama*, ed. Elizabeth Burns and Tom Burns (Harmondsworth: Penguin, 1973), 86.

27. Ronald Reagan, quoted in *TV Guide*, March 20–26, 1982, 6.

28. Dick Kleiner, "TV question box," *Columbus Citizen-Journal*, March 6, 1981, 16.

29. Ernst Bloch, "Happy End, Seen Through and Yet Still Defended," *The Principle of Hope*, trans. Neville Plaice, Stephen Plaice, and Paul Knight (Cambridge, Mass.: MIT Press, 1986), 443.

30. Bloch, "Happy End," 443. In a recent book, Walter Hinck measures the "potential of hope" in three centuries of German drama. See Walter Hinck, *Theater der Hoffnung: Von der Aufklärung bis zur Gegenwart* (Frankfurt am Main: Suhrkamp 1988).

31. *Gespräche mit Gerhard Hauptmann*, ed. Joseph Chapiro (Berlin: S. Fischer, 1932), 162.

32. Peter Szondi, *Theorie des modernen Dramas* (Frankfurt am Main: Suhrkamp, 1963), 72–73.

33. See Szondi, *Theorie*, 72–73.

34. Walter Hinck, *Vom Ausgang der Komödie: Exemplarische Lustspielschlüsse in der europäischen Literatur* (Opladen: Westdeutscher Verlag, 1977), 10.

35. Quoted in Louis Sheaffer, *O'Neill: Son and Artist* (Boston: Little, Brown, 1973), 67.

36. Quoted in Murray Krieger, "Tragedy and the Tragic Vision," in *On King Lear*, ed. Lawrence Danson (Princeton: Princeton University Press, 1981), 148. See also Henry J. Schmidt, "The Language of Confinement: Gerstenberg's *Ugolino* and Klinger's *Sturm und Drang*," *Lessing Yearbook* 11 (1979): 179.

37. See Henry J. Schmidt, "The Language of Rationality: Leisewitz's *Julius von Tarent*," in *Theatrum Mundi: Essays on German Drama and German Literature*, ed. Edward R. Haymes (Munich: Wilhelm Fink, 1980), 37.

38. Herrnstein Smith, *Poetic Closure*, 262.

39. Cf. Herrnstein Smith, *Poetic Closure*, 121n; Rachel Blau DuPlessis, *Writing beyond the Ending: Narrative Strategies of Twentieth-Century Women Writers* (Bloomington: Indiana University Press, 1985), 4ff.

40. See Elaine Marks and Isabelle de Courtivron, eds., *New French Feminisms: An Anthology* (Amherst, Mass.: University of Massachusetts Press, 1980), 36–37; Julia Kristeva,

interview with Xavière Gauthier, 166; Claudine Herrmann, "Les coordonnées féminines: Espace et temps," 172; Hélène Cixous, "The Laugh of the Medusa," 248, 259. See also Case, *Feminism*, 129.

41. Kermode says that endings are in a "quasi-grammatical class": "But just as, in the understanding of sentences, we may grasp the whole by perceiving the significance of parts, so the weight of the ending may be distributed among *Eindruckspunkte* which are not in themselves terminal" (Frank Kermode, "Sensing Endings," in "Narrative Endings," *Nineteenth-Century Fiction* 33, no. 1 [June, 1978]: 154).

42. Sources for quotations of drama endings are listed following the notes.

43. These epilogues often fulfilled the ritual of deference before the patron, anticipating and deflecting possible displeasure. An example of the celebration of self-abasement to which all artists in a feudal culture were subject is the epilogue spoken at court appended to Marlowe's *The Jew of Malta*.

> It is our fear, dread sovereign, we have been
> Too tedious; neither can't be less than sin
> To wrong your princely patience. If we have,
> Thus low dejected, we your pardon crave.
> And if ought here offend your ear or sight,
> We only act and speak what others write.

44. Quoted in Kermode, *Sense of Ending*, 22.

45. Alvin B. Kernan, "*King Lear* and the Shakespearean Pageant of History," in *On* King Lear, ed. Lawrence Danson (Princeton, N.J.: Princeton University Press, 1981), 22–23.

46. Comedies often conclude with the clear recognition that the action has played itself out: a promise is made to narrate events unknown to several of the characters but not to the audience. The imminent repetition of familiar material signals to the spectators that whatever follows is no longer interesting, and they are to turn their attention elsewhere, namely back to their own reality.

47. Letter to Schröder, July 4, 1787, in Friedrich Schiller, *Briefe*, ed. Gerhard Fricke (Munich: Carl Hanser, 1955), 119.

48. Freidrich Schiller, "Nänie," in *The Penguin Book of German Verse*, ed. Leonard Forster (Baltimore: Penguin, 1957), 242.

49. Thomas Mann, *Doctor Faustus*, trans. H. T. Lowe-Porter (New York: Vintage, 1971), 491.

50. See Herrnstein Smith, *Poetic Closure*, 206–7.

51. See also the concise final stage direction of Müller's *The Battle*: "*Over the dead bodies begins the struggle of the survivors for bread.*"

52. See also the famous example of title inversion at the end of Shakespeare's *Romeo and Juliet*.

53. Gerd Kremer, "Die Struktur des Tragödienschlusses," in *Die Bauform der griechischen Tragödie*, ed. Walter Jens (Munich: Wilhelm Fink, 1971), 118.

54. The tableau of Strindberg's *The Ghost Sonata* invokes Boecklin's well-known painting, *The Island of the Dead*.

55. Similarly, Heiner Müller's *Hamletmaschine*: "*Ophelia remains onstage, motionless in white wrapping paper.*"

56. Volker Klotz, *Geschlossene und offene Form im Drama* (Munich: Carl Hanser, 1962), 12.

57. Raymond Williams, *Modern Tragedy* (1966; rev. London: Verso, 1979), 55. Moreover, an unresolved ending can become as conventional and mannered—and thereby lose its original provocative quality—as any ending that celebrates the values that allow a particular society to cohere.

58. Examples include the numerous Amphitryon dramas, Shakespeare's *Comedy of Errors*, and Mozart/Da Ponte's *Don Giovanni*, in which the melodramatic punishment of the sinning Don is juxtaposed against Leporello's comic fear, followed by Leporello's unraveling of the action, "high" and "low" reconciliations (Don Ottavio/Donna Anna, Masetto/Zerlina), who then join forces to sing the final moral. Such a multitude of resolutions resemble the repetition of the final chord in a classical symphony.

59. A. Tol'stoi, "Piataia simfoniia Shostakovicha" [Shostakovich's *Fifth Symphony*], *Izvestiia* (December 28, 1937), 3 (translated by Laurel E. Fay).

60. Solomon Volkov, *Testimony: The Memoirs of Dmitri Shostakovich* (New York: Harper and Row, 1979), 183.

61. Cf. Terry Eagleton: "The work's insights, as with all writing, are deeply related to its blindnesses: what it does not say, and *how* it does not say it, may be as important as what it articulates; what seems absent, marginal, or ambivalent about it may provide a central clue to its meanings" (*Literary Theory*, 178).

62. In the second version of the play, her subjugation is intensified by a marriage ceremony, to which the Rittmeister even sardonically invites the audience.

63. In a novel variant, Handke silences the *audience* in his *Denouncing the Public*; after the actors' final obeisance, "You were welcome here. We thank you. Good night," the audience's traditional response is turned against it: ". . . *Wild applause and whistles are directed at the audience through loudspeakers . . . until the audience leaves.*"

64. Reinhold Schneider, *Winter in Wien: Aus meinen Notizbüchern 1957–58*, in *Gesammelte Werke*, ed. Josef Rast (Frankfurt am Main: Insel, 1978), 10:245.

65. See Susan McClary, "Talking Politics during Bach Year," *Music and Society: The Politics of Composition, Performance, and Reception*, ed. Richard Leppert and Susan McClary (Cambridge: Cambridge University Press, 1987), 17–19.

66. Williams, *Modern Tragedy*, 45, 56. See also Case, *Feminism*, 116–17.

67. Cf. Blau DuPlessis, *Writing*, 3; McClary, "Talking Politics," 17.

68. Like numerous other contemporary critics of drama, Hinck pays insufficient attention to class, gender, and race when assessing the utopian potential of German drama in his *Theater der Hoffnung*. In contrast, Alice Walker's observation about narrative prose endings offers a more concrete social perspective.

> For the most part, white American writers tended to end their books and their characters' lives as if there were no better existence for which to struggle. The gloom of defeat is thick.
>
> By comparison, black writers seem always involved in a moral and/or political struggle, the result of which is expected to be some kind of larger freedom. Perhaps this is because our literary tradition is based on the slave narratives, where escape for the body and freedom for the soul went together, or perhaps this is because black people have never felt themselves guilty of global, cosmic sins. (Alice Walker, *In Search of our Mothers' Gardens* [New York: Harcourt Brace Jovanovich, 1983], 5)

69. Raymond Williams, *Marxism and Literature* (Oxford: Oxford University Press, 1977), 116. See also Fredric Jameson, *The Political Unconscious* (Ithaca, N.Y.: Cornell University Press, 1981), 106: "[G]enres are essentially literary *institutions*, or social contracts between a writer and a specific public, whose function is to specify the proper use of a particular cultural artifact."

70. Blau DuPlessis, *Writing*, ix-xi.

71. Williams, *Marxism and Literature*, 155.

72. Julia Kristeva, quoted in Ulrike Strauch, "Antwort über Antwort auf die Frage: Gibt es eine weibliche Ästhetik?" *Frauen sehen ihre Zeit*, Katalog der Literaturausstellung des Landesfrauenbeirates Rheinland-Pfalz (Mainz, 1984), 81; italics added.

73. At the conclusion of Jameson's *The Political Unconscious* (296), he calls for a synthesis of the Marxist "negative hermeneutic" of ideological analysis with "a Marxist positive hermeneutic, or a decipherment of the Utopian impulses of . . . cultural texts." Therefore an *"instrumental"* or *"functional"* method for describing cultural texts" should be "coordinated with a *collective-associational* or *communal* reading of culture." It is not clear to me how an ideological reading is distinguishable from an "anticipatory" one, for the utopian moment is itself an expression of ideology, therefore time bound and subject to ideological criticism. Nonetheless, Jameson's dual hermeneutic helps illustrate the tensions and contradictions that an analysis of endings should uncover and sustain.

74. Bloch, "Happy End," 517.

75. See Schmidt, "Language of Rationality," especially 31.

76. See "Maschine der Freiheit: Ruth Berghaus und Heiner Müller über Theater," interview with Sigrid Neef, *Tageszeitung*, March 22, 1989, 14.

Chapter 2

1. Michel Foucault, *Madness and Civilization: A History of Insanity in the Age of Reason*, trans. Richard Howard (New York: Vintage, 1973), 84.

2. Foucault, *Madness*, 248.

3. Foucault, *Madness*. 252–53.

4. See Friedrich II's edict of 1784, quoted in Jürgen Habermas, *The Structural Transformation of the Public Sphere: An Inquiry into a Category of Bourgeois Society*, trans. Thomas Burger (Cambridge, Mass.: MIT Press, 1989), 25.

5. See Habermas, *Structural Transformation*, 46–48. See Karin A. Wurst's exemplary study of the sociology of the family during the German Englightenment in *Familiale Liebe ist die "wahre Gewalt": Die Repräsentation der Familie in G. E. Lessings dramatischem Werk* (Amsterdam: Rodopi, 1988), especially 31.

6. See Erich Fromm, "Sozialpsychologischer Teil," *Studien über Autorität und Familie*, ed. Max Horkheimer (Paris: F. Alcan, 1936), 88.

7. See Karl S. Guthke, *Das deutsche bürgerliche Trauerspiel* (Stuttgart: Metzler, 1972), 34; Wurst, *Familiale Liebe*, 12–32.

8. I am retaining the German term *Sturm und Drang* because the conventional English equivalent, Storm and Stress, has become hopelessly inadequate. Stress is now a seemingly universal malaise in postindustrial society, rather than the creative urge and its concomitant emotional turmoil that the word *Drang* originally connoted. The

following remarks pertain primarily to the dramas of Gerstenberg, Leisewitz, Klinger, Goethe, and Schiller. The impact of *economic* factors on individual autonomy comes to the fore in the social dramas of Lenz, which will be discussed in chap. 3.

9. See Fritz Martini, "Die feindlichen Brüder: Zum Problem des gesellschaftskritischen Dramas von J. A. Leisewitz, F. M. Klinger und F. Schiller," *Jahrbuch der deutschen Schillergesellschaft* 16 (1972): 234.

10. Martini, "Die feindlichen Brüder," 236.

11. Fromm, "Sozialpsychologischer Teil," 79–80.

12. See Ernst Bloch, "Entfremdung, Verfremdung," in *Literarische Aufsätze* (Frankfurt am Main: Suhrkamp, 1965), 281.

13. Cf. Johann Wolfgang von Goethe: "Oh, if I weren't writing dramas now I would perish" (letter to the Countess of Stolberg, March 7–10, 1775; Johann Wolfgang von Goethe, *Goethes Werke, Briefe*, ed. Karl Robert Mandelkow [Hamburg: Wegner, 1960], 1:179).

14. The conflict was, in fact, dramatized during the Sturm und Drang era in L. P. Hahn's *Rebellion in Pisa* (1776). See Heinrich Wilhelm von Gerstenberg, *Ugolino*, ed. Christoph Siegrist (Stuttgart: Reclam, 1966), 152. Quotations from *Ugolino* derive from this edition.

15. Heinrich Wilhelm von Gerstenberg, "Briefe über Merkwürdigkeiten der Literatur," in *Sturm und Drang: Kritische Schriften*, ed. Lambert Schneider (Heidelberg: Lambert Schneider, 1963), 49. Subsequent quotations refer to this edition.

16. See Andreas Huyssen, *Drama des Sturm und Drang: Kommentar zu einer Epoche* (Munich: Winkler, 1980), 98.

17. See Klaus Gerth, *Studien zu Gerstenbergs Poetik* (Göttingen: Vandenhoeck and Ruprecht, 1960), Palaestra, n. 231: 45, 53.

18. Letter to Gotthold Ephraim Lessing, May or June, 1768. G. E. Lessing, *Sämtliche Schriften*, ed. Karl Lachmann and Franz Muncker (Leipzig, 1885ff.), 19:256 (henceforth abbreviated LM).

19. Lessing, LM, 19:254.

20. "I looked in the faces of my sons without saying a word . . . nor answered all that day nor the night after. . . . That day and the next we stayed all silent" (Dante Alighieri, *The Divine Comedy: Inferno*, trans. and comment by John D. Sinclair (New York: Oxford University Press, 1961), canto 33, 407).

21. Respectively from Guthke, *Trauerspiel*, 32; Peter Szondi, *Die Theorie des bürgerlichen Trauerspiels im achtzehnten Jahrhundert*, ed. Gert Mattenklott (Frankfurt am Main: Suhrkamp, 1973), 99–100; Lessing, LM, 7:68.

22. Ernst Karl Ludwig Ysenburg von Buri, *Ludwig Capet oder der Königsmord*, quoted in Guthke, *Trauerspiel*, 16.

23. See Szondi, *Die Theorie Trauerspiels*, 128.

24. For greater elaboration of the following observations, see Henry J. Schmidt, "The Language of Confinement: Gerstenberg's *Ugolino* and Klinger's *Sturm und Drang*," *Lessing Yearbook* 11 (1979): 165–97.

25. Passivity is overcome only once, when the eldest son Francesco finds a gap in the tower and escapes into the night, but hope of release is grotesquely thwarted when he is delivered back into the tower—alive, but soon to die of poison—in a coffin.

26. See Guthke, *Trauerspiel*, 33; and Gert Mattenklott, *Melancholie in der Dramatik des Sturm und Drang* (Königstein/Ts: Athenäum, 1985), 29.

27. Szondi, *Die Theorie Trauerspiels*, 90. See also Gerd Stein, "Genialität als Resignation bei Gerstenberg," in *Literatur der bürgerlichen Emanzipation im 18. Jahrhundert*, eds. Gert Mattenklott and Klaus R. Scherpe (Kronberg/Ts.: Scriptor, 1973), 110; Wolf Lepenies, *Melancholie und Gesellschaft* (Frankfurt am Main: Suhrkamp, 1972), 98.

28. See Peter Uwe Hohendahl, "Empfindsamkeit und gesellschaftliches Bewußtsein: Zur Soziologie des empfindsamen Romans am Beispiel von *La Vie die Marianne, Clarissa, Fräulein von Sternheim* und *Werther*," *Jahrbuch der deutschen Schillergesellschaft* 16 (1972): 199, 204. To say, therefore, that the Rousseauistic preoccupation with the inner mechanisms of the psyche, typical for the entire Sturm und Drang, was simply compensatory for the writers' inability/unwillingness to indulge in social observation and critique minimizes the socially progressive, even subversive aspects of the eighteenth-century "cult of feeling." (See Hans J. Haferkorn, "Zur Entstehung der bürgerlich-literarischen Intelligenz und des Schriftstellers in Deutschland zwischen 1750 und 1800," in *Deutsches Bürgertum und literarische Intelligenz 1750–1800*, ed. Bernd Lutz [Stuttgart: Metzler, 1974], 185.)

29. See Szondi, *Die Theorie Trauerspiels*, 110. Johann Gottfried Herder's extremely perceptive analysis of *Ugolino* in the *Allgemeine deutsche Bibliothek* (11 [1770], quoted in Siegrist, *Ugolino*, 74–86) praises the drama primarily for this reason. As Bruce Duncan points out, Gerstenberg's professed intent was to portray "the fact of suffering, not its cause" (Bruce Duncan, "'Ich platze!' Gerstenberg's *Ugolino* and the Mid-Life Crisis," *Germanic Review* 53 [1978]: 13).

30. One example: crazed by hunger, Anselmo prepares to sink his teeth into the flesh of his dead mother (who was delivered into the tower in a second coffin). The inanimate yet morally enlightened coffin rebels by falling shut. As daring (or reckless) as these effects are, they remain focused on character and emotion without lapsing into sensationalism. See the subsequent section on Wagner for a discussion of this difference.

31. Cf. the conclusion to Goethe's *Egmont*, cited in chap.1.

32. Quoted in Montague Jacobs, *Gerstenberg's "Ugolino": Ein Vorläufer des Geniedramas* (Berlin: E. Ebering, 1898), 49.

33. Dante, *Divine Comedy*, 408–9.

34. February 25, 1768; Lessing, LM 17:246. See also Robert R. Heitner, *German Tragedy in the Age of Enlightenment* (Berkeley: University of California Press, 1963), 390–92; Richard Sheppard, "Lessing, Gerstenberg, and *Ugolino*," *Forum for Modern Language Studies* 7 (1971): 60–67 (Sheppard's thesis of Gerstenberg the revolutionary versus Lessing the reactionary seems far too simplistic to be useful); and Duncan, "'Ich platze!' " 13–19.

35. Lessing, LM, 10:121.

36. Lessing, LM, 19:254; italics added.

37. Lessing, LM, 19:254–55; italics added. Significantly, Gerstenberg originally wrote "on a note of resignation" instead of "on a note of submission to fate."

38. Fromm, "Sozialpsychologischer Teil," 121.

39. Lessing, LM, 19:247–48.

40. Lessing, LM, 19:254.

41. "An Herrn Conferenzrath Gähler," Heinrich Wilhelm von Gerstenberg, *Vermischte Schriften von ihm selbst gesammelt und mit Verbesserungen und Zusätzen herausgegeben in drei Bänden* (Altona: Hammerich, 1815), 1:29–30. The letter is dated December 10, 1812.

42. Letter to Gähler, *Vermischte Schriften*, 1:13, 15. Klaus Gerth writes that Gerstenberg's literary productivity extended from 1759 to 1771, after which his personal fortunes declined and he was unable to create anything of abiding literary interest until his death more than fifty years later. (See Klaus Gerth, "Heinrich Wilhelm von Gerstenberg," in *Deutsche Dichter des 18. Jahrhunderts: Ihr Leben und Werk*, ed. Benno von Wiese [Berlin: Schmidt, 1977], 393.) Only two performances of *Ugolino* appear to have taken place during his lifetime, namely in Berlin in 1769 by Döbbelin's theater troupe while Gerstenberg was in Denmark. The play's four characters were played by Döbbelin, his wife, daughter, and son (See Jacobs, *Gerstenberg's "Ugolino"*, 116–18).

43. Gerstenberg conscientiously footnoted the monologue as preparatory for a conclusion that was to deviate from the first edition (*Vermischte Schriften*, 1:474–76).

44. *Vermischte Schriften*, 1:505. A portion of the final scene is reprinted in Siegrist, *Ugolino*, 69–71.

45. *Stella, ein Schauspiel für Liebende, von J. W. Göthe. Sechster Akt.* Its author was Johann Georg Pfranger, a preacher at the Meiningen court. See Julius W. Braun, ed., *Goethe im Urtheile seiner Zeitgenossen*, (Berlin: Luckhardt, 1883), 1:275–76, 282–84, 318.

46. *Stella, Numer* [sic] *zwey. Oder Fortsetzung des Götheschen Schauspiels Stella, in fünf Acten* (Frankfurt and Leipzig, 1776); see Braun, *Goethe*, 288–91. In 1798, August von Kotzebue published a "corrective" to *Stella* in the form of a full-length drama, set on a desert island, titled *La Peyrouse*. He creates a morally acceptable ménage à trois that functions as a family by day but separates the two women from the man at night. See Heinz-Dieter Weber, "Stella oder die Negativität des Happy End," in *Rezeptionsgeschichte oder Wirkungsästhetik*, ed. Heinz-Dieter Weber, (Stuttgart: Klett-Cotta, 1978), 158–59.

47. *Freywillige Beyträge zu den Hamburgischen Nachrichten aus dem Reiche der Gelehrsamkeit* (Hamburg), February 23, 1776, in Braun, *Goethe*, 242–44. Goeze's influence was sufficient to cause the play to be banned on Hamburg stages.

48. *Berlinisches Litterarisches Wochenblatt* (Berlin), March 30, 1776, in Braun, *Goethe*, 252–53. The critic concludes almost plaintively: "Our wish [in making these suggestions] was only that [the author] might in the future consent to tread a less paradoxical path" (253). A seemingly more urbane critic from another Berlin journal wondered "whether [Cäcilie and Stella] could sustain this harmony permanently, or whether they might not make faces at each other from time to time while saying 'good morning,' or whether the European Fernando could love equally and perpetually both of these so attractive women?" (*Berlinische Nachrichten von Staats- und Gelehrten Sachen* [Berlin], February 22, 1776, in Braun, *Goethe*, 240).

49. "Über das deutsche Theater" (1815), quoted in Hans Gerhard Gräf, ed., *Goethe über seine Dichtungen* (Frankfurt am Main: Rütten und Loening, 1908), vol. 2, no. 4, 203–4. *Stella* was performed in Weimar in 1806; the revised version appeared in 1816 in the *Zweite Gesamtausgabe* with the subtitle, "A Tragedy."

50. See Weber, *Rezeptionsgeschichte*, 154; Lothar Pikulik, "Stella: Ein Schauspiel für Lie-

bende," *Goethes Dramen. Neue Interpretationen,* ed. Walter Hinderer (Stuttgart: Reclam, 1980), 95.

51. See Pikulik, "Stella," 97.

52. His ambivalent rapport with his sister Cornelia is mirrored in his famous characterization of Frau von Stein: "Ach, du warst in abgelebten Zeiten / Meine Schwester oder meine Frau." See Sigrid Damm, *Cornelia Goethe* (Frankfurt am Main: Insel, 1988), 154–55, 200.

53. *Stella: Ein Schauspiel für Liebende,* in Johann Wolfgang von Goethe, *Goethes Werke,* vol. 4, ed. Wolfgang Kayser (Hamburg: Wegner, 1960), 319 (henceforth abbreviated *HA* [*Hamburger Ausgabe*]; further quotations from this edition).

54. "Über das deutsche Theater," in Gräf, *Goethe,* 204.

55. A perceptive critic wrote in 1776 that "Stella speaks like Cäcilie, Cäcilie like Stella, and both together like Fernando . . ." (*Freywillige Beyträge zu den Hamburgischen Nachrichten aus dem Reiche der Gelehrsamkeit* [Hamburg], April 2, 1776, in Braun, *Goethe,* 263).

56. See Georg-Michael Schulz, "Goethes *Stella*": Wirrnisse der Liebe und Gottes Gerechtigkeit," *Germanisch-Romanische Monatsschrift* 60 (1979): 419.

57. See Peter Pfaff, *Das Glücksmotiv im Jugendwerk Goethes* (Heidelberg: Winter, 1965), 66.

58. Johann Wolfgang von Goethe, *The Sorrows of Young Werther,* trans. Catherine Hutter (New York: New American Library, 1962), 42. Cf. also Goethe to Auguste von Stolberg, August 3, 1775: "Accursed fate, which will not allow me a position between extremes. I'm either focused upon, clinging to a point or swept up by all four winds!" *HA, Briefe,* 1:189.

59. This is the only segment of the first printed version that Goethe felt compelled to alter when *Stella* was republished in 1787. In the latter, Fernando's motivation for leaving his women was considerably toned down; the estate manager gives a more detailed exposition and downgrades Fernando's self-obsessed longings to "a concealed restlessness." I quote this passage at some length because Wolfgang Kayser reproduces it inadequately in the *Hamburger Ausgabe.* Text quoted from *Der junge Goethe,* ed. Hanna Fischer-Lamberg (Berlin: De Gruyter, 1973), 5:92–93; cf. *HA,* 4:328–29, 557.

60. Like Wild in Klinger's *Sturm und Drang* and Major von Berg in Lenz's *The Tutor,* he views war as a form of therapy, even self-humiliation, as he willingly sides with the forces of oppression.

61. See Pikulik, "Stella," 99.

62. Cf. Gerstenberg's comment (cited previously) about not hacking apart the "knot" of his drama by ending it in a suicide.

63. See Bernd Fischer, "Goethes *Clavigo*: Das Melodrama des Bildungsbürgers im Trauerspiel des Sturm und Drang" *Goethe-Yearbook* 5 (1990): 47–64, in which he shows that *Clavigo*'s trajectory through act 4 leaves open the possibility of its ending as a sentimental comedy, *Geniedrama,* political tragedy, middle-class tragedy, or sentimental melodrama.

64. See Pfaff, *Das Glücksmotiv,* 69.

65. Even though Goethe used illustrative stories, rational advisers, and so forth in other works of this period such as *Werther* and *Clavigo,* these Enlightenment intrusions into sentimental and Sturm und Drang milieus fail to change the course of the outcome. When a transformation does occur, as in *Stella,* the denouement — which, nota bene,

takes place at night—is so ambiguous and abbreviated that it strains credibility. Thus, when Goethe wanted to eradicate residual contradictions once and for all, he had to bypass the Enlightenment and really "go for Baroque" with an operatic allegory such as Egmont's final vision of freedom.

66. In his breathtaking contemporary staging of the play at the Deutsches Theater in East Berlin, Alexander Lang takes Goethe's deconstruction of Enlightened male authority to its logical conclusion. After the parable, Fernando throws himself with exaggerated gestures repeatedly at the feet of the women. They march off resolutely without him, and he screams in pain as the stage darkens. Just before the curtain falls a large red neon heart lights up before him—"Herz," by now a cliché, reveals itself as a tyrant rather than a savior.

67. See Pfaff, *Das Glücksmotiv*, 71: "One senses how Goethe attempted to comprehend his play across the distance of decades, how he indeed rediscovered his intent and motives but could no longer bring them to dramatic life and thus wrote only descriptive commentary instead of dynamic sentences. . . . [One sees] with what reluctance Goethe approached the adaptation and how little it did justice to the spirit of his youthful work." At nearly the same time as Goethe, Klinger looked back on his early works and mused: "I don't know if it is necessary and advantageous to recast the all-too-daring products of genius into a more reasonable—that is, colder—form: the poet always looks like he has castrated himself just to appear agreeable and modest" (*Betrachtungen und Gedanken, Erster Theil*, Friedrich Maximilian Klinger, *Werke* [Leipzig: Fleischer, 1832], 11:298).

68. See the reference to Gellert's *The Affectionate Sisters* in chap. 1.

69. The *Stella* of 1775 remains ambivalent about power relationships within male-female unions. In 1776, however, Goethe wrote an even briefer drama, *Die Geschwister*, in which the triumph of male dominance is absolute. Believing herself to be the sister of the merchant Wilhelm, Marianne is wholly submissive to him. It transpires that he has been testing her worthiness, and when she goes so far as to reject her suitor for Wilhelm's sake, he reveals that they are not brother and sister and can marry each other. Marianne utters exclamations of joy at her "reward," and the curtain falls. Like his eventual revision of *Stella*, Goethe's *Die Geschwister*—most likely meant to be a reproach of his insufficiently dependent sister (see Damm, *Cornelia Goethe*, 206–9)— erases emancipatory impulses that threaten convention.

70. Original text in Heinrich Leopold Wagner, *Die Kindermörderin* [based on the first edition, 1776], ed. Jörg-Ulrich Fechner (Stuttgart: Reclam, 1969) (henceforth referred to as *Kinder*). Quotations are identified by act in parentheses. Translated into English by Betty Senk Waterhouse as *The ChildMurderess* in *Five Plays of the Sturm und Drang* (Lanham, Md.: University Press of America, 1986), 97–144; translations derive, with occasional alterations, from this edition.

71. Letter to Heribert von Dalberg, July 15, 1782, in Friedrich Schiller, *Schillers Briefe*, ed. Fritz Jonas (Stuttgart: Deutsche Verlags-Anstalt, 1892–96), 1:64.

72. In his recent book, Walter Hinck arrives at a similar judgment. See his *Theater der Hoffnung: Von der Aufklärung bis zur Gegenwart* (Frankfurt am Main: Suhrkamp 1988), 31.

73. See e.g., Johannes Werner, *Gesellschaft in literarischer Form: H. L. Wagner's "Kindermörderin" als Epochen- und Methodenparadigma* (Stuttgart: Klett, 1977), 108–9.

74. September 28, 1778; published in *Deutsches Museum* 2, no. 11 (November 1778):

478–80, quoted in *Kinder*, 146. Calas was tortured and executed during the anti-Huguenot hysteria in France, and Beverley was a figure in Edward Moore's *The Gambler*.

75. Preface to K. G. Lessings adaptation (1777), quoted in *Kinder*, 94–95.
76. Schlosser, *Deutsches Museum*, quoted in *Kinder*, 146.
77. *Frankfurter Gelehrte Anzeigen* (1777), 100–108, quoted in *Kinder*, 137–43.
78. Preface to the 1779 edition of Wagner's dramas, quoted in *Kinder*, 121–23. The adaptation was prepared for a performance by Seyler's troupe in Frankfurt am Main.
79. For a thorough analysis of the "reading-play vs. stage-play" controversy, see Edward J. Weintraut, "The Reception History of Goethe's *Götz von Berlichingen:* 1771–1815" (Ph.D. diss., Ohio State University, 1984).
80. *Kinder*, 122–23.
81. *Kinder*, 133. As noted above, the original conclusion already manifested didactic tendencies. East German playwright Peter Hacks produced an adaptation of the play in 1957 that ends with the discrediting of all the male figures. Evchen sets out like a Schillerian heroine to cope with the world on her own.
82. Huyssen considers the revised ending to be a satire of pre–Sturm und Drang theatrical form (Huyssen, *Drama*, 177).
83. See Ruth Freydank, *Theater in Berlin: Von den Anfängen bis 1945* (Berlin: Henschelverlag, 1988), 102–15.
84. To call the revised ending "triviality nearly beyond parallel," as Werner does, obscures the significance of this ideological shift and seems more to express the critic's feeling of betrayal than an objective assessment of the result (see Werner, *Gesellschaft*, 111). I see few parallels, however, between Wagner's alteration and Schiller's revision of his *The Robbers* for the Mannheim stage (1781–82); the latter had distinct philosophical and aesthetic motives for attempting to bring his "undisciplined" work into line with his views on the social function of drama, as expressed, for example, in his "The Stage Viewed as a Moral Institution" (1784).
85. Helga Stipa Madland's thesis that Sturm und Drang depictions of infanticide were written to intimidate women is appropriate for Wagner's *Evchen Humbrecht*, but I would not agree that it applies to all contemporaneous treatments of the theme. See her "Infanticide as Fiction: Goethe's *Urfaust* and Schiller's 'Kindsmörderin' as Models," *German Quarterly* 62 (1989): 27–38.

Chapter 3

1. See Henry J. Schmidt, "The Language of Rationality: Leisewitz's *Julius von Tarent*," in *Theatrum Mundi: Essays on German Drama and German Literature*, ed. Edward R. Haymes (Munich: Fink, 1980), 35–36.
2. Friedrich Maximilian Klinger, *Storm and Stress*, in *Five Plays of the Sturm und Drang*, trans. Betty Senk Waterhouse (Lanham, Md.: University Press of America, 1986), 148.
3. See Gert Mattenklott, *Melancholie in der Dramatik des Sturm und Drang* (Königstein/Ts: Athenäum, 1985).
4. Klaus R. Scherpe, "Dichterische Erkenntnis und 'Projektemacherei': Widersprüche im Werk von J. M. R. Lenz," *Sturm und Drang*, ed. Manfred Wacker (Darmstadt: Wissenschaftliche Buchgesellschaft, 1985), 279–314.

5. Jakob Michael Reinhold Lenz, *Werke und Briefe in drei Bänden*, ed. Sigrid Damm (Leipzig: Insel, 1987), 3:265 (subsequent references in the text are to this edition). See also Sigrid Damm's outstanding biography, *Vögel, die verkünden Land. Das Leben des Jakob Michael Reinhold Lenz* (Berlin: Aufbau, 1985).

6. Friedrich von Hagedorn's first collection of poetry, for example, was subtitled "A Sampling of the Results of Poetic Leisure Hours."

7. The title derives from a novel by the Danish author Eric Pontoppidan: *Menoza, an Asiatic Prince, who Traveled Through the World Looking for Christians, but Found Little of What he Sought*. This orthodox Protestant work had been translated into German in 1742. Translations from this play are my own; translations from the other two derive, with occasional alterations, from Jakob Michael Reinhold Lenz, *The Tutor* (Waterhouse, *Five Plays*, 1–55), and *The Soldiers* (57–95). Act and scene are given in parentheses. See also J. M. R. Lenz, *The Tutor, The Soldiers*, trans. William E. Yuill (Chicago: University of Chicago Press, 1972).

8. On this point there is critical consensus; see, for example, Scherpe, "Dichterische Erkenntnis," 294; Walter Hinderer, "Lenz: *Der Hofmeister*," in *Die deutsche Komödie*, ed. Walter Hinck (Düsseldorf: Bagel, 1977), 86; Leo Kreutzer, "Literatur als Einmischung: Jakob Michael Reinhold Lenz," in *Sturm und Drang: Ein literaturwissenschaftliches Studienbuch*, ed. Walter Hinck (Königstein/Ts: Athenäum, 1978), 224; Andreas Huyssen, *Drama des Sturm und Drang: Kommentar zu einer Epoche* (Munich: Winkler, 1980), 168; Hans-Günther Schwarz, *Dasein und Realität: Theorie und Praxis des Realismus bei J. M. R. Lenz* (Bonn: Bouvier, 1985), 61; Martin Rector, "Götterblick und menschlicher Standpunkt: J. M. R. Lenz' Komödie *Der neue Menoza* als Inszenierung eines Wahrnehmungsproblems," *Jahrbuch der deutschen Schillergesellschaft* 11 (1990): 205.

9. J. M. R. Lenz, *Der Hofmeister: Synoptische Ausgabe von Handschrift und Erstdruck*, ed. Michael Kohlenbach (Basel: Stroemfeld/Roter Stern, 1986), 68, 82 (henceforth referred to as *Hofmeister*).

10. Wilhelmine's parents are both quintessentially middle class ("Biederling") and, for reasons of plot, of the lower aristocracy ("von").

11. March 6, 1779; Johann Wolfgang von Goethe, *Goethes Werke*, vol. 5, ed. Josef Kunz (Hamburg: Wegner, 1960), 403.

12. His redefinition of comedy and tragedy in his "Notes on the Theater" and other writings has been extensively analyzed. See the bibliography in Hans-Gerd Winter, *J. M. R. Lenz* (Stuttgart: Metzler, 1987), 80.

13. See Ruth Freydank, *Theater in Berlin: Von den Anfängen bis 1945* (Berlin: Henschelverlag, 1988), 102–15.

14. One cannot count Friedrich Ludwig Schröder's 1781 adaptation of *The Tutor*, which eliminated many major characters and transformed the entire work into a sentimental comedy.

15. McInnes has demonstrated how this principle operates in act 1, scene 5 of *The Soldiers*. See Edward McInnes, "Kommentar," J. M. R. Lenz, *Die Soldaten: Text, Materialien, Kommentar*, ed. Edward McInnes (Munich: Hanser, 1977), 113–14.

16. Lenz's father figures are particularly prone to such distractions. In the final scene of *The Tutor*, Major von Berg can hardly contain his enthusiasm over his newly found grandson, but he *"throws the child on the sofa"* upon hearing of a potential suitor for

his daughter. Herr von Biederling (*The New Menoza*, 3, 5) is planting trees while he exchanges incriminations with Herr von Zopf. On the verge of challenging Zopf to a duel, he is immediately placated by Zopf's present of silkworm eggs, which are in turn nearly destroyed when von Biederling happens to think of asking Zopf about his long-lost son.

17. For example: does the Councillor von Berg have one or two sons? Why does Babet claim to be the Countess Diana's mother in *The New Menoza*? Why does Gustav hang himself? Concerning two inconsistencies in *The Tutor*, I would like to add my assessment to the ongoing debate about them.

1. Does Gustchen's illegitimate child undergo a sex change between 5, 1 and 5, 12? At the conclusion of the former scene, Martha picks up the screaming baby after Läuffer has dropped it and pacifies it with the words, "Suschen, mein liebes Suschen" (or "Sußchen" or "Sussichen" in the original manuscript [*Hofmeister*, 130]). This could either be the diminutive of a girl's name ("Susie") or a neutral term of endearment ("Sweetie"). In his annotations to *The Tutor*, Friedrich Voit offers several possible explanations for the latter term (Friedrich Voit, ed., *Erläuterungen und Dokumente: Jakob Michael Reinhold Lenz: Der Hofmeister* [Stuttgart: Reclam, 1986], 52). In Lenz's dramatic fragment, "Magisters Lieschen," Lieschen refers first to "unser armes Sußchen," then to "das Bild *unserer* kleinen Sußchen" (*Werke*, 1:590–91). This grammatical error makes the child unmistakeably female, and although this proves nothing conclusively about the situation in *The Tutor*, one could speculate that Lenz thought of Gustchen's baby as female – at first – as well. Did Lenz associate its destitute, weak state with femaleness and its later status as an heir with maleness?

2. Is Läuffer really the father of Gustchen's child? Claus O. Lappe has maintained that he could not be because, in 4, 2, he and Gustchen appear to have been parted for a year (Claus O. Lappe, "Wer hat Gustchens Kind gezeugt? Zeitstruktur und Rollenspiel in Lenz' *Hofmeister*," *Deutsche Vierteljahrsschrift* 54 [1980]: 14–46). Lappe suggests Pätus as the father; responding to Lappe, Jan Knopf proposes Seiffenblase (Jan Knopf, "Noch einmal: Pätus. Zur Vaterschaft in Lenz' *Hofmeister*," *Deutsche Vierteljahrsschrift* 54 [1980]: 517–19). Hans-Gerd Winter thinks that Lenz did mean one year but that the father remains unnamed and irrelevant, the main issue being Gustchen's status as a whore (Inge Stephan and Hans-Gerd Winter, *"Ein vorübergehendes Meteor"? J. M. R. Lenz und seine Rezeption in Deutschland* [Stuttgart: Metzler, 1984], 159). Finally, Helmut Schmiedt hypothesizes that Lenz, who was naive about many things, may not have known how long a pregnancy takes (Helmut Schmiedt, "Wie Revolutionär ist das Drama des Sturm und Drang?" *Jahrbuch der Deutschen Schillergesellschaft* 29 [1985]: 52). But, in 1776, Lenz did write a satiric poem about "Leopold Wagner, Author of the Drama about Nine Months" (*Werke*, 3:208), i.e., *The Child-Murderess*, which states at the outset that the action takes place over nine months. Be that as it may, the key line expressing Läuffer's recognition or nonrecognition of the child is his "Wie? dies wären nicht meine Züge?" before he drops it and faints (5, 1). Lappe and others read it as: "Eh? This isn't my likeness." instead of "Isn't this my likeness?" meaning that Läuffer is surprised to discover that the baby does *not* resemble him. In the original manuscript, Lenz's intention on this vital point is unmistakable: the line reads, "Eh, aren't these my lineaments? The crease on my forehead, the line of my mouth[?]" (*Hofmeister*, 130). Changing these to negatives would

make no sense. So Läuffer remains the father, which *does* make sense, despite Lenz's error about the year. But with respect to the child's apparent sex change, Lappe nonetheless deserves credit for discovering a hilarious new dimension of the word *Versöhnung*.

18. Walter Hinck, *Das deutsche Lustspiel des 17. und 18. Jahrhunderts und die italienische Komödie* (Stuttgart: Metzler, 1965), 339; likewise Hinck, "Zur Analyse des Stücks," in *Jakob Michael Reinhold Lenz: Der neue Menoza*, ed. Walter Hinck (Berlin: De Gruyter, 1965), 89.

19. Lenz's anticipation of Brecht's *Verfremdungseffekt* is obvious here. A foreshadowing of the open-minded and analytic Brechtian spectator occurs in Lenz's fragment, "For [Heinrich Leopold] Wagner," in which he contrasts two types of dramas via a popular eighteenth-century image—gardens: "There are two types of gardens, one that can be surveyed in one glance, the other that one traverses gradually as in nature, going from one diversion to another. Likewise there are also two types of drama . . . one presents everything simultaneously and coherently and is thus easier to survey, in the other one must climb up and down as in nature" (*Werke*, 2:673).

20. See Karl S. Guthke, *Geschichte und Poetik der deutschen Tragikomödie* (Göttingen: Vandenhoeck and Ruprecht, 1961), 51–72.

21. For more extensive discussions of both terms, see chap. 5 as well as Henry J. Schmidt, *Satire, Caricature, and Perspectivism in the Works of Georg Büchner* (The Hague: Mouton, 1970).

22. Peter Szondi, *Die Theorie des bürgerlichen Trauerspiels im achtzehnten Jahrhundert*, ed. Gert Mattenklott (Frankfurt am Main: Suhrkamp, 1973), 163–64.

23. *The Soldiers*, however, is less strictly denotative; that is, certain situations, objects, and gestures function in a more conventionally symbolic way. The first appearance of Stolzius, for example, is so deeply ironic that it is difficult not to conclude that Lenz was parodying the traditional dramatic hero. Technically, Stolzius could be the play's leading romantic male role, since he is the suitor of the main female character. Yet he comes to dramatic life *"with bandaged head,"* saying "Mother, I don't feel well!" Marie Wesener's personality and situation are aptly characterized by the "quivering brooch" that her father tries to sell to Desportes. Her grandmother's song about young girls as playthings sung or "croaked" during Marie's sport with Desportes in the next room has the connotative, transrealistic power of the Grandmother's fairy tale in Büchner's *Woyzeck*.

24. René Girard, *J. M. R. Lenz: Genèse d'une Dramaturgie du Tragi-Comique* (Paris, Klincksieck, 1968), 282.

25. See, for instance, Mattenklott, *Melancholie*, 166, and John Osborne, *Jakob Michael Reinhold Lenz: The Renunciation of Heroism* (Göttingen: Vandenhoeck and Ruprecht, 1975), 128.

26. Scherpe, "Dichterische Erkenntnis," 300–301; Stephan and Winter, *Lenz*, 164–65.

27. Stephan and Winter, *Lenz*, 164.

28. A dramatist can try to redefine ethical balance, but always at the risk of alienating a smaller or larger portion of his or her audience. Lenz was aware that certain aspects of reality would be considered shocking if they were portrayed in art, and he claimed to be unafraid of the consequences (see *Werke*, 3:326).

29. Cf. Horst Albert Glaser, "Heteroklisie – der Fall Lenz," in *Gestaltungsgeschichte und Gesellschaftsgeschichte*, ed. Helmut Kreuzer (Stuttgart: Metzler, 1969), 148; Huyssen, *Drama*, 167. In "Zerbin or The New Philosophy" (1775) Lenz describes a man who does commit suicide as atonement for seducing and abandoning a young girl, executed for concealing an illegitimate pregnancy. Zerbin deliberately caused her misfortune, so his death can be considered just. See Girard, *Lenz*, 287.

30. It is unclear to me whether Lenz intended this monologue to have an explanatory/affective function, as in Enlightenment drama, or whether it parodies this function. Since I believe that Lenz was trying to win sympathy for Läuffer in these final scenes, I incline toward the first possibility.

31. This option was taken up by Schröder in his bowdlerization of the play; see n. 14.

32. Winter mentions this passage but relates it only to Läuffer (Stephan and Winter, *Lenz*, 157).

33. See Stephan and Winter, *Lenz*, 165.

34. See n. 17.

35. The reunion of Marie Wesener and her father in *The Soldiers* is far bleaker, in keeping with their more serious transgressions. She is not granted a husband, and her father's rehabilitation is dependent on the generosity of aristocrats.

36. See, for example, his agonizingly poignant note to his father during his mental breakdown while living with Pastor Oberlin in 1778: "Father! I have sinned before heaven and before you and am now no longer worthy of being called your child" (*Werke*, 3:568).

37. See Walter Hinck, *Theater der Hoffnung: Von der Aufklärung bis zur Gegenwart* (Frankfurt am Main: Suhrkamp 1988), 34.

38. An additional resemblance to *Stella* occurs in a note in which Lenz contemplated a different plot or perhaps a sequel to the play: Seraphine takes Strephon into her house, but inwardly he rebels and finally "says that he cannot endure it any longer and leaves [like Fernando!] with great relief" (*Werke*, 1:751).

39. Cf. Huyssen, *Drama*, 172; Stephan and Winter, *Lenz*, 164.

40. Cf. Lappe, "Wer hat," 43; Stephan and Winter, *Lenz*, 162–63; Barbara Becker-Cantarino, "Jakob Michael Reinhold Lenz: Der Hofmeister," *Interpretationen: Dramen des Sturm und Drang* (Stuttgart: Reclam, 1987), 53–54.

41. See Sigrid Damm, *Cornelia Goethe* (Frankfurt am Main: Insel, 1988), 219–20; as well as Silvia Bovenschen, *Die imaginierte Weiblichkeit: Exemplarische Untersuchungen zu kulturgeschichtlichen und literarischen Präsentationsformen des Weiblichen* (Frankfurt am Main: Suhrkamp, 1980).

42. Klaus Theweleit maintains that moral reformers tend to demand from those of inferior social standing an idealized morality that delegitimates authority but contradicts the actual needs of the lower classes. See Klaus Theweleit, *Männerphantasien* (Hamburg: Rowohlt, 1980), 1:380.

43. Rector, "Götterblick," 200; see also Helga Stipa Madland, *Non-Aristotelian Drama in Eighteenth Century Germany and its Modernity: J. M. R. Lenz* (Bern: Peter Lang, 1982), 118; Karin Wurst, intro. to Lenz anthology, 15–20, typescript.

44. See Helga Stipa Madland, "Gesture as Evidence of Language Skepticism in Lenz's *Der Hofmeister* and *Die Soldaten*," *German Quarterly* 57 (1984): 546–57.

45. In a letter to Achim von Arnim, Clemens Brentano wrote that the play "rumbles and roars and is nonetheless so empty and so full" (Clemens Brentano, *Briefe*, ed Friedrich Seebaß [Nürnberg: Hans Carl, 1951], 1:302–3).

46. See Rector, "Götterblick," 208. Christoph Hein omits these scenes in his recent adaptation of the play (*Cromwell und andere Stücke* [East Berlin: Aufbau, 1981] 225–97). Similarly in *The Soldiers*, the action of the first act is interrupted for a discussion of the social advantages and disadvantages of theatrical entertainment (1, 4).

47. See Girard, *Lenz*, 336. Performing just the last two scenes with marionettes could produce, I think, an interesting estrangement effect.

48. Girard, *Lenz*, 399. The play's final lines have themselves been subjected to "reform" by those who find them impractical: Kreutzer suggests replacing them with lines from Lenz's essay, "which would sound a good deal more serious" (Leo Kreutzer, "Literatur als Eimischung: Jakob Michael Reinhold Lenz," in *Sturm und Drang: Ein literaturwissenschaftliches Studienbuch* [Kronberg/Ts.: Athenäum, 1978], 227). In his adaptation of the play, Heinar Kipphardt lets the discredited philosopher Pirzel speak the lines while others mock him (Heinar Kipphardt, *Die Soldaten nach J. M. R. Lenz*, in *Stücke II* [Frankfurt am Main: Suhrkamp, 1974], 251–52). Ironically, Lenz's "outlandish" idea of a bordello for soldiers was recommended for the American military as recently as 1970 (see "Government-Issue Girls?" *Playboy* 17, no. 2 (February, 1970): 42.

49. Approximate translation; the syntax of both versions is unclear.

50. See, as one example among many, Stephen and Winter, *Lenz*, 158, 164.

51. See Paul Michael Lützeler's description of the effect in Lenz's time of edicts prohibiting soldiers to marry ("Jakob Michael Reinhold Lenz: *Die Soldaten*," *Interpretationen: Dramen des Sturm und Drang* [Stuttgart: Reclam, 1987], 143–44).

52. See Rector, "Götterblick," 206.

53. In contrast to Goethe, Lenz saw a justification for social revolutions in nature: "I'm not opposed to local upheavals within republics, as are most philosophers who recommend the spirit of tranquility, which deadens one's sense of one's powers. . . . [D]issension in republics and the treaties that follow are as beneficial for the political sphere as a thunderstorm is for the physical sphere" (*Werke*, 3:536).

54. Alan C. Leidner, "The Dream of Identity: Lenz and the Problem of *Standpunkt*," *German Quarterly* 59, no. 3 (1986): 397.

55. Ernst Bloch, *The Principle of Hope*, trans. Neville Plaice, Stephen Plaice, and Paul Knight (Cambridge, Mass.: MIT Press, 1986), 416; translation slightly altered.

56. Bloch, *Principle of Hope*, 415–18; translation slightly altered.

Chapter 4

1. Quotations from Büchner's works are from Georg Büchner, *Complete Works and Letters*, trans. Henry J. Schmidt, ed. Walter Hinderer and Henry J. Schmidt (New York: Continuum, 1986). References in the text to plays are by act and scene, otherwise page numbers, using the abbreviation *CWL*.

2. Louis Adolphe Thiers, *Histoire de la Révolution Française* (Paris, 1823–27) and *Unsere Zeit, oder geschichtliche Übersicht der merkwürdigsten Ereignisse von 1789–1830*, ed. Carl Strahlheim (Stuttgart, 1826–30). See also Ilona Broch, "Die Julia und die Ophelia der

Revolution: Zu zwei Frauenfiguren in *Dantons Tod*," in *Georg Büchner: 1813-1837: Revolutionär, Dichter, Wissenschaftler*, ed. Susanne Lehmann, Stephen Oetterman, Reinhard Pabst, and Sibylle Spiegel (Basel and Frankfurt am Main: Stroemfeld/Roter Stern, 1987), 241-46.

3. *Danton's Death* 4, 1; *Julius Caesar* 2, 4.

4. From Shakespeare's source, Plutarch's *Lives of the Noble Grecians and Romans*, trans. Sir Thomas North (1579). Quoted in William Shakespeare, *The Tragedy of Julius Caesar*, in *The Modern Reader's Shakespeare*, ed. Henry Norman Hudson (New York: Bigelow, Smith, 1909), 8:98. Another literary model is *Egmont's* Klärchen, who poisons herself while Egmont awaits his end in prison.

5. Juliet dies, to be sure, of a self-inflicted stab wound. Concerning Julie's "Come, dearest priest" when she produces her vial, Broch indicates a similarity to Juliet's "Come, vial" and to Faust's "Come down, you glass of crystal purity." See Broch, "Die Julia," 242.

6. Dorothy James, *Georg Büchner's* Dantons Tod: *a Reappraisal* (London: Modern Humanities Research Assn., 1982.), 21. She justly takes my *Satire, Caricature, and Perspectivism in the Works of Georg Büchner* (The Hague: Mouton, 1970) to task on this account.

7. James, *Büchner's* Dantons Tod, 27.

8. Karl Viëtor interprets this approvingly as an example of "unconscious correspondence to nature" (Karl Viëtor, *Georg Büchner: Politik, Dichtung, Wissenschaft* [Bern: Francke, 1949], 147), which testifies to the endurance of gender stereotyping based on the nature/intellect dichotomy of preromantic philosophy. Not until recent decades was there much objection in German secondary literature to the belief that women's self-abasing subservience to men was "natural" and hence an enhancement of their aesthetic appeal.

9. James, *Büchner's* Dantons Tod, 25, 24.

10. "Here . . . arises in this gloomy tragedy of fatalistic necessity the idea of freedom, in which the extinct world of idealistic belief would have perceived humankind's divinity" (Viëtor, *Büchner*, 148). For William H. Rey, a woman's suicide offers "the purest possibility of human fulfillment — when it is accomplished in the spirit of love" William H. Rey, *Georg Büchners* Dantons Tod: *Revolutionstragödie und Mysterienspiel* (Bern: Lang, 1982), 111.

11. Cf. Burghard Dedner, "Legitimationen des Schreckens in Georg Büchners Revolutionsdrama," *Jahrbuch der deutschen Schillergesellschaft* 29 (1985): 374.

12. Critical commentary on Büchner has readily fallen in line with, for example, a chapter heading such as: "Woman's Naive Security in her Vegetative Substance" (Gustav Beckers, *Georg Büchners* Leonce und Lena: *Ein Lustspiel der Langeweile* [Heidelberg: Winter, 1961], 111).

13. That is, a *Fatalismusbrief*, as it is so often called by literary critics.

14. *CWL*, 261 et passim, 295. His psychological reaction to "imprisonment" in Giessen resembles, down to numerous linguistic parallels, that of Danton in jail. Compare, for example, his second extant letter to Minna Jaeglé (*CWL*, 258-59) to *Danton's Death* 4, 5.

15. Heinz Fischer, *Georg Büchner: Untersuchungen und Marginalien* (München: Bouvier, 1972), 81. See also Heinz Fischer, *Georg Büchner und Alexis Muston: Untersuchungen zu einem Büchner-Fund*, (Munich: W. Fink, 1987), 272, 274.

16. The only letters from her hand that have survived were written after Büchner's death. Several of Büchner's acquaintances, in particular Caroline and Wilhelm Schulz, praised her character and devotion to her fiancé.

17. Cf. Dolf Oehler, "Liberté, Liberté Chérie: Männerphantasien über die Freiheit; Zur Problematik der erotischen Freiheits-Allegorie," in Georg Büchner: Dantons Tod: Die Trauerarbeit im Schönen, Ein Theater-Lesebuch, ed. Peter von Becker (Frankfurt am Main: Syndikat, 1980), 102.

18. See Reinhold Grimm, "Coeur und Carreau: Über die Liebe bei Georg Büchner," Georg Büchner I/II, ed. Heinz Ludwig Arnold (Munich: Text + Kritik, 1982), 299–326. Klaus Theweleit singles out Büchner as one of the few German authors who did not present to his readers an idealized image of femaleness. See Klaus Theweleit, Männerphantasien (Reinbek and Hamburg: Rowohlt, 1980), 1:295–97. For the political significance of Heine's erotic poetry see Jost Hermand, "Erotik im Juste Milieu: Heines 'Verschiedene,' " in Heinrich Heine. Artistik und Engagement, ed. Wolfgang Kuttenkeuler (Stuttgart: Metzler, 1977), 86–104.

19. For an example of such a study with respect to Lessing's dramas, see Karin Wurst's Familiale Liebe ist die "wahre Gewalt": Die Repräsentation der Familie in G. E. Lessings dramatischem Werk (Amsterdam: Rodopi, 1988).

20. Hermand, "Erotik," 101.

21. Christa Wolf, "'Shall I Garnish a Metaphor with an Almond Blossom?': Büchner-Prize Acceptance Speech," trans. Henry J. Schmidt, New German Critique 23 (Spring/Summer, 1981), 6. However, Wolf consigns Danton and his colleagues without differentiation to the "citadel of reason," overlooking the occasional similarity of their sensibilities to those of the women.

22. Cf. Dedner, "Legitimationen," 352.

23. See Henri Poschmann, Georg Büchner: Dichtung der Revolution und Revolution der Dichtung (Berlin and Weimar: Aufbau, 1985), 116.

24. Poschmann, Büchner, 116.

25. Johann Wolfgang von Goethe, Die Leiden des jungen Werthers, letter of May 22.

26. "The creativity of [their] sentence making realizes itself as a shaping of the world to which those sentences relate" (Martin Swales, "Ontology, Politics, Sexuality: A Note on Georg Büchner's Drama Dantons Tod," New German Studies 3 [1975]: 122).

27. William H. Rey is among the numerous critics who have maintained that Büchner creates "a tender lyrical language . . . that floats above all of life's contradictions" (Rey, Büchner's Dantons Tod, 111). But the elimination of contradictions would signify a relapse into epigonal romanticism. For a contrary view, see Poschmann: "[Büchner's] play rotates phenomena in a way . . . that contradiction becomes apparent and they lose their false simplicity" (Büchner, 102). The statement could also apply to Lenz's dramaturgy.

28. This scene and the beginning of scene 9 recall the gravedigger scene in Hamlet.

29. For an elaborate scene-by-scene analysis, see Alfred Behrmann and Joachim Wohlleben, Büchner: Dantons Tod, Eine Dramenanalyse (Stuttgart: Klett, 1980), 126–36.

30. See Grimm, "Coeur und Carreau," 304.

31. A prime example of a "profiteer" from death is the artist David, who sketches victims in order to capture "the last spasms of life in these villains" (2, 3).

32. Peter Michelsen, "Die Präsenz des Endes: Georg Büchners *Dantons Tod*," *Deutsche Vierteljahrsschrift* 52, no. 3 (1978): 487.
33. See Thomas Michael Mayer, "Büchner und Weidig–Frühkommunismus und revolutionäre Demokratie: Zur Textverteilung des 'Hessischen Landboten,' " in *Georg Büchner I/II*, ed. Arnold, esp. 108–36.
34. Quoted in Peter von Becker, "Die Trauerarbeit im Schönen: 'Dantons Tod'–Notizen zu einem neu gelesenen Stück," in *Büchner*: Dantons Tod, ed. von Becker, 89.
35. The quotation continues: "as if that to which great art had given shape was now thought to be conquered and resolved by the class struggle. Such pessimism prevails even in literature that thematizes revolution: Büchner's *Danton's Death* is a classical example." Quoted in von Becker, *Büchner*: Dantons Tod, 75.
36. See Dedner, "Legitimationen," 352.
37. See Karl Marx, *The Eighteenth Brumaire of Louis Bonaparte* (New York: International, 1963).
38. Renate Zuchardt, "'Wagt!' lehrt uns Danton: Vorschläge zur szenischen Realisierung des Büchner-Dramas," *Theater der Zeit* 14, no. 9 (1959): 14, 18–19. In his Mercury Theatre (New York, 1938) production of the play, Orson Welles–who played St. Just–placed his speech at the conclusion for dramatic effect. See John Houseman, *Run-Through: A Memoir* (New York: Simon and Schuster, 1972), 379–90. See also Henry J. Schmidt, "Büchner in Amerika: Ein Überblick," in *Georg Büchner*, ed. Henri Poschmann (Bern: Peter Lang, forthcoming).
39. Walter Benjamin, *Ursprung des deutschen Trauerspiels* (Frankfurt am Main: Suhrkamp, 1972), 148–49.
40. "Had Büchner ended the drama directly after the execution, the effect of the ending would have been similar to the effect of K's death at the end of Kafka's *The Trial*: a passive, meaningless death as a final, none-too-surprising confirmation of the worldview that has been suggested throughout the work" (Herbert Lindenberger, *Georg Büchner* [Carbondale: Southern Illinois University Press, 1964], 53).
41. Wolf, "Shall I Garnish," 7.
42. *Hamlet* 4, 5. Male literary predecessors also seem to have left their mark: Lucile's "Everything may live, everything, the little fly there, the bird. Why not he?" recalls King Lear's despair over Cordelia's corpse: "Why should a dog, a horse, a rat, have life, / And thou no breath at all?" (*King Lear* 5, 3). Likewise her "I suppose we must bear it" evokes Goethe's "wild youth" who was stung by "the rose in the meadow," and he "just had to bear it." (My thanks for these references to Jerry Wasserman and Ingrid Oesterle.) Like Goethe himself (see chap. 2), Büchner does not classify emotional response according to gender.
43. Williams maintains that this nostalgia is "a nostalgia for prerevolutionary society," implying not a reactionary but an idealized, stable world. See Raymond Williams, "Georg Büchner: A Retrospect," in *Drama from Ibsen to Brecht* (New York: Oxford University Press, 1971), 234.
44. This mood is emphasized by critics who seize upon the "atmospheric" qualities of the final scenes involving Julie, Danton, and Lucile in order to cloud the drama's political issues with vague emotionalism. See, for example, Michelsen, who calls the atmospheric mood the "medium . . . that envelops the soul like a veil of music"

("Die Präsenz," 493). Similarly, the play's conclusion does not allow one to absolutize love as the *only* "positive message"; see Helmut Krapp, *Der Dialog bei Georg Büchner* (Darmstadt: Gentner, 1958), 121.

45. *Georg Büchners Sämtliche Werke und Briefe*, ed. Fritz Bergemann (Leipzig: Insel, 1922), 677; *Georges Büchner: La Mort de Danton*, ed. Richard Thieberger (Paris: Presses Universitaires de France, 1953), 148.

46. Cf. Lacroix: "The asses will bray 'Long live the Republic!' as we go by" (4, 5). As Hans-Georg Werner points out, these phrases have degenerated into slogans that have lost their ethical correlatives. See Hans-Georg Werner, *"Dantons Tod* im Zwang der Geschichte," *Studien zu Georg Büchner*, ed. Hans-Georg Werner (Berlin and Weimar: Aufbau, 1988), 47–48.

47. At the conclusion of Alexander Lang's production of the play at the Deutsches Theater (East Berlin), two clownish representatives of the "folk" stroke her cheek tenderly before they lift her slightly off the floor and dance toward the back of the stage, to piano improvisations on the "Marseillaise." The back curtain lifts for the first time, revealing blackness, and the three dance off into the void as the curtain falls. The unexpected intimacy, even lightness of this finale serves to make the contrast to the Revolution's brutal reality yet more poignant. See *Dantons Tod von Georg Büchner: Eine Dokumentation der Aufführung des Deutschen Theaters Berlin 1981*, ed. Michael Funke (East Berlin: Verband der Theaterschaffenden der DDR, [1983]), 179–81.

48. Thiers, *Unsere Zeit*, supplement vol. 5, 84, quoted in Broch, "Die Julia," 244.

49. Thiers, *Unsere Zeit*, 12, 156–57, quoted in Walter Hinderer, *Büchner-Kommentar zum dichterischen Werk* (München: Winkler, 1977), 128.

50. "The unfortunate [Lucile] Desmoulins died with a courage worthy of her husband and his character. Since Charlotte Cordai and Madame Roland, no victim had inspired a more tender interest and more sorrowful regrets" (Thiers, *Unsere Zeit*, 6, 235, quoted in Büchner, *La Mort de Danton*, ed. Richard Thieberger, [Paris: L'Arche, 1953], 52).

51. Ironically, the historical Camille Desmoulins demanded the death penalty for this offense in his *Le Vieux Cordelier*. See Broch, "Die Julia," 244.

52. "Our legislatures are a satire against good sense" (*CWL*, 250 [letter of April 5, 1833]) – the result of "republican" idealism and aristocratic concessions in Büchner's Hesse-Darmstadt. See also Büchner's letter to Edouard Reuss (*CWL*, 253–54 [August 31, 1833]), recently discovered by Jan-Christoph Hauschild.

Chapter 5

1. The author was Bruno Wille, a founder of the *Freie Volksbühne*. See Manfred Brauneck, *Literatur und Öffentlichkeit im ausgehenden 19. Jahrhundert* (Stuttgart: Metzler, 1974), 34–35.

2. Bertolt Brecht, "Notizen über realistische Schreibweise," *Schriften zur Literatur und Kunst 2, Werkausgabe* (Frankfurt am Main: Suhrkamp, 1967), 19:364.

3. Gerhart Hauptmann, *The Weavers*, trans. Frank Marcus (London: Eyre Methuen, 1980). All subsequent quotations from the drama refer to this volume.

4. Brecht, "Notizen," 366.

5. Conversation with C. F. W. Behl, quoted in Gerhart Hauptmann, *Die Weber*, ed. Hans Schwab-Felisch (Frankfurt: Ullstein, 1959), 110.

6. Fontane claimed that Hauptmann's concluding act sacrifices the rebellion for the sake of a tragic conclusion—"expiation through death, destruction of a sinner"— which, however, was necessary for a proper distancing from the destructiveness of revenge (Theodor Fontane, September 26, 1894, quoted in Helmut Praschek, *Gerhart Hauptmanns* Weber: *Eine Dokumentation* [East Berlin: Akademie, 1980], 196–97). Brian Holbeche sees a formal-dramaturgical problem in act 5: "the need to compensate for the impossibility of presenting an action of such force and magnitude within the limits of the Naturalist set" (Brian Holbeche, "Naturalist Set and Social Conflict in Hauptmann's *Die Weber*," *Australasian Universities Modern Language Journal* 56 [November 1981]: 188).

7. Konrad Haenisch reported: "In a letter to me, Hauptmann himself expressly called *The Weavers* his '*profession of faith in Christianity*' and confirmed that he had derived *from this religion* 'the purely Christian idea of pity, upon which my *Weavers* are based' " (quoted in Praschek, *Hauptmanns* Weber, 365.) See also Hauptmann's testimony transmitted by his lawyer to the Deutsches Theater in 1894: "one may well call it a crime against art that the Christian and the universally human feeling called pity helped create my drama" (quoted in Praschek, *Hauptmanns* Weber, 329). In 1943, referring in a conversation with C. F. W. Behl to *The Weavers*, he claimed: "A bit of the spirit of the Sermon on the Mount is in my writing as a whole" (quoted in Praschek, *Hauptmanns* Weber, 333).

8. See Hauptmann's "Im Fragment einer Rede (1922)," quoted in Praschek, *Hauptmanns* Weber, 331. The focus on repentance and on pious acceptance of the human condition was perhaps influenced as well by Tolstoy's *The Power of Darkness*, in which a multitude of gruesome crimes culminate in a fervent plea for spiritual solace.

9. Critics have often asserted that his piety places him on higher moral ground than the rebels, that through him Hauptmann is denouncing their claim to legitimacy. See e.g., Hans M. Wolff, "Der alte Hilse," *Das Leid im Werke Gerhart Hauptmanns*, ed. Karl S. Guthke and Hans M. Wolff (Bern: Francke, 1958), 65–73; William H. Rey, "Der offene Schluß der *Weber*: Zur Aktualität Gerhart Hauptmanns in unserer Zeit," *German Quarterly* 55, no. 2 (1982): 141–63. Rey insists that the rebels are morally disqualified by their actions and repeatedly condemns their "lack of dignity."

10. "A woman who stood at the door of her house two hundred paces away sank down without moving. . . . A girl on her way to knitting lessons fell to earth riddled with bullets." Schwab-Felisch, ed., *Die Weber*, 146.

11. Gerhart Hauptmann, *Hannele*, trans. Charles Henry Meltzer (New York: Doubleday, 1908), 102. Cf. Heine's *Germany: A Winter's Tale*: "She sang the old abnegation tune, / The lullaby Heaven simpers / To lull the People back to sleep, / When that lummox whines and whimpers." (*The Complete Poems of Heinrich Heine*, trans. Hal Draper [Boston: Suhrkamp/Insel, 1982], 484).

12. Rey magnifies this to "fear of global catastrophe," incorporating *The Weavers* into the "ice-age spirit" of the 1970s and 1980s. See Rey, "Der offene Schluß," 160.

13. Brauneck, *Literatur*, 51.

14. Brauneck, *Literatur*, 51.

15. *Germania*, October 2, 1894, quoted in Brauneck, *Literatur*, 69; italics in original.
16. *Der Reichsbote*, September 28, 1894, quoted in Brauneck, *Literatur*, 226.
17. *Deutsche Warte*, September 27, 1894; Brauneck, *Literatur*, 226.
18. Walther Kiaulehn, *Berlin: Schicksal einer Weltstadt* (Munich and Berlin: Biederstein, 1958), 456; Erich R. Schmidt, *Meine Jugend in Groß-Berlin: Triumph und Elend der Arbeiterbewegung 1918–1933* (Bremen: Donat, 1988), 115.
19. Christine Heiss, "Hauptmanns *Weber* auf deutschen Bühnen der USA im neunzehnten Jahrhundert," *German Quarterly* 59, no. 3 (1986): 367, 371.
20. Gerhart Hauptmann, "Das Abenteuer meiner Jugend (1929–1935)," quoted in Praschek, *Hauptmanns* Weber, 323.
21. Gerhart Hauptmann to Charles Henry Meltzer, *New York World*, February 18, 1894, quoted in Praschek, *Hauptmanns* Weber, 329.
22. Gerhart Hauptmann, "Das zweite Vierteljahrhundert," quoted in Praschek, *Hauptmanns* Weber, 324.
23. Throughout his life, Hauptmann attempted to mitigate the unexpectedly powerful antiestablishment impact of *The Weavers* by claiming that his drama was nontendentious. "The less politically biased a drama is, the higher it stands" (Gerhart Hauptmann, *Die Kunst des Dramas: Über Schauspiel und Theater*, ed. Martin Machatzke [Berlin: Ullstein, 1963], 24). When Ernst Toller reprimanded Hauptmann with: "I thought I was talking to the author of *The Weavers!*" Hauptmann asserted, *"The Weavers* is a nontendentious drama" (quoted in Praschek, *Hauptmanns* Weber, 362).
24. See, for example, *Der Reichsbote*, September 28, 1894, quoted in Brauneck, *Literatur*, 226; *Hamburger Nachrichten*, October 1, 1894, quoted in Schwab-Felisch, ed., *Die Weber*, 204.
25. Max Baginski, "Gerhart Hauptmann unter den schlesischen Webern," quoted in Schwab-Felisch, ed., *Die Weber*, 170.
26. See Johann N. Schmidt's outstanding discussion of the theory, history, and reception of melodrama in *Ästhetik des Melodramas: Studien zu einem Genre des populären Theaters im England des 19. Jahrhunderts* (Heidelberg: Carl Winter, 1986). See also Peter Brooks, *The Melodramatic Imagination: Balzac, Henry James, Melodrama, and the Mode of Excess* (New York: Columbia University Press, 1985); James L. Smith, *Melodrama* (London: Methuen, 1973); and Thomas Elsaesser, "Tales of Sound and Fury: Observations on the Family Melodrama," *Monogram* 4 (1972): 2–15. The distinction between drama and melodrama becomes yet more obscure when one considers that any drama with a cast of more than a handful of characters must resort to character simplification if it is to distinguish between psychologically complex primary figures and purely functional secondary figures. The latter represent, like caricature, a distillation of essentials, sustaining the "proper" hierarchical structure both of the plot and of the society being portrayed. See Henry J. Schmidt, *Satire, Caricature, and Perspectivism in the Works of Georg Büchner* (The Hague: Mouton, 1970), esp. 32–37.
27. See Brooks, *Melodramatic Imagination*, 205–6; and Elsaesser, "Tales," 2.
28. Schmidt, *Ästhetik*, 256. After the first performances, several critics noted the roots of Hauptmann's play within the melodramatic tradition: "It is basically patterned after the good old model that the fabricators of French sensationalist melodramas relied on for their lasting successes. Starving children, pale-cheeked women, hardhearted factory owners, permeated by the muffled grumbling of the oppressed,

which finally swells to a mighty revolutionary outcry. In Paris's Ambigu- and Chatelet-Theaters this kind of mass-audience showpiece was produced by the dozens, and they rarely failed to have a powerful effect on the spectators' tear ducts" (*Das Kleine Journal*, September 26, 1894, quoted in Brauneck, *Literatur*, 227). Cf. also Maximilian Harden in *Die Zukunft*, March 11, 1893: "The tragedy? I'd rather say: the melodrama, the new type that operates with more sophisticated artistic devices and refined techniques, but which cannot conceal its origins. . . . When *The Weavers* are performed in Paris, then one might be reminded of Victor Hugo's *Les Miserables* or even Sue's *Mystères de Paris* . . ." (quoted in Schwab-Felisch, ed., *Die Weber*, 194). Raymond Williams asserts that "[t]here was nothing in the new naturalist or realist drama of the 1880s which, in terms of the vulgarity of low life or of the violence of events, was new to the English nineteenth-century theatre, and especially to the melodrama" (Raymond Williams, "Social Envirnoment and Theatrical Environment: The Case of English Naturalism," in *English Drama: Forms and Development*, ed. Marie Axton and Raymond Williams [Cambridge: Cambridge University Press, 1977], 213).

29. Brooks claims that in the modern era, melodrama opposes "the . . . 'decentering' of modern consciousness, its lack of a central plenitude. It is arguable that melodrama represents a refusal of this vertiginous but possibly liberating decentering, a search for a new plenitude, an ethical recentering. . . . The anxiety of man's prodigious revolutionary freedom . . . is dealt with . . . through the promise of a morally legible universe . . ." Brooks, *Melodramatic Imagination*, 200–201.

30. Schmidt, *Ästhetik*, 223, 226.

31. According to Raymond Williams, English melodrama "preserved, as the foundation of its conventions, providential notions of the righting of wrongs, the exposure of villainy, and the triumph or else the apotheosis of innocence"—characteristics related in his view to the "social and moral consciousness which was to inform serious naturalism" (Williams, "Social Environment," 214).

32. Cf. the reaction in the *Berliner Tageblatt* of September 26, 1894 to the premiere: "The outward display of shouting, screaming, singing, bell ringing, drumming, and shooting was in and of itself exciting, sensational. Who could resist it?" (quoted in Brauneck, *Literatur*, 227).

33. Schwab-Felisch, ed., *Die Weber*, 104–5.

34. The tendency among some postwar critics to interpret the play as an expression of an existentialist philosophy of suffering obscures this reformist impulse. See, for example, Hans M. Wolff, William H. Rey, and Karl S. Guthke, "Die Bedeutung des Leids im Werke Gerhart Hauptmanns," in *Das Leid im Werke Gerhart Hauptmanns*, 11–50.

35. Fontane interpreted this open-ended dualism as "a double warning, directed toward upper and lower ranks, appealing to the conscience of both sides" (quoted in Praschek, *Hauptmanns* Weber, 197).

36. See Brauneck, *Literatur*, 217, 82.

37. Conversation with C. F. W. Behl, quoted in Praschek, *Hauptmanns* Weber, 334.

38. Peter Sprengel, *Gerhart Hauptmann: Epoche—Werk—Wirkung* (Munich: Beck, 1984), 96.

39. See Andreas Huyssen, "The Politics of Identification: 'Holocaust' and West German Drama," *New German Critique*, no. 19 (Winter, 1980): 124.

40. Flannery O'Connor, "The Fiction Writer and His Country," in *Collected Works*, ed.
    Sally Fitzgerald (New York: Library of America, 1988), 806.

Chapter 6

 1. Marieluise Fleisser, "Das dramatische Empfinden bei den Frauen," in *Gesammelte
    Werke*, ed. Günther Rühle (Frankfurt am Main: Suhrkamp, 1989), 4:409 (abbrevia-
    tion: *GW*. Subsequent references in the text are to this edition).
 2. Marieluise Fleisser, "Das ist mir vollkommen natürlich, wie ich schreib," interview
    with Rainer Wagner, *Main-Echo Aschaffenburg*, May 21, 1973.
 3. Letter to Rainer Roth (undated, 1971), quoted in Günter Lutz, *Marieluise Fleißer: Ver-
    dichtetes Leben* (Munich: Obalski and Astor, 1989), 9.
 4. Letter to Rainer Roth (January 12, 1972), quoted in Wend Kässens and Michael Töte-
    berg, " '. . . fast schon ein Auftrag von Brecht': Marieluise Fleissers Drama *Pioniere
    in Ingolstadt*," in *Brecht-Jahrbuch 1976*, ed. John Fuegi, Reinhold Grimm, Jost Her-
    mand (Frankfurt am Main: Suhrkamp, 1976), 111.
 5. Walter Dimter, "Die ausgestellte Gesellschaft: Zum Volksstück Horváths, der
    Fleisser und ihrer Nachfolger," in *Theater und Gesellschaft: Das Volksstück im 19. und
    20. Jahrhundert*, ed. Jürgen Hein (Düsseldorf: Bertelsmann, 1973), 233; italics in
    original.
 6. Günther Rühle, "Leben und Schreiben der Marieluise Fleisser aus Ingolstadt," *GW*
    1:17.
 7. Cf. Günther Rühle, "Die andere Seite von Ingolstadt. Wirkung und Umfang des
    Fleißerschen Werkes," in *Marieluise Fleisser: Anmerkungen Texte Dokumente*, ed.
    Friedrich Kraft (Ingolstadt: Donau Kurier, 1981), 62–63; Wend Kässens and Michael
    Töteberg, "Psychodrama und Literaturbetrieb: Kontexte zu Marieluise Fleissers
    Stück *Der Tiefseefisch*," in *Marieluise Fleisser: Der Tiefseefisch, Text, Fragmente, Materi-
    alien*, ed. Wend Kässens and Michael Töteberg (Frankfurt am Main: Suhrkamp,
    1980), 186.
 8. See Sue-Ellen Case, *Feminism and Theatre* (London: Macmillan, 1988), 124.
 9. In notes to her play *The Deep-Sea Fish*, presumably contemporaneous to "Women's
    Sensibility for Drama," Fleisser combines a traditionally female symbol with an un-
    characteristic image of coercion: "A plot [of a drama] must be a funnel that sucks up
    the inescapable ending." She continues with a classical precept that contradicts the
    dramaturgy of her most successful plays: "A scene must inevitably result from an-
    other, which it must never precede" (*Der Tiefseefisch*, 154).
10. See chap. 1. See also Case, *Feminism*, esp. 129ff.
11. The correspondences between the fictional account "Avantgarde" (1962; second
    quotation) and factual accounts such as "Two Premieres" (1947; first quotation) are
    close enough to warrant viewing the short story as a largely accurate description of
    Fleisser's experiences. The impact of Brecht's method on the authorship and text of
    Soldiers in Ingolstadt will be discussed in detail subsequently.
12. See Sabine Kebir, *Ein akzeptabler Mann? Brecht und die Frauen* (Köln: Pahl-Rugenstein,
    1989), 66.
13. Interview with Rainer Wagner.
14. Marieluise Fleisser, *Pioniere in Ingolstadt* (Berlin: Arcadia Verlag, 1929). Page num-

bers refer to this edition; the copy in the Marieluise Fleisser Archive in Ingolstadt contains numerous handwritten corrections. The text differs only slightly from that of the original typescript (2.a.1. in Eva Pfisters register of the archive holdings; see Eva Pfister, "Der Nachlaß von Marieluise Fleisser," *Maske und Kothurn* 26 [1980]: 293–303; references to Archive holdings are abbreviated MFA). Günter Rühle gives a scene-by-scene précis in *GW*, 1:442–44.

15. Neither *Fegefeuer in Ingolstadt* nor *Pioniere in Ingolstadt* have been published in English; translations are, therefore, my own. I believe that calling Fleisser's second play "Pioneers in Ingolstadt" would be misleading, especially for a U.S. audience.

16. "Durch Brecht kam ich zu den 'Pionieren in Ingolstadt,'" *Ingolstädter Zeitung*, July 12, 1973. Within her convent, however, she had certainly learned about regimentation, as her early prose works indicate. And for that matter, not only the garrison town Ingolstadt but the convent itself offered her opportunities to observe the military long before she began work on the play, for wounded soldiers were quartered at the convent during her stay.

17. *Materialien zum Leben und Schreiben der Marieluise Fleisser*, ed. Günther Rühle (Frankfurt am Main: Suhrkamp, 1973), 349.

18. While omitting any mention of Fleisser, Brecht's diary contains numerous disparagements of women, individually and generically. Sissi Tax provides a sampling (Sissi Tax, *Marieluise Fleisser: Schreiben, Überleben, Ein biographischer Versuch* [Basel: Stroemfeld/Roter Stern, 1984], 61, 135), and Klaus Theweleit discusses what he calls Brecht's "anti-whore-syndrome" (Klaus Theweleit, *Männerphantasien* [Reinbek/Hamburg: Rowohlt, 1980], 1:170). Yet Brecht's relationships with women, including Fleisser, were by no means entirely exploitative, as Sabine Kebir attempts to demonstrate in *Ein akzeptabler Mann? Brecht und die Frauen*.

19. Fleisser used the Bavarian "Korl" in V1 and V3. That a Prussian soldier acquires a Bavarian name and speaks Bavarian-inflected German shows to what extent the play is conceived from the perspective of an Ingolstadt resident. "Korl" becomes "Karl" in the Berlin version (V2).

20. The "tableau" created by these photographs is intentionally ironic, making an image of happy harmony appear permanent when it is obviously fleeting. In V1, Berta and Karl admire their "large and quite dreadful" photo; in V2 there is no longer any talk of an engagement, thus the photo is simply a keepsake, which Fleisser underscores in V3 with a soldier's comment: "Then at least she'll have you on paper" (*GW*, 1:184). (My thanks to Ann Blackler for pointing out the connection between the photographs and a tableau.)

21. Rühle misreads this passage and ascribes it to Fabian (*GW*, 1:446). I will return to this inspired mistake below.

22. Marieluise Fleisser, *Pioniere in Ingolstadt* (Berlin: Arcadia Verlag, 1929). Reprinted in *GW*, 1:187–222 with the subtitle: "Comedy in Twelve Scenes." Version 2 is, in fact, the second *extant* draft. Its predecessor, the uncut version used for the first Berlin performance, is lost.

23. Ironically, today these traits would be considered feminine—yet authoritarianism can still creep in if they are inflicted upon others in a hierarchical setting such as a theatrical company.

24. Letter to Günther Rühle, February 9, 1965, MFA III.10, 3.

25. In a letter to Dr. H. G. Göpfert she described her relationship to V2: "Various sentences I don't recognize at all. Actors improvised passages that were transformed into absurdly literary German. The text also contains alterations that I was compelled to produce from one day to the next in my utterly exhausted condition; I can't produce anything in a hurry. . . . I never saw the text again before it was published for theatrical performance. . . . I refuse to identify myself with the Arcadia-Verlag text" (February 5, 1960, quoted in Tax, *Marieluise Fleisser*, 273–74).

26. This phenomenon has been often documented; see Fleisser's short story, "The Maid's Hour" (*GW*, 3:25–31) and Theweleit's comments on this "Wilhelminian heritage" that persisted into the Weimar Republic (*GW*, 1:172–73).

27. See Botho Strauß, "Bürgerdämmerung auf der Bühne," *Theater Heute* 11, no. 4 (1970): 18.

28. "Ich schreibe Leben – aus Betroffenheit: Gespräch mit Marieluise Fleisser," interview with Thomas Thieringer, *Süddeutsche Zeitung* January 9, 1974, 8. In her works as a whole, they mark a stage in the development of her female fictional characters. See Susan L. Cocalis, "Weib ohne Wirklichkeit, Welt ohne Weiblichkeit: Zum Selbst-, Frauen- und Gesellschaftsbild im Frühwerk Marieluise Fleissers," in *Entwürfe von Frauen in der Literatur des 20. Jahrhunderts*, ed. Irmela von der Lühe (Berlin: Argument, 1982), 66.

29. Letter to H. J. Weitz, quoted in Eva Pfister, "Eine Wirklichkeit mußte sie haben: Über den Aufbruch der Marieluise Fleisser," *Marieluise Fleisser: Anmerkungen Texte Dokumente*, 66. See also Lutz, *Marieluise Fleisser*, 150–51.

30. Once again Brecht's and Feuchtwanger's influence is evident: the relationship between an English king and his favorite closely resembles that between Edward II and Gaveston in Brecht/Feuchtwanger's Marlowe adaptation, *The Life of Edward the Second of England*, which impressed Fleisser deeply in the mid-1920s.

31. Fleisser claimed that Karl's final line derived from Brecht – not Brecht-the-playwright but Brecht-the-private-person apparently indulging in Baal-like bluster.

32. See Moray McGowan, *Marieluise Fleisser* (Munich: Beck, 1987), 45–46, 61; see also Cocalis, "Weib," 67.

33. Roland Gall, quoted in Fleisser, *Der Tiefseefisch*, 7.

34. Strauß, "Bürgerdämmerung," 18.

35. Walter Benjamin, "Nochmals: Die vielen Soldaten," in *Gesammelte Schriften*, ed. Tillman Rexroth (Frankfurt am Main: Suhrkamp, 1972), 4:1, 462.

36. Typescript of V2, MFA VI.2.a.1, 29–31.

37. Theweleit, *GW*, 1:221. The contemporaneous *Freikorps* soldiers, whose writings Theweleit analyzes in his *Männerphantasien*, were not nearly as sexually active as Fleisser's Pioneers but were often similarly misogynist. Their descriptions of women "waver between intensive interest and cool indifference, aggressiveness and worship, hatred, fear, alienation, and desire" (*GW*, 1:33).

38. My qualifications arise from his occasional uncharacteristic lapses into the rhetoric of Roelle, a character in Fleisser's *Purgatory*.

39. See the quotation from Theweleit in *GW*, n. 24.

40. McGowan, *Marieluise Fleisser*, 36–37.

41. Walter Benjamin noted that Lorre "delved into the schizophrenic world of a small-town moron" ("On *Soldiers in Ingolstadt*," in *Gesammelte Schriften*, 4:2, 1208).

42. Contrary to Lutz's view, comedy *intensifies* rather than conflicts with Fleisser's "empathy for the plight of her incomprehending characters" (Lutz, *Marieluise Fleisser*, 87).

43. Only a fragment of this scene remains in scene 6 of V2.

44. One provocation that both Brecht and Ernst Josef Auricht, the producer, sidestepped was retaining the Prussian identity of the Pioneers. Auricht is reported to have said: "If I present Prussian Pioneers like that on stage, I'll be stoned" (*Materialien*, 115–16). Brecht relocated the drama in a pre-World War I setting with Bavarian Pioneers, fueling thereby the Berliners' scorn for the provincial south. A further affront to Ingolstadt sensibilities was his comment on the play, published in the theater's newspaper: "The comedy *Soldiers in Ingolstadt* depicts the manners and customs of deepest Bavaria. It offers a fine opportunity to study certain atavistic and prehistoric emotions. Thus the primeval form of love has been preserved quite intactly in it, like certain primordial flowers in limestone deposits" (*Materialien*, 62). Besides Peter Lorre, the production featured Lotte Lenya as Alma. The nominal director was Jacob Geis; set designs were by Caspar Neher.

45. Marieluise Fleisser, *Pioniere in Ingolstadt*, first published in *Theater Heute* 9, no. 8 (1968): 52–60, and *Spectaculum*, 13 (Frankfurt am Main: Suhrkamp, 1970), 87–126. Reprinted in *GW* 1:127–85 with the subtitle, "Comedy in Fourteen Scenes."

46. Letter to Rainer Roth, January 12, 1972, quoted in McGowan, *Marieluise Fleisser*, 117; see also *Materialien*, 348 *GW* 1:447.

47. Her good friend, the actress Therese Giehse, commented about Fleisser in an interview: "She always wants to revise everything, because she thinks it's old-fashioned. That's nonsense, but she won't believe it. Nothing is old-fashioned if it's really good" (quoted in Lutz, *Marieluise Fleisser*, 194).

48. "Brecht had suggested [the lines]. To me, though, they seemed quite incredible for a father" (*GW*, 1:448).

49. "12. Szene," MFA VI.2.d, 1–2.

50. Kässens and Töteberg, " '. . . fast schon,' " 114–16. See also Moray McGowan, "Kette und Schuß: Zur Dramatik der Marieluise Fleißer," in *Marieluise Fleisser*, ed. Heinz Ludwig Arnold (Munich: Text + Kritik, 1979), 13.

51. Donna L. Hoffmeister, *The Theater of Confinement: Language and Survival in the Milieu Plays of Marieluise Fleisser and Franz Xaver Kroetz* (Columbia, S.C.: Camden House, 1983), 45, see also 47.

52. Barbara Stritzke, *Marieluise Fleisser, "Pioniere in Ingolstadt,"* (Frankfurt am Main: Lang, 1982), 79.

53. *Materialien*, 239, 245, 248. See also Kässens and Töteberg, " '. . . fast schon,' " 115–16.

54. MFA VI.1.b, quoted in McGowan, *Marieluise Fleisser*, 30.

55. Fleisser, *Der Tiefseefisch*, 143.

56. Into the 1960s she was recommending to young authors that they consult Freytag's *The Technique of Drama* as a "good old household remedy" (Letter to Heinz Piontek, January 18, 1964, quoted in Lutz, *Marieluise Fleisser*, 148).

57. Bertolt Brecht, *Werkausgabe* (Frankfurt am Main: Suhrkamp, 1967), 15:150–51. Cf. also his postcard to her in 1948: "We really need the fearless realism of *Soldiers* now, when the bloodsuckers are shitting in their pants. Regards, Brecht" (quoted in Günther Rühle, "Die andere Seite," 82).

58. Ulrike Prokop, quoted in Tax, *Marieluise Fleisser*, 49.
59. Donna Hoffmeister makes this point with respect to Fleisser's narrative prose: "The narrator of this story will sometimes adopt the persona of judge, only to revert without any transition to a perspective of empathy, and the reader is left to oscillate between the two standpoints" ("Growing Up Female in the Weimar Republic: Young Women in Seven Stories by Marieluise Fleisser," *German Quarterly* 56 [1983]: 402); see also McGowan, *Marieluise Fleisser*, 154. Kurt Pinthus wrote in 1928, "One could venture the paradox that of all contemporary writers, Fleisser offers the most simple, folklike language and yet the most complex feelings" (*Materialien*, 371). Cf. also Walter Benjamin, "On *Soldiers in Ingolstadt*," 1208.
60. The final line of *The Deep-Sea Fish* is: "I'll never let anyone devour me again," upon which the Fleisser persona breaks off a self-destructive relationship (Fleisser, *Der Tiefseefisch*, 136). As Theo Buck points out, "being devoured" is a central metaphor in Fleisser's works. See Theo Buck, "Dem Kleinbürger aufs Maul geschaut: Zur gestischen Sprache der Marieluise Fleisser," in *Marieluise Fleisser*, ed. Heinz Ludwig Arnold, 41.
61. I wish to thank the Berlin Studio Archive of Zweites Deutsches Fernsehen for allowing me to view a copy of this production.
62. V1 is nearly inaccessible and, as indicated earlier, Rühle's summary is not entirely reliable. Michael Töteberg's "Die Urfassung von Marieluise Fleissers *Pioniere in Ingolstadt*," *Maske und Kothurn* 23 (1977): 119–21, is extremely brief. Of particular importance for the evolution of V2 from V1 are Fleisser's as yet undeciphered notes in the MFA's Arcadia Verlag copy of V1.
63. Marieluise Fleisser, *Ingolstädter Stücke: Fegefeuer in Ingolstadt. Pioniere in Ingolstadt* (Frankfurt am Main: Suhrkamp, 1977) only contains V3.
64. Günther Rühle, "Von Soldaten und Dienstmädchen," *Theater Heute* 17, no. 4 (1976): 14.

Chapter 7

1. An example would be Gustav Gründgens' filmed production of Goethe's *Faust*, a staple among West Germany's cultural exports.
2. Interview with Heiner Müller, *Lieb' Georg*, a television documentary about Georg Büchner, dir. Konrad Herrmann, DDR1, 1988. I wish to thank Dr. Henri Poschmann for providing me with a copy of this film.
3. See "Author's Note" and Sue-Ellen Case, "Notes on Directing *Cement*," in Heiner Müller, *Cement*, *New German Critique*, supplement to no. 16 (Winter, 1979): 67, 79–80.
4. Heiner Müller, *Gesammelte Irrtümer: Interviews und Gespräche* (Frankfurt am Main: Verlag der Autoren, 1986), 130, and *Verkommenes Ufer Medeamaterial Landschaft mit Argonauten*, Heiner Müller, *Herzstück* (Berlin: Rotbuch, 1983), 101.
5. Müller, *Verkommenes Ufer*, 101.
6. For another, see Henry J. Schmidt, "Brecht's *Turandot*: 'Tuis' and Cultural Politics," *Theatre Journal* 32, no. 3 (1980): 289–304.
7. An instructive contrast prevails in the contemporary West Berlin theater scene: the Grips Theater, whose progressive plays for young people have attracted a large and loyal adult audience as well, continues to reach new heights of success, whereas the

heavily subsidized yet sporadically attended state theaters grope for a sense of identity and purpose.

8. Edward W. Said, *Beginnings: Intention and Method* (Baltimore: Johns Hopkins University Press, 1978), 5.

9. *Gespräche mit Gerhard Hauptmann*, ed. Joseph Chapiro (Berlin: S. Fischer, 1932), 162.

Sources of Quoted Drama Endings

When not otherwise indicated, German dramas are quoted in my translations; note references are to the original texts.

Aeschylus. *The Eumenides*. Trans. Richmond Lattimore, *Oresteia*. Chicago: University of Chicago Press, 1953, 171.

Arbuzov, Alexei. *It Happened in Irkutsk*. Trans. Rose Prokofieva, in *Drama in the Modern World: Plays and Essays*, ed. Samuel A. Weiss. Boston: D. C. Heath, 1964, 545.

Beckett, Samuel. *Krapp's Last Tape*. New York: Grove, 1960, 28.

Beckett, Samuel. *Waiting for Godot*. New York: Grove, 1954, 61.

Brecht, Bertolt. *Der aufhaltsame Aufstieg des Arturo Ui* (The Resistible Rise of Arturo Ui). In *Gesammelte Werke*. Frankfurt am Main: Suhrkamp, 1967, 4:1835.

Brecht, Bertolt. *Das Badener Lehrstück vom Einverständnis* (The Baden Learning Play on Consent). In *Große kommentierte Berliner und Frankfurter Ausgabe*, ed. Manfred Nössig. Berlin and Frankfurt am Main: Aufbau/Suhrkamp, 1989), 3:46.

Brecht, Bertolt. *Trommeln in der Nacht* (Drums in the Night). In *Große kommentierte Berliner und Frankfurter Ausgabe*, ed. Hermann Kähler (Berlin and Frankfurt am Main: Aufbau/Suhrkamp, 1989), 1:229.

Chekhov, Anton. *Uncle Vanya*. Trans. Stark Young. In *Best Plays by Chekhov*. New York: Modern Library, 1956, 135.

Euripides. *Medea*. Trans. Rex Warner. In *Three Great Plays of Euripides*. New York: New American Library, 1958, 71.

Frisch, Max. *Als der Krieg zu Ende war* (When the War Was Over). In *Stücke 1*. Frankfurt am Main: Suhrkamp, 1972, 257.

Gellert, Christian Fürchtegott. *Die zärtlichen Schwestern* (The Affectionate Sisters). Ed. Horst Steinmetz. Stuttgart: Reclam, 1969, 85.

Goethe, Johann Wolfgang von. *Egmont*. Trans. Theodore H. Lustig. In *Classical German Drama*, ed. Victor Lange. New York: Bantam, 1963, 212.

Goethe, Johann Wolfgang von. *Faust, I & II*. Trans. Charles E. Passage. Indianapolis: Bobbs-Merrill, 1965, 413.

Goethe, Johann Wolfgang von. *Götz von Berlichingen*. In *Goethes Werke*, vol. 4, ed. Wolfgang Kayser. Hamburg: Wegner, 1960, 175.

Grabbe, Christian Dietrich. *Don Juan und Faust*. In *Werke und Briefe*, ed. Alfred Bergmann. Darmstadt: Wissenschaftliche Buchgesellschaft, 1960, 513.

Hebbel, Friedrich. *Maria Magdalene*. Stuttgart: Reclam, 1962, 87.

Gandersheim, Hrotsvitha von. *Dulcitus*. Ed. Karl Langosch Stuttgart: Reclam, 1964, 19.

Ibsen, Henrik. *Rosmersholm*. Trans. Ann Jellicoe. In *Four Modern Plays*, ed. Henry Popkin. New York: Holt, Reinhart and Winston, 1961, 77.

Ionesco, Eugène. *The Future is in Eggs or It Takes All Sorts to Make a World*. Trans. Derek Prouse. In *Rhinoceros and Other Plays*. New York: Grove, 1960, 141.

Ionesco, Eugène. *Rhinoceros*. Trans. Derek Prouse. In *Rhinoceros and Other Plays*. New York: Grove, 1960, 107.

Kroetz, Franz Xaver. *Heimarbeit* (Cottage-Work). In *Gesammelte Stücke*. Frankfurt am Main: Suhrkamp, 1972, 66.

Lessing, Gotthold Ephraim. *Nathan the Wise*. Trans. Theodore H. Lustig. In *Classical German Drama*, ed. Victor Lange. New York: Bantam, 1963, 133.

Lillo, George. *The London Merchant*. In *Eighteenth-Century Plays*. New York: Modern Library, 1952, 340.

Lorca, Federico Garcia. *The House of Bernarda Alba*. Trans. James Graham-Luhán and Richard L. O'Connell. In *Drama in the Modern World: Plays and Essays*, ed. Samuel A. Weiss. Boston: D. C. Heath, 1964, 317.

Miller, Arthur. *Death of a Salesman*. In *A Treasury of the Theater*, ed. John Gassner. New York: Simon and Schuster, 1956, 1099.

Ostrovsky, Alexander. *The Thunderstorm*. Trans. Florence Whyte and George Rapall Noyes. In *World Drama*, ed. Barrett H. Clark. New York: Dover, 1933, 641.

Pirandello, Luigi. *Each in His Own Way*. Trans. Arthur Livingston. In *Naked Masks: Five Plays by Luigi Pirandello*, ed. Eric Bentley. New York: Dutton, 1952, 361.

Pirandello, Luigi. *Henry IV*. Trans. Edward Storer. In *Naked Masks: Five Plays by Luigi Pirandello*, ed. Eric Bentley. New York: Dutton, 1952, 208.

Plautus. *Poenulus, or the Little Carthaginian*. Trans. Janet Burroway. In *Five Roman Comedies*, ed. Palmer Bovie. New York: Dutton, 1970, 262.

Sartre, Jean-Paul. *Kean*. Trans. Kitty Black. In *The Devil and the Good Lord and Two Other Plays*. New York: Vintage, 1960, 279.

Shakespeare, William. *King Richard II*. Ed. Peter Ure. London: Methuen, 1969, 180.

Shakespeare, William. *The History of Troilus and Cressida*. Ed. Daniel Seltzer. New York: New American Library, 1963, 183.

Sophocles. *Oedipus at Colonus*. Trans. Robert Fitzgerald. In *The Oedipus Cycle*. New York: Harcourt, Brace, and World, 1949, 170.

Sophocles. *Oedipus Rex*. Final lines translated by Francis M. Dunn.

Stoppard, Tom. *Jumpers*. New York: Grove, 1972, 81.

Stoppard, Tom. *Travesties*. New York: Grove, 1975, 98–99.

Toller, Ernst. *Hinkemann*. In *Prosa, Briefe, Dramen, Gedichte*. Reinbek bei Hamburg: Rowohlt, 1979, 273.

Toller, Ernst. *Die Maschinenstürmer* (The Machine-Wreckers). In *Prosa, Briefe, Dramen, Gedichte*. Reinbek bei Hamburg: Rowohlt, 1979, 227.

Toller, Ernst. *Masse-Mensch* (Mass Man). In *Prosa, Briefe, Dramen, Gedichte*. Reinbek bei Hamburg: Rowohlt, 1979, 168.

Wagner, Richard. *The Flying Dutchman*. In *The Opera Libretto Library*. New York: Crown, 1980, 32.

Wedekind, Frank. *Frühlings Erwachen* (Spring's Awakening). Ed. Georg Hensel. Stuttgart: Reclam, 1971, 70.

Williams, Tennessee. *The Glass Menagerie*. In *A Treasury of the Theater*, ed. John Gassner. New York: Simon and Schuster, 1956, 1059.

Wolf, Friedrich. *Die Matrosen von Cattaro*. Ed. Klaus Hammer. Leipzig: Reclam, 1988, 78.

Index